THEATRE:
THE SEARCH FOR STYLE

THEATRE:
THE SEARCH FOR STYLE

MASTER DIRECTORS ON STYLE:
chekhov - to - kabuki - to - musical comedy

by
JOHN D. MITCHELL, Ed.D.
President,
Institute for Advanced Studies
in the Theatre Arts

NORTHWOOD INSTITUTE PRESS
Midland, Michigan 48640

PN
2053
.M55

First Edition

© 1982 by Northwood Institute Press

LCN 81-85193   ISBN 0-87359-028-7

Printed in the United States of America

DEDICATION

For Theodore Fuchs, a friend and a teacher of theatre without equal.

TABLE OF CONTENTS

Pg.

* capa y spada
* * le corselet de fer
* * * sturm und drang
* * * * verfremdungseffekte

ILLUSTRATIONS

by

Donald Chang, John Daniel Mitchell,
and Lorenzo T. Mitchell

Donald K. Chang: Born in Peking, China, Master of Fine Arts, Pratt Institute, New York City. Senior Lecturer in Chinese, Department of East Asian Languages and Cultures, Columbia University, New York City. Exhibition of Photographs in New York City. Featured in an article on photography in Camera 35.

John Daniel Mitchell: Mr. Mitchell was graduated from Muhlenberg College with a bachelor's degree in science. As scientist-artist, his research in ecology has taken him to three continents. With his brother Lorenzo T. Mitchell, he has had several exhibitions of his paintings and drawings and he collaborated on line drawings for THE WILD BOAR FOREST.

Lorenzo T. Mitchell: Lorenzo Mitchell has studied art at Skidmore College. His work ranges from pastel to water color to oil painting. His works are in private collections. He has exibited with his brother John and contributed illustrations to THE WILD BOAR FOREST. The brothers are sons of the author.

FOREWORD

I am so happy this book has been written by John D. Mitchell, who understands so well the meaning of style in the theatre. John was way ahead of his time in forming IASTA in New York, where professional actors had the chance to work with top directors from such countries as China, Japan, Italy, France and to learn, through working with them, the meaning of style.

European actors have a tradition of National theatres and repertory theatres where they can watch and perform in the classics. Here in this country there is very little opportunity to work in this area, except in a few fine regional theatres. Our theatre is more naturalistic in writing and performing.

I remember well, as a young girl (already sure I would be an actress) seeing in Paris, Michel Saint-Denis's production of "The Rape of Lucrece" with his company "The Compagnie des Quinze"—it changed my understanding of the theatre! The simplicity and beauty of the direction and production with such style, was a revelation.

When Michael Chekhov, founder of the second Moscow Theatre came to perform on Broadway with his company, in Russian, his sense of style was breathtaking. I was able to found, with him, the Chekhov Theatre Studio at Dartington Hall in England and then to move it to Ridgefield, Connecticut, where we formed a company. Chekhov's training included a great deal of work and exercises on style, which gave us a sense of freedom and joy in performing plays. Later, at IASTA I had the rare opportunity of playing Racine's "Phèdre" under the direction of the brilliant actor, director of the "Comédie-Française," Paul-Émile Deiber, a real challenge as at that time he did not speak a word of English! Paul-Émile said that Racine was like an "iron corset" with all the emotion inside. This was very hard, but fascinating to work on, so different from American openness and freedom.

This book I know will be a wonderful help to everyone in the theatre: actors, writers, designers, directors and to the general public as well. A brilliant introduction to understanding the meaning of style.

Los Angeles and New York City   —Beatrice Straight
January, 1982   Recipient of the Oscar as
                                        Supporting Actress in the film NETWORK

ACKNOWLEDGEMENTS

The manuscript of the interviews, the exchange of letters with the writer, the speeches of the stage directors while they were in residence at IASTA, represented, not a mole-hill, but a mountain, seemingly.

The writer wishes to express very sincere thanks and a very real sense of indebtedness to Claudia Webster Robinson, former Professor of Dramatic Production, School of Speech, Northwestern University. Her spontaneous enthusiasm for the work and her eager offer to assist in the shaping and the distillation of the interviews proved to be invaluable.

The writer wishes to acknowledge certain friends and colleagues who have contributed richly to this book and to whom I am indebted for their continuous encouragement and enthusiasm. Among them are C. George Willard; Donald Chang and Roger Yeu whose collaboration with the writer in Chinese studies has been indispensible; Miyoko Watanabe, Professor Richard Strassberg of UCLA, Professors Benito Ortolani and Samuel L. Leiter in Japanese studies, Gala Ebin in Russian studies.

Thanks are due Aida Alvarez, Peter Blaxill, William Burdick, Bonnie Crown, George Drew, Christine Edwards, Robert Epstein, Hugh Harter, Mary W. John, Elena Karam, Bettina L. Knapp, Charles Lara and his father, Nuvart Mehta, Toni Mendez, John W. Mitchell, my wife Miriam, Mary Morris, Colette Nivelle, William Packard, Mary Jean Parsons, Richard Philp, Eva Prina, Vera Roberts, Arnold Tager, and Abbott von Nostrand of Samuel French, all of whose friendship, work in theatre, and support, proved helpful and encouraging.

John E. Booth, author of ACTORS ON ACTING, and of the Twentieth Century Fund, was among the first to read the manuscript; his enthusiasm and suggestions were invaluable.

Publishers and editors have been helpful in granting permission to quote from the writers' articles; among the publications are EDUCATIONAL THEATRE JOURNAL, PLAYERS MAGAZINE, EQUITY MAGAZINE, and FIRST STAGE.

Thanks are due Gil Forman, who saw the project through from inception to completion.

The writer also wishes to thank Irene Shawtell, Edward P. Godek, Jr.; and William G. Harkey, and Virginia Morrison for their commitment to the book and their editorial creativity.

INTRODUCTION

American Musical Comedy is among the most recent national styles of theatre to have established itself as a unique style. Although they may seem poles apart, the format of Peking opera is strikingly similar to American Musical Comedy: dialogue, song, virtuosity in movement. (Peking opera is more appropriately designated as capital drama; a true translation of its Chinese appellation. It is *not* opera, in the Western use of the word.) The performing of both are highly charged with energy.

The Elizabethan and Jacobean plays, like the 'capital dramas' of China, were performed on a bare, thrust stage. The imagery of the dialogue took the place of settings and stage properties. The extensive use of battle scenes of both Shakespeare's plays and Peking operas necessitated that the actors be skilled in the martial arts.

Shakespeare's theatre was a popular theatre; likewise, from its inception, Kabuki theatre of Japan was popular theatre. Both theatres appealed; e.g. through use of rich and elaborate costumes under sumptuary laws. Although the Jacobean plays and Kabuki plays were performed, geographically worlds apart, they were of the 17th century, and they have on the surface a striking similarity in the use of violence, blood and rhetoric.

The Golden Age of Theatre of Spain is parallel in time with the Elizabethan and Jacobean theatres of England. It has been said that under the Empire, Provincial Spain was more Roman than Rome. Small wonder that the plots, characters and gags of classical Spanish comedy evolved, as did those of Italian *commedia dell'arte*, out of the Roman comedies of Plautus and Terence.

Molière learned his craft from the Italian *commedia dell'arte* actors resident in Paris. The influence of *commedia* shaped the 18th century theatres of both France and England.

Noh has special interest to us of the West because like the ancient Greek theatre it has a chorus. Performances of Greek drama, like those of the Noh plays, combine in a veritable seamless style mime, dance, music, song, and poetic speech. Like attic theatre, masks are used in the Noh theatre of Japan. Although present day performers of Noh skirt talk of religion in their theatre, the disciplines under which the actors train and perform suggest a religious order. This aspect prompts comparison, not only with the plays of ancient Greece, but with the Sanskrit plays of India and the medieval plays of Europe.

The 'iron corset' of Neo-classic French theatre accounts for the economy, exactness and detail of the plays of Feydeau, which are aptly characterized as being 'swiss watches.'

The social protest and multi-scened structure of Brecht's seemingly revolutionary theatre has its roots in the 18th century German theatre of Goethe and Schiller.

Polish nationalistic theatre is deeply slavic, as is the theatre of Chekhov. Each is concerned with presenting reality.

The circle has come full, for the plays of Chekhov and the realistic style of acting it set in motion has had the greatest impact on 20th century theatre, and particularly on the style of American theatre.

For more than two decades, under the aegis of the Institute for Advanced Studies in the Theatre Arts (IASTA), the author and American and foreign stage directors have collaborated in a search for styles of theatre. Many of the directors have also been distinguished actors. Under rehearsal and performance conditions at the Institute in New York, the rich diversity of theatre styles was demonstrated, illuminated and observed.

The late Michel Saint-Denis, an advisory director and mentor for the Institute since its inception, had devoted his life to THEATRE: THE REDISCOVERY OF STYLE, the title of his book. As a convert to Saint-Denis' conviction that style is the heart of theatre, the author, through follow-up interviews with these master directors, sought explicit definitions of eighteen major styles of theatre. To that end, each of the directors was invited to respond to a set of questions, as applicable to the style of his national theatre. To capture nuances respecting so subtle and elusive a thing as style, each artist was interviewed and taped in his native language.

Few directors adhered strictly to the questions posed, nor was any, as on a bed of Procrustes, forced to fit the questions. Kita Sadayo of the Japanese Noh Theatre responded to some of the questions with, "That is a Western question to which I, obviously, have no answer!" The very nature of the culture out of which the style of theatre or the temperament of the artist had evolved resulted in illuminating departures.

It is the hope of the author that the readers will feel the sweep of the Institute's Search for Style—taking the reader around the world and in and out of the past and into the present. A first impression might be the differences in styles of the theatre as presented and analyzed by these master directors. It is a fact that a heady diversity of styles exists: a style of deceptive simplicity and innocence characterizes both the Medieval and the Sanskrit; ebullience and theatricality, the Kabuki and the Spanish Golden Age; a hard brilliance, logicality, sheen and intensely pent up passion, the French Neo-Classical style.

One might go on citing diversities and, ultimately, what is most likely to strike our reader is that there are many areas of agreement among the master stage directors and actors as to the universal aspects of style.

Of the master directors who came to the Institute to direct the American actor, most had little or no knowledge or awareness of the other directors' national theatre. The realism of Chekhov seems a world apart from Kabuki, however, Yuri Zavadski's dictum: "but the artist has somehow to understand from within that which he *knows*" is a tenet of acting as well of Onoe Baiko VII. When Paul-Emilé Deiber of Comedié-Française says in the interview that Racine's language, his verses, will do much of the work for the actor, Deiber may seem to have known—but certainly did not— the approaches to style of Blatchley, Devine and O'Donovan. "True style is determined by the time, the period, by the complexities of human relationships, by the particular author and what is most important to him," will be found in the interview with Yuri Zavadski. Echoes of that conviction about styles of theatre are to be found in each of the interviews.

John D. Mitchell

A HISTORY OF THE SEARCH FOR STYLE

In the beginning there were five, including the author John D. Mitchell, who founded the Institute for Advanced Studies in the Theatre Arts (IASTA). Soon after, two more joined the founding five to make it seven in all. Each was an American who had worked in professional theatre. Each desired a role in an institution which was directed towards enhancing and enriching the American theatre.

For many days and many nights they conversed as to what they should found; out of the hours of talking came a realization that they shared a belief that the "method" style of acting was not the only approach to theatre. All had traveled extensively and had seen the work of foreign counterparts in Europe and Asia and in other parts of the world. Indeed, they had a hunch that the Actors' Studio interpretation of Stanislavski's method of acting did not always work; in fact they had witnessed that the method acting had never worked for many of the world's classics. They believed with Bernard Berenson that art enhances life—and this surely included the theatre arts—that "just as Vintners take aged and prime vintage to enhance the grape just pressed from ordinary grapes" an infusion of great classics of the world into American theatre could enhance contemporary American playwrighting, acting, directing, designing.

As the group of founders began to bring into focus what they wanted to do they realized a need for a lawyer, preferably a knowledgeable, theatrical lawyer. At this point, John F. Wharton joined the group. He responded to an invitation to become Chairman of the Board of Trustees. There were many hours of discussion with him as to what should be the structure and the program and the goals of an Institute for Advanced Studies in the Theatre Arts. (For a long time, it did not have that title.) The group had been advised by various persons not to use the word *international* because that could put off—so some said—foundations and individuals. There was a conviction on the part of some that Americans were still, underneath, isolationists.

As the group talked with John Wharton they began to see that one of the things they wanted to do had a parallel with the Institute for Advanced Studies in Princeton, New Jersey. The goal might have been phrased as a desire to bring riches from abroad. Or, when the writer invited the Pulitzer-prize winning playwright William Inge to become a trustee he began his explanation of the Institute with the statement: "We want to make the impossible possible! We want to enable American actors to have experiences, as if they were actors of theatres of the world, to work under stage directors of the Comédie-Française, the Old Vic, the Moscow Art Theatre, the Kabuki-za, etc."

The writer completed his doctoral dissertation, *The Traveling Seminar as an Educational Experience,* which grew out of several study tours of the Theatre Arts which he had organized and led. The study tours in different years traveled to Europe, around the world, and to the Soviet Union. The format of these traveling theatre seminars was to meet and to discuss with colleagues in theatre abroad, to observe rehearsals and classes of theatrical training schools, and to attend as many performances of plays, operas, and ballet as possible.

During these five years of study tours, it became apparent that most young theatre professionals were unable to avail themselves of the unique experiences offered by the traveling theatrical study tours abroad. They did not have the money. This realization prompted the writer to shift the focus (and the group agreed to it) to bring riches from abroad. The hope was that in this way young theatre professionals and the young who aspired to become theatre professionals in New York could have the stimulating experiences of rehearsal and classes under masters of theatres from all parts of the world.

As a means to fostering improved international relations and understanding, the young institute set out to provide a setting in which persons who shared a common discipline; e.g. the arts of the theatre, might for a measure of time work together under a common discipline toward a shared goal. This aspiration helped the group evolve a plan.

Of the group, Gala Ebin had worked with The Theatre Guild, with a repertory company founded by Eva Le Gallienne, Margaret Webster, and Cheryl Crawford. Gala had been born in Russia, educated in Poland, and was a graduate of Vassar College in the United States. She had a command of a number of languages, and they proved valuable to the work of the Institute. She had observed much theatre in the United States, as well

2

as abroad.

Robert Epstein had had a successful background in business and a profound advocational interest in music, theatre, and the graphic arts.

Gearge Drew, a member of the Stage Designers Union, had worked both as an actor and as a designer of sets and costumes in the professional theatre. He had acted with a number of repertory groups; e.g. The Brattle Theatre of Boston.

Miriam Mitchell had been educated in theatre at the School of Speech, Northwestern University, and had acted in community theatre and had taught theatre. She later became a member of Actors Equity.

The writer had acted, directed, taught theatre, and had worked for the broadcasting networks and for play publishers. He had traveled extensively abroad observing theatre. His study tours abroad had expanded his knowledge and awareness of styles of theatre in Europe and in Asia.

Mary W. John had created an important regional professional theatre in Milwaukee, and George Willard had acted since childhood.

The members of the group were aware that their colleagues in theatre, when employed and even when unemployed, devoted their resources and time to taking classes. They were seeking a "stretch" through taking acting classes, fencing lessons, voice lessons, dance classes. Their's was an unstructured and haphazard pattern.

One of the goals that came out of the group's discussions was to offer not only a place, but indeed a studio theatre and advanced professional training to enable all actors to come and do what they'd always been doing—in a structured pattern. An incident of the 50's stimulated a basic idea. Actor Richard Burton had become well known to the theatre community in New York for his triumphs in acting in Shakespeare's plays in England; Burton was performing on Broadway in a play, TIME REMEMBERED, with the American star Helen Hayes. (This was a French play by the playwright Jean Anouilh.) There had been an item in the theatrical column in the New York Times that a group of actors had approached Mr. Burton and had asked him if he would agree to give them classes, to coach them in scenes from Shakespeare's plays. He was flattered and pleased and agreed to do it. As one recalls, on Tuesdays and Thursdays (there are no matinees on those days) they met with Mr. Burton

3

and worked on a style for Shakespeare.

One of the corporations owning theatres in New York agreed to let them have the use for their work with Mr. Burton, one of the stages which was free from performances at the time. This spontaneous desire, which had manifested itself on the part of American actors in New York, suggested to the founders of the Institute that it might be a viable goal for the Institute to send invitations to great master-actors and/or directors to come from abroad to direct members of the Institute in a classical play of the country of the director. The Institute wanted to reveal to colleagues-in-theatre, styles, in some cases over 400 or more years old, that were still accessible to actors and directors: for example, the actors of the Comédie-Française had inherited an acting tradition and style from Molière's troupe.

In retrospect it was fortuitous that in the 50's there were the Fullbright Grants for study abroad. More than the founding group had predicted these Fullbright scholarships in theatre proved a part of the destiny that shaped the Institute's ends. Many returning Fullbright scholars who had studied theatre in England, Italy, France, Germany, and even Japan came spontaneously to the Institute for Advanced Studies in the Theatre Arts to continue their advanced professional training in the classics.

The Institute soon realized that the Fullbright program had been a 2-way street, indeed. Great actor-directors like Jacques Charon had toured the USA on Fullbright grants. It made for warm friendships for the United States as well as admiration for their American colleagues in theatre. These actors and directors as visitors from abroad had observed that some directors, some teachers and some actors were often ignorant of the style of the foreign classics that they were presenting to their American audiences. Out of a pride in their own culture and a reverence for their great writers, these directors like Jacques Charon were strongly motivated to direct American actors and by so doing to share with American directors, playwrights and actors the style as they knew it, appropriate to Molière, Shakespeare, Schiller, Kabuki, etc.

Forms of Asian theatre like Japan's Kabuki and Noh, and China's Peking opera embraced the performing arts of acting, singing, dancing, martial arts, poetry. They were in a sense total theatre or, as one may label them in contemporary jargon, multimedia, theatrical events. These Asian classics suggested parallels to the complex styles of the ancient Greek Theatre and the Elizabethan theatre. Not only were these Asian theatre plays fascinating in their own right, but they also deserved being performed in English translation by American actors for American audiences. Since the Institute had had aspirations to create an environment in which theatrical works might prove to have a catalytic impact on American playwrights, directors, choreographers, composers and designers, this infusion of Asian styles into the American style of theatre was a subtle but a significant goal which the Institute for Advanced Studies in the Theatre Arts had set itself. Had not the Japanese wood block prints in the 19th century a profound impact on the impressionist painters of France and America?

The visiting directors from abroad were urged by the Insitute, as a goal, to direct the plays with American actors as much as they would in their theatres at home. Thus, the goal was to enable, hopefully, American playwrights, designers, directors and other actors to experience the world classics *as if*—through magic—they were hearing and understanding Chekhov—in Russian!

In the planning stages, it was decided that work under a foreign master-director would be open rehearsals, for in 1959, during daily visits to Brecht's Berliner Ensemble, the writer had observed that Brecht had set an example at his theatre in Berlin for open rehearsals for qualified professionals, enabling not only actors but also directors and playwrights on a day-to-day basis to watch a work in progress. Brecht hoped to combat, as he said, the mystique of closed professional rehearsals. Thus, IASTA members had the privilege to follow rehearsals through dress rehearsal and performance. Performances were for invited professional audiences. (However, the production of these international classical plays excited great interest in the communities of nationals living in New York, communities of nationals represented by the play; e.g. the Polish. The Institute found it too cruel not to extend invitations to other professionals and nationals of the country of the director to these invited performances.)

Gala Ebin called to the attention of the Institute that she had become aware that a professional theatre in Los Angeles, California, was using actors who were regularly employed in films and television. By casting the play, three deep, they were always assured that no film or television conflict on a particular evening would prevent them from giving a performance. Thus, the director of this "off-Broadway" Hollywood theatre directed three casts.

From the beginning of IASTA's international classical theatre program at IASTA the commitment was to cast all of the plays at least two deep. (In the case of the short Kabuki play, NARUKAMI (THUNDER GOD) the director from Japan's Kabuki-za cheerfully agreed to rehearsing three sets of actors!) Not only was there assurance that all performances would take place, but it also enlarged the spread of opportunity, enabling more actors in New York to have 'stretch' through working in a classical play under a master director from abroad.

January 1, 1960, the Institute began its programs and work shops for advanced professional training.

The Institute for Advanced Studies came into existence as an Institute early in 1959. It was fortunate in having been granted, at first, a provisional charter by the Regents of the University of the State of New York. (Later, IASTA proved itself and was granted a permanent charter by the Regents of New York State.)

In 1959, careful plans were laid for a research trip by a team of the Institute to go around the world observing how actors are trained professionally in the vocational schools of theatre in Europe and Asia; how their colleagues in foreign countries rehearse and how they perform. (The result of this six month's research trip in the field around the world has been compiled, edited, and bound and is part of the archives of the Institute for Advanced Studies in the Theatre Arts. An abstract of it became a master's thesis at the University of Denver, which is in the library of the University of Denver, and is also available upon request from the Institute.)

The research trip started in England and included France, Italy, Germany, Sweden; the team then flew over the North Pole to Japan where Asian forms of theatre, Kabuki and Noh, were studied in depth. The goal of the research trip was to provide a basis for advanced professional training back in New York at the Institute. The trip also proved to be a scouting for stage directors and actors, as directors, who would be able and interested in teaching the style of their national theatre to professional actors, playwrights, and stage directors at the Institute in New York.

In a former bank building on 42nd Street, which had not been used since the depression of 1932, IASTA converted the premises into a studio theatre, a dance studio and classrooms. The response from the theatre community of New York was immediate. There was cooperation from the producers of Broadway shows; many served on audition committees as a means by which the young professional actors of New York were able to become members enrolled in the Institute.

Part of the philosophy of the Institute was that there be no tuition. The founders had felt that there was a risk in tuition, namely, that less talented actors might at length buy their way into enrollment into the Institute. The Institute felt the need to have the very best of American talent to present to foreign master directors from abroad. By the same token the founders of the Institute also felt that there was risk that many might not adequately respect something which was given to them free. Therefore, after each applicant had been interviewed and had successfully passed an audition by a committee of producers of the New York theatre, each paid a registration fee.

Using guidelines for international programs of the United States State Department and the Fullbright Committee at the Institute for International Education, IASTA offered its visiting directors from abroad a per diem out of which they paid for their hotel, bought their Broadway theatre tickets, and paid for their meals. They also received an honorarium. They had their transportation paid for by the Institute by air across the Atlantic or Pacific. Most of the directors from abroad agreed to travel tourist. A great spirit of cooperation, working together in a common discipline was a remarkable aspect of this era. Quite recently the violinist, Isaac Stern, following his trip to China, said that his conviction was that the way to learn about a country for him was to meet and work with its professionals.

THE SEARCH BEGINS

GERMAN ROMANTICISM: Schiller; the Institute opened its doors in January of 1960. Willi Schmidt, a German director from Berlin, started the workshop program by putting into production with American actors a play of the great classical German writer, Friedrich Schiller. To celebrate the 200th anniversary of the birth of Friedrich Schiller the director had picked the play LOVE AND INTRIGUE. No translation existed, and this was the first of many translations commissioned by the Institute. The actor-playwright who made the translation from German into English was able to be on hand to work in close collaboration with the director from abroad. Professor Willi Schmidt, who was both a stage director and a scene designer, was able to speak English. However, he did wish to have always on hand an interpreter while he was rehearsing the actors.

The fact that 90% of the stage directors from abroad did not speak English did not deter the Institute from inviting them to come and direct. Interpreters, as in the case of Professor Schmidt, were provided for all.

Unexpected dividends resulted from the courageous adventures to invite a director who did not speak English. Each director, at first, communicated with his actors with the help of an interpreter. (A few actors did know the French, or the Spanish, or the Italian of the visiting director.) However, a very subtle thing became apparent during the 4-6 week period of rehearsal; there began to develop a non-verbal type of communication between actors and their stage director. One can only speculate, but it may be that a subtle style of the foreign classic was communicated on a non-verbal level.

In the first season of the Institute for Advanced Studies there proved to be five major classical theatre productions. This was much in excess of what the Institute had planned, and what was to be undertaken in later seasons by IASTA.

MOLIÈRE: The German classic was followed by a French classic, Molière's THE MISANTHROPE which was directed by Jacques Charon of the Commédie-Française.

CHEKHOV: Molière was followed by a production of Anton Chekhov, in honor of the 100th anniversary of the birth of Chekhov. Chekhov holds the mirror up to reality in a very special way. With what depth of understanding the actors of the Moscow Art Theatre and the Vakhtangov Theatre are able to evoke from Russian audiences smiles, chuckles and even belly laughs. Was it that Ivan and Ivanova recognized themselves in Chekhov's characters and were amused as well as moved?

The goal at the Institute for Advanced Studies in the Theatre Arts was to entertain American audiences in the same way. But how? Most English-speaking performances of Chekhov have been either too turgid or too uneventful to hold the interest of the average theatregoer for long. Perhaps the clue to the success of those Russian performances was the remarkable ambiance permeating every aspect of the productions.

Yuri Zavadski was invited to America to direct THE CHERRY ORCHARD. The New York Times reported that he spent an entire day's rehearsal on the first seven lines of the script. This painstaking evocation of a period and an environment culminated in a performance to which the audience responded as if they were Russians hearing the text in Chekhov's native tongue.

Since this was a director from the Soviet Union, it was only possible to effect this exchange under the treaty of cultural exchange that had recently been signed between the United States and the Soviet Union. In the terms of the treaty, Yuri Zavadski came to IASTA to direct American actors; Norris Houghton, as an exchange visitor, went to the Soviet Union to research, once again, the performing arts there. Norris Houghton, a member of IASTA's advisory council, had written MOSCOW REHEAR-SALS between the wars.

The outcome of Norris Houghton's return visit to Russia was a second book on theatrical life and productions in the Soviet Union. The title of the book is RETURN ENGAGEMENT. This, too, was the first of many books which have come out of the work at the Institute for Advanced Studies in the Theatre Arts. In this first season of workshops at the Institute, the stage directors from abroad who were leaving often were on hand to be met by the director who was coming in. It proved to be a very tight schedule.

The summer of 1960 was a relaxed period for the staff at the Institute and for the writer. He and his wife went to South America to research the theatre in Latin America; for in collaboration with the American Theatre Association, a program had been instituted to encourage translations into English of Latin American plays. The awards were for two translations into English of two Latin American plays and one children's theatre play; the awards came to be known as the Rosamond Gilder Awards.

In the fall of 1960, the great Kabuki actor Onoe Baiko VII came to direct

American actors in a Kabuki play, NARUKAMI (THUNDER GOD). Baiko's being able to come to the United States proved to be a saga of persistence and frustrations; there had been the greatest of difficulties in convincing the heads of the Kabuki-za, where Onoe Baiko was one of the stars of Kabuki, that they should allow one of their great actors to come to the United States to direct Kabuki. They feared the creation of rival Kabuki troupes in America would result and compete with their troups! After two years of negotiation he was able to realize *his* wish to come to America; this was the first time Mr. Baiko and his wife had left their own country of Japan.

This pioneer production of a Kabuki play, translated into English and performed by American professional actors attracted a great deal of attention in the United States and back in Japan.

RESTORATION THEATRE: Very close, indeed, on the heels of the last performances of the Kabuki play, NARUKAMI, came from London stage director George Devine. As founder of the Royal Court Theatre, grave responsibilities rested on the shoulders of Mr. Devine. An invitation had been extended to Mr. Devine to come to IASTA as early as 1959. There was a friendly exchange of letters and Mr. Devine was not optimistic that he would be able to find in his busy life and in the schedule of his dynamic theatre time to come to IASTA. In the spring of 1960, Mr. Devine directed a play on Broadway A TASTE OF HONEY. Shortly thereafter, from London, Mr. Devine let the Institute know that there was a period in the winter when he could come and would like to come.

Although the Institute had not planned to have in one calendar year five productions, the opportunity to have Mr. Devine of the Royal Court Theatre was such a temptation the Institute stretched itself and agreed to his coming. His Congreve's THE WAY OF THE WORLD proved to be a remarkable production.

GREEK TRAGEDY: In 1950, the writer had sat on the Pentelic marble rises of a Greco-Roman theatre (Herodes Atticus) to witness a dress rehearsal of OEDIPUS performed by Greek actors of Athens' National Theatre. To the rear and above the audience rose the Parthenon on the Acropolis; to the left, some hundred yards away, were the ruins of the Theatre of Dionysus where the first production of OEDIPUS was performed. Under a full moon, as the male chorus of OEDIPUS chanted, sang, moved, and danced across the marble orchestra floor, addressing themselves directly to the spectators, the small hairs on the neck and head rose and the flesh tingled. In 1952, the Greek National Theatre's production of ELEKTRA and OEDIPUS, as directed by Dimitrios Rondris, had similar impact on American audiences.

The Greek actors and their directors would seem to have succeeded in getting in touch with the passionate and profound feelings of the characters, welling up out of the unconscious; e.g. Sophocles has depicted the behaviour of psychological derangements, the fanaticism of an Elektra, fixated on her father—and her brother Orestes; it was not without good reason that Freud laid Sophocles under contribution for naming of the Oedipus complex. Might not its counterpart be the Elektra complex? These insane and obsessed people of Sophocles all display a perverse kind of nobility. *

In the Renaissance the rediscovery of Greek Tragedy triggered a revival of theatre—and led to the creation of opera. Down through the ages, the phenomenon and theatrical device of the chorus in attic drama had inspired, but had eluded contemporary playwrights; e.g. Eugene O'Neill, Robinson Jeffers.

It now seemed appropriate for IASTA to take on the challenge of the chorus of the tragedies of the Attic dramatists. Dimitrios Rondiris, a former director of the Greek National Theatre, came from Athens, Greece. His choice of a play to direct for IASTA was Sophocles' ELEKTRA. Since it was of prime importance, it necessitated creating, as in the ancient Greek theatres in Greece, an acting area large enough to accommodate the chorus as a unit in front of a low platform stage on which the actors could perform as required by the action of the tragedy. It proved possible to move the seats of the studio theatre back into the dance studio area by opening up folding doors that separated the dance studio from the theatre proper. Thus was achieved the appropriate playing area for a performance of Sophocles' ELEKTRA.

Upon his return to London, George Devine wrote IASTA that he had

---

*Wilson, Edmund, THE WOUND AND THE BOW. New York: Oxford University Press, 1965.

11

been proud to bring into existence an American company that, in his opinion, could continue to perform 18th century plays. Thus, early in 1961, George Devine's letter prompted the Institute to set in motion a plan to create a summer theatre, which would enable some of the actors who had had a unique experience working under master directors from abroad, to recreate their roles before a public, paying audience.

IASTA decided to lease for the summer season the Wharf Theatre on the Island of Nantucket. An advance work group from the Institute went early in the Spring to Nantucket to prepare publicity, the theatre, and to organize a Nantucket Advisory Council for the summer season. This was the first of IASTA's International Classic Theatre Festivals.

It proved to be an ambitious schedule; the season was of eight weeks' duration, and in the eight week period eight international classics were presented, including the American play, THE HEIRESS, a play adapted from Henry James' novel WASHINGTON SQUARE.

The accounting firm for the Institute had been very skeptical that a summer theatre offering classics to a summer colony on the Island of Nantucket would find an audience. As it turned out, the Wharf Theatre sold most of its tickets each week in the small 100-seat theatre.

It was a very intensive experience for actors, directors, and producers and staff. For example, the week that Congreve's THE WAY OF THE WORLD was being performed evenings, the daytime hours for resident company were spent rehearsing the next week's classic which was Schiller's LOVE AND INTRIGUE.

The pattern that evolved left little free time for anyone. When the curtain came down on a Saturday night performance, the crew worked through the night taking down the set and building and creating a set for the subsequent play. Sunday afternoon was also allotted for a dress rehearsal of the play for the week; Sunday night a final dress rehearsal for an invited audience of young people: the waiters and waitresses—college students—were invited to come for the small amount of 50¢ to see the final dress rehearsal. This evening came to be the most exciting of the week, for the youthful audience was a responsive one and the house was full.

Ironically, the Nantucket Advisory Council for IASTA and residents of the Island of Nantucket did not come forth to provide a subsidy for subsequent seasons; therefore the Institute did not return to Nantucket to put on a summer theatre festival. This was regrettable since residents, young people, and tourists of the Island had been enthusiastic about the season and had attended the plays.

PEKING OPERA: The British scholar A. C. Scott had written a number of books on Peking Opera; he had seen IASTA's pioneer production of Kabuki at the Institute. When he was invited to collaborate with the Institute to pioneer in producing, with Peking Opera actors, as directors, a Peking opera in English, he responded with enthusiasm. Up until IASTA's Kabuki he admitted that he had been dubious that a performance of Peking opera in English would achieve the style of the original. The Institute enabled Mr. A. C. Scott to return to Hong Kong; there he and the brother and sister Peking opera actors, Hu Hung-Yen and Hu Yung-Fang, arranged for the costumes and properties for the short Peking opera THE BUTTERFLY DREAM. A. C. Scott's decision to choose the popular opera THE BUTTERFLY DREAM was based on the fact that it has always been a popular opera with Chinese audiences, and it involves a small amount of singing. His decision was to cut the singing.

The flexibility of the IASTA studio theatre, designed by George Drew, enabled the IASTA professional actors to perform on a thrust stage. For centuries the teahouse stage of China was a platform stage; not too different in some respects from Shakespeare's stage. The teahouse platform stage, regrettably no longer exists in China.

IASTA'S BUTTERFLY DREAM (HU DIE MENG) was the first of its productions to be performed in the Coolidge Auditorium of the Library of Congress in Washington, D.C.

At that time A. C. Scott was in the United States under a grant from the Rockefeller Foundation; his association with the production of THE BUTTERFLY DREAM and his work at the Institute brought the Institute to the attention of the Rockefeller Foundation, which provided a grant to enable the Institute for two years to bring directors from regional theatres and from college and university theatres to be assistant or associate directors to the visiting master-directors from abroad.

COMMEDIA DELL'ARTE: Early in 1962, Giovanni Poli came to the Institute for Advanced Studies in the Theatre Arts to direct Carlo Gozzi's

THE GREEN BIRD. The play was of his choice, and it enabled him to instruct American actors, directors, playwrights in the style of Commedia dell'Arte. The fact that no existing translation of Gozzi's comedy existed in English, and the original text was in Italian and Venetian dialect proved to be another challenge to the Institute. However, the challenge was met; the play was performed before invited audiences and filmed. Among the many from across the country who saw the production and were filled with wonder, was Professor Campton Bell, Head of the Theatre Department of the University of Denver.

POLISH THEATRE: In 1959, in Warsaw, the research team of the Institute saw a remarkable production of Brecht's THE THREE PENNY OPERA in the theatre of the Polish director, Erwin Axer. Gert Weymann in 1959 in Berlin, had provided an introduction to Erwin Axer. While chatting with stage director Axer, the writer had learned that Axer had worked in East Berlin with Bertolt Brecht.

IASTA cabled an invitation to Axer to come to IASTA, as visiting Polish director to direct American actors in a play by Brecht!

Upon reflection, Axer wrote back that since he was Polish, he would come to the Institute to direct a Polish classic. Thus, Erwin Axer introduced IASTA to a distinct and significant international style of theatre: nationalism as theatre. THE WEDDING of the Polish playwright Wsypianski proved to be a viable, entertaining and moving drama.

The Nantucket season of 1961 made the directors of IASTA aware that American actors welcomed an opportunity to perform as in repertory, in the classical plays of Molière, Schiller, Chekhov. Indeed, It had always been a goal of the Institute to give the American actor, who had had advanced professional training in styles of theatre, an opportunity to act the classics before paying, public audiences.

That first summer season on Nantucket, the Institute had tested the *gestalt* theory of psychologists: "the whole is greater than the sum of the parts." The gamble to test the *gestalt* concept arose out of the writer's having seen the Piccolo Teatro of Milan perform THE SERVANT OF TWO MASTERS of Goldoni in Bergamo Italy; when the Italian troupe of actors performed at the City Center in New York, backstage afterwards the writer complimented an actor of the company for his performance, adding that

14

he'd seen the actor perform in Bergamo, Italy. The actor smiled and said, "No, I just joined the company a few weeks before the tour to America; I am *not* an actor of Milan; I am a Roman actor."

The excellence of his performance and the ensemble work of the company in the comedy THE SERVANT OF TWO MASTERS made a deep impression on the writer. Obviously, a nucleus of the Piccolo Teatro's own actors was able, in a small space of time, to take actors into the company and shape a new actor and transmit the style to him and make him an integral part of the ensemble.

The Nantucket experience tested if it is possible to revive a production of a classic with just a nucleus of the actors who had had the original direction from the master-director from abroad. The Nantucket season assured IASTA that it was possible to revive a classic and to achieve ensemble acting, to retain the style of the original New York production!

For the summer of 1963, the University of Denver's Professor Bell invited IASTA to come and perform an International Classical Theatre Festival on the Denver campus. His enthusiasm for IASTA's commedia production triggered another chapter in the IASTA program. There were subsequent festivals in Denver in 1965 and 1966, and as adjunct to the 1966 season in Denver, the Institute responded to an invitation from the Institute for Humanistic Studies, Aspen, Colorado, to bring two of its classical plays to be performed in Aspen.

Two seminars were in progress that summer at the Institute for Humanistic Studies: Classics of the Western world and the Classics of Asia. The two plays taken up to Aspen out of the repertory of the Denver festival were the neoclassic play, PHÈDRE by Racine and the Peking opera THE BUTTERFLY DREAM. (The actors and directors of the two productions were invited to participate in seminars.)

LOPE DE VEGA: The names of Lope de Vega and Calderon of Spain's Golden Age of Theatre are known to theatre folk, but productions of their dramas and comedies are strikingly absent from the repertories of regional theatres, university theatres, Broadway and off-Broadway theatres. What was it about the plays of Lope de Vega and Calderon, reputedly the giants, that bestowed upon their age the appellation Golden? Many may talk of "cape and sword" drama *(capa y spada)*, but what is its style?

Nineteen sixty-two was the 400th anniversary of the birth of the Spanish playwright Lope de Vega. Thorton Wilder had suggested to the Institute that it produce Lope de Vega's THE KNIGHT FROM OLMEDO. José Tamayo of the Bellas Artes Theatre came from Madrid to direct the IASTA actors in this play. Circumstances enabled the company to perform the play on the very birthday October 25, 1962, of Lope de Vega in the Coolidge Auditorium of the Library of Congress in Washington, D.C.

BRECHT: Directors of the Institute had met the German playwright and stage director Gert Weymann. In 1962, he was in New York under a Ford Foundation grant. He had worked with Brecht in Berlin; through the cooperation of the Ford Foundation it was possible to invite Gert Weymann to direct Bertolt Brecht's THE GOOD WOMAN OF SZECHWAN.

MARIVAUX: The first directors to respond to an invitation from the Institute for Advanced Studies in Theatre Arts to come to the United States to direct American actors proved to be excellent recruiters for subsequent directors from the theatres of their countries. Jacques Charon encouraged his fellow actor and director Robert Manuel of the Comédie-Française to come in the spring of 1963 to direct Marivaux's THE FALSE CONFESSIONS.

SANSKRIT: The writer had seen Mrinalini Sarabhai give a lecture demonstration of Indian dance at Asia House, in New York. Through correspondence with her, he invited her to come to IASTA to reconstruct a style for a Sanskrit play. Correspondence established that they shared a conviction that through the unbroken continuity of style of classical Indian dance, it could be possible to rediscover the style for such a play as THE VISION OF VASAVADATTA by Bhasa.

At the Library of Congress performance of IASTA's production of THE VISION OF VASAVADATTA, critics and audiences fell under the spell of the play. Some few came away thinking they had seen Indian actors and dancers performing a Sanskrit classic.

SHAKESPEARE: Having successfully celebrated the anniversary of the birth of the Spanish playwright Lope de Vega, the Institute was especially eager to celebrate the 400th anniversary of the birth of William Shakespeare. George Devine recommended John Blatchley, who had worked with him at the Royal Court Theatre. How fortuitous it was that it was possible to present John Blatchley's production of MACBETH on the stage of the Coolidge Auditorium of the Library of Congress, Washington, D.C., on April 23, 1964, the Bard's very birthday. The flexibility of IASTA's Studio Theatre enabled the play to be performed on a thrust stage. The newspaper coverage of the performance of MACBETH characterized it as a performance "performed as the Elizabethans had seen it."

NOH THEATRE: An American wit has quipped: Noh Theatre is no theatre. Throughout its long history Noh has been a theatre for aristocrats. It is static, painfully slow and lacking in dramatic actions. Even today it is not a popular theatre in Japan. Spectators, young and old, follow the play with a libretto in their laps to provide a translation into modern Japanese.

If, as Aristotle decreed, drama is an action exciting pity and fear, could the elements of dance, music, dialogue and acting found in Noh ever take their place beside other great theatres of the world?

IASTA sought an answer to this question by producing a Noh play in English on a Noh stage under the direction of master Noh actors. Kita Sadayo (surnames are given first in Asia) of the traditional Noh Theatre of Japan came to the Institute with an assistant Tomoeda Akiyo, from the Noh Theatre. This was the first time a 16th generation actor from the Noh Theatre had directed a Noh play in English translation. The choice of play was dictated by the desire to do the Noh "ancestor" of the Kabuki play which the Institute had produced in 1960. THE ONE HORNED HERMIT (IKKAKU SENNIN) is the Noh play from which the actors of the Kabuki Theatre had devised the play which is called THE THUNDERGOD (NARUKAMI). The plot is very much the same, but each illustrates the diversity of styles of the Noh Theatre and the Kabuki Theatre.

Through the Japan Society of New York and the State Department of the federal government, funds were allocated to assist the Institute to carry out this exchange program with Japan. To match the movement and the music of the Noh play the poet, William Packard was invited to assist the directors in fashioning into English verse the translation, which had earlier been commissioned by the Institute. While in Japan, the writer had discussed with Sadayo Minoru, the head of the troupe, the need for a taping of the IKKAKU SENNIN music for the New York production. A problem arose: the writer learned that the Noh musicians stated that they could not make a tape of the music, because they got their cues *from* the actors. What to do?

The following day Sadayo Kita and his father had solved the problem. In a Tokyo studio, the Noh actors and their musicians made a tape of the play. Then, the musicians put on head phones in the same studio, took their cues from the actors via the tape, and thus they were able to make a tape of the music *without the voices of the actors* who were performing in Japanese.

By scrupulously reproducing the rehearsal and performance situation of a Noh play, IASTA attempted to bring the text to life as if for a Japanese audience who could understand the text. The production's success with actors, directors, playwrights and paying audiences in New York and Denver resulted largely from the fact that the story was now accessible. Embellished by rich, beautiful costumes, masks, movement, verse and music, ONE-HORNED HERMIT was indeed an action. Binding all these elements together, however, was the skill and concentration demanded of the participants.

CALDERON DE LA BARCA: John Davis Lodge, former United States Ambassador to Spain, wrote, "Our Spanish past constitutes a significant part of our American heritage. THE PHANTOM LADY of Calderon, like any world classic, is fully within the grasp of the American actor. It should provide the audiences privileged to witness it with an enjoyable, stimulating and enlightening experience in the theatre."

José Luis Alonso responded to an invitation sent to his theatre in Madrid to direct the American professional IASTA actors in Calderon's comedy.

MEDIEVAL THEATRE: It had long been a desire of the Institute to research the style for a medieval play. The medieval play EVERYMAN is often produced, and the Dutch director Johan De Meester had directed a festival production of EVERYMAN. He had come to be recognized throughout Europe as a master of the style of the medieval drama. Each summer in Delft for many consecutive years his EVERYMAN was performed. De Meester accepted the invitation of the Institute to direct the medieval classic, which all Dutch children study in their elementary and secondary schools, MARY OF NIJMEGHEN.

FRENCH NEO-CLASSICISM: In 1965, the Institute embarked upon an ambitious project: to perform in English Racine's PHÈDRE under the direction of Paul-Émile Deiber of the Comédie-Française.

A verse translation of Racine's PHÈDRE existed in the Iambic pentameter, the five beat verse used by William Shakespeare and most English Poets. The original French play of Racine is in Alexandrines. Paul-Émile Deiber of the Comédie Française expressed his egerness to direct American professional actors in the celebrated play of Racine, PHÈDRE; however, before coming, he insisted that the PHÈDRE be in an English translation of Alexandrines, a verse length of 12 feet. Once again, IASTA turned to William Packard.

Later Packard said, "I had only two months in which to complete my translation of PHÈDRE. If there had been time, I would have had a nervous breakdown."

In the production two stars of America theatre and films, Beatrice Straight and Mildred Dunnock were cast, as was an excellent supporting cast of American professional actors. The Institute felt this was the time to take a production of a classic to the public. Money was contributed which enabled the Institute to move the production to a professional off-Broadway theatre in Greenwich Village.

The reviews in the newspapers were such that the morning after the opening, lines of future audiences seeking tickets wound around the block. IASTA's PHÈDRE ran for 100 performances off-Broadway; French director Deiber said that he'd gone through the archives of the Comédie Française in France (which plays in repertory) and found that it took 16 years for the Comédie Française to perform PHÈDRE 100 times for public audiences.

Through foundation money it was possible to respond to an invitation to bring the production to England to play at a festival at Dartingdon Hall in Devon, England. There was in progress at the same time in London at the American Embassy a festival of American arts. A phone call from America to the Cultural Officer at the American Embassy in London prompted Ambassador Bruce to add the PHÈDRE to the week of festival events. Thus, PHÈDRE was performed in London and was reviewed favorably by the London Times.

JACOBEAN: In some respects the post-Elizabethan era, often referred to as the Jacobean Period, and the later half of the 20th century are strikingly parallel. Both ages seem characterized by a pre-occupation with destruction and a general loss of optimism. The Jacobean Period's pathological fascination with violence and crime is reflected in the plays of its most famous author, John Webster.

Concurrently with the off-Broadway performances of PHÈDRE, Desmond O'Donovan, of the National Theatre of England, directed the challenging Jacobean play John Webster's THE DUCHESS OF MALFI. It was in IASTA's repertory of plays for the 1965 International Classical Theatre Festival in Denver.

KABUKI WITH A CHORUS: In 1965, the celebrated actors of the Kabuki, Matsumoto Kirshiro VIII and Nakamura Matagoro II, came from Japan to direct a Kabuki classic KANJINCHO (THE SUBSCRIPTION LIST). It was of keen interest to the Institute to explore the use of a chorus in a Kabuki play.

FRENCH FARCE: As a result of his acclaim for his directing of PHÈDRE with American actors, Paul-Émile Deiber had been invited, in 1966, to stage new productions of opera for the Metropolitan Opera in New York. Thus, while he was directing an opera for the Metropolitan Opera, it proved possible for him to direct a 19th century French classic Labiche's GLADIATOR'S: 30 MILLIONS.

AN AUTO SACRAMENTALE: The Institute had come to feel identification with off-Broadway's Greenwich Mews Theatre. IASTA's production of PHÈDRE and its revival of THE BUTTERFLY DREAM had played there. For the first time IASTA joined with a Spanish language off-Broadway theatre, which had settled in the Greenwich Mews, to produce a religious play of the Golden Age of Spain, an auto sacramentale. No translation existed, so the writer collaborated with Aida Alvarez of the Institute to make a translation of Valdivielso's THE HOUSE OF FOOLS. This production marked a departure for IASTA, for director Miguel Narros from Madrid agreed to direct one cast of professional American actors, performing in English, and the resident company of Spanish speaking actors, performing in the original Spanish of THE HOUSE OF FOOLS.

In 1973, for a second time IASTA took a troupe of American actors to perform abroad. H.S.H. Princess Grace of Monaco invited the Institute to revive a small-scale Broadway musical. Many of the original cast of YOUR OWN THING performed in Monaco's opera house as a part of an international arts festival.

A PARTNER IS ADDED

This occasion was the first major joint venture for the Institute for Advanced Studies in the Theatre Arts and Northwood Institute. The event was both happy and fortunate, for it led to a close working relationship between the two institutes, working under an arts endowment which has enabled both to promote education and advanced professional training in the arts and arts management.

The Institute had realized very early that working actors employed in theatre, films, and television, would not be able to commit themselves to long term classes; e.g. the usual 16 week academic semester. Therefore, IASTA classes were set up to last for 5, at most, 6 weeks meeting once or twice a week in late afternoon hours. The courses were scheduled to accommodate actors' lifestyle and those actors who had part time employment when not working in the theatre. The late hours proved to be attractive to the teachers of these courses, for the teachers of the classes were usually recruited from among the enrolled members of the Institute; many were directors, older actors, playwrights; e.g. Mark Connelly taught an advanced seminar for writers.

After the Institute had been in session for two years, Frank Rowley of IASTA decided to offer a type of seminar not available any where else, a seminar for aspiring producers. His goal was to invite as teachers of the seminar the leading producers of Broadway and off-Broadway.

A news story—not an advertisement—was placed in Variety, the trade publication for show business. Response for this kind of business management training was immediate. The seminar was a 'hit.' Enrollment was to capacity for IASTA's studio theatre.

Mr. Rowley, as assistant to the president of IASTA, had asked busy Broadway producers, theatrical lawyers, company managers, for example, of the Shubert chain of theatres to teach the seminar on producing.

At first, some were reticent, saying, "I've never taught. I don't know how to teach!" Mr. Rowley assured them, "Make an opening statement. Questions will come from the young producers. The 'teaching' will take care of itself." The seminar met once a week for six weeks. Those shy producers from Broadway enjoyed teaching so much that Mr. Rowley often had to end the seminar session by turning off the lights in the auditorium.

A decade later IASTA in collaboration with Northwood Institute created the Musical Theatre Studio, which for six years has been taking place in the month of June on the Texas campus of Northwood Institute, outside of Dallas. Like the earlier seminar of IASTA in New York, it features leading professionals from the American theatre as guests teachers. It meets daily, six days a week from 10 a.m. to 4 p.m. (then a lunch break). It is fully accredited by the North Central Association. The program grants three semesters of college credit. However, enrollment for credit is optional. Performers get a critique of their skills when they audition; they learn to negotiate a contract; work with agents, and through personal counsel learn how to market their talent. Composers and writers have their work critiqued.

The "masters" from Broadway cover the following areas: composing and writing a musical, producing a musical, business management as it relates to a production and creative personnel. Many of the students from previous Studios are now working professionally in New York and around the country.

Adjunct to this seminar, there is always a *work-in-progress*, a new musical. Composers and writers are in residence. Rehearsals with those enrolled in the Musical Theatre Studio are held from 4 p.m. to 10 p.m. and there are two performances of the work-in-progress. Each of the two performances is critiqued by a Broadway master.

As an abstract to the Musical Theatre Studio, the Institute for Advanced Studies in the Theatre Arts, in collaboration with Northwood Institute offers *Actors Ladder*. Actors Ladder each year takes place in New York City. As designed for young professional workers in the theatre residing in New York, the applicants are screened and 35 students are enrolled; *Actors Ladder* meets for five sessions. Producers, company managers, production stage managers, casting directors, talent agents, choreographers take the young professionals through a diagnostic clinic; they are encouraged to audition as if they were on the stage of a Broadway theatre before the producers of a commercial play or musical. What can never happen in a true audition on Broadway does happen in *Actors Ladder* as part of the training on how to market your talent: the performers are given a critique of the material they've used, their techniques in auditioning. Thus, the masters of Broadway give the young professionals an analysis in depth of their auditioning skills. In addition to advanced professional training in the practical problem of auditioning, those who teach Actors Ladder give training in job seeking and the business side of their profession as performers.

In 1983, the Institute for Advanced Studies in the Theatre Arts in association with Northwood Institute celebrates its 25th anniversary. During a period of two and one half decades, IASTA produced over 23 world classics, presented four international classical theatre festivals, produced plays off Broadway, brought a number of plays for the first time into English translation. Some of which have been published, and are in anthologies as well.

Through its association with Northwood Institute, IASTA has been able to make use of its archives of films and tapes and thus make available to the nation, aspects of classical theatre. They serve as materials and background to: THEATRE: THE SEARCH FOR STYLE.

AMERICAN MUSICAL THEATRE

"energy as theatre"

D.C.

JACK EDDLEMAN, Broadway actor-singer-dancer, performed in 18 of the Institutes international classical productions; enabling him to act in 11 of the styles of theatre discussed in this volume. Among the master directors from abroad under whom he achieved 'a stretch' as a young professional actor in New York were José Luis Alonso, John Blatchley, Johann de Meester, Kita Sadayo, Robert Manuel, José Tamayo.

Today, Mr. Eddleman continues to perform in musicals, opera, and plays throughout the United States and in Canada. However, he is best known as a director of opera. In 1973, he staged the revival of the American musical YOUR OWN THING for IASTA, in Monaco's International Performing Arts Festival. Mr. Eddleman staged LA PERICHOLE for the San Francisco opera, and Mozart's LE NOZZE DI FIGARO for the Cincinnati Summer Opera where he also played Koko in their festival production of Gilbert and Sullivan's MIKADO.

He is on the roster of directors of the New York City Opera; and for the opening of the 1979-80 season adapted and directed the revival of NAUGHTY MARIETTA.

As a director, as well as a performer, Jack Eddleman has said, "I was one of the Broadway 'gypsies' singing and dancing in musicals who through participation in IASTA became educated in styles ranging from Chekhov and Congreve and *commedia dell'arte* to Noh to Kabuki to Shakespeare.

"I learned the importance of the performing space, and how an actor displaces space through his body.

"In a modern play the actor requires less space. The larger the play, the more stylized, the bigger the emotions of the characters, the more of that space the actor has to displace with his being, not just with his body.

"I learned that charisma and talent are not enough to get an actor through a performance of a play of Shakespeare, of Molière, of Congreve, or of the Noh theatre. Fortunately, as a dancer, I had learned discipline. As a singing-actor I had begun to train my instrument. I learned that an actor, also has to have vocal and rhythmical resources *and* breath, for these skills are demanded when one performs classical plays. The dancer has always known that on-going training is essential. Performing in the classics taught me, as an actor, that I, too, had to have a dedication to on-going training.

"An actor does not move and talk in a play by Arthur Miller as he must move and talk in a play of Congreve or Shakespeare or Calderon. There is a different sound to the words, let alone the costume.

"Clothes reflect the manners, morals and the movement of an age. How much the audience see of the outline of the body tells the audience *and* the actor whether there's sensuality in the period or whether the period is repressed.

"As I learned at IASTA, the silhouette of the costume dictates the way the actor should move, and relate to other characters of the play.

"Until I worked with Blatchley of the Royal Shakespeare Company, Manual of the Comédie-Française, Kita of the Noh theatre of Japan, and other IASTA guest directors, I might have agreed with many actors who think of style as posing on stage. I learned that pretty stage pictures do not necessarily reveal style. True style is a vivid, organic, living thing on stage."

LEHMAN ENGEL, musical director for 170 musicals, has been a major force in the American theatre since his first Broadway assignment as musical director of the Group Theatre's production of JOHNNY JOHNSON in 1936. Composer, conductor, and author, Engel is a Tony Award winner, head of the B.M.I. Musical Theatre Workshop, and writer of numerous articles and books including planning and producing THE MUSICAL SHOW and THE AMERICAN MUSICAL THEATRE. Lehman Engel has participated in the Musical Theatre Studio of the Institute for Advanced Studies in the Theatre Arts.

INTERVIEW WITH LEHMAN ENGEL

Q. How do you choose and define the style for a production of a musical comedy?

Engel: You, above all else, must allow the composer to speak for himself. You don't superimpose anything on him; you don't subtract anything from *his* music. The style is his. It's personal, and it really has to do much more with what and who he is than it does with the period and the locale of the show. For example, MY FAIR LADY takes place in

England; THE KING AND I takes place in Siam; OKLAHOMA in Oklahoma territory, but basically they have one thing in common; all are American musicals. This means that the style of performance, of staging, of singing, of orchestra playing, etc., is the same in all of them. By that I mean, in America, all musicals are rhythmical; the music goes at whatever pace is required, which may be slow or fast. But it 'goes'; it keeps moving. I don't think the style of a musical should be tied to the country it's supposed to take place in or the period it's supposed to take place in. Richard Strauss wrote ELEKTRA, which takes place roughly six centuries before Christ; and SALOME which was at the time of Christ, and DER ROSENKAVALIER which is set in 18th century. The musical texture is the same for all of them; it is Richard Strauss.

Mozart wrote a wonderful opera based on a French play by Beaumarchais, THE MARRIAGE OF FIGARO. Mozart was German; the play was set in Spain. Now, you don't hear one castanet; you don't hear one guitar; you hear 18th century Mozartian music.

Rossini wrote an opera based on another play by Beaumarchais, and called it THE BARBER OF SEVILLE. It was also set in Spain, but Rossini's opera was pure Italian.

If you're an American, it's a mistake to think you should write Spanish music because a musical is to take place in Spain. An American can't write Spanish music; he can write ersatz Spanish music in five minutes, but it's much harder as every composer knows, to write one's own music at its very best. FIDDLER ON THE ROOF is not Russian music of 1900. There is nothing British about the music of MY FAIR LADY. They are first and foremost, brilliant American musicals.

Q. How did the American musical evolve?

Engel: Well, let's take it back to its origin, when Victor Herbert, an Irishman, set out to revive Viennese operetta in New York around 1900. Victor Herbert had a very well-defined style, but he never wrote a Viennese operetta. His operettas were simpler—much simpler; his songs shorter; the demands on the orchestra, the chorus, and the singers' ability were less, far less for Viennese operetta. What it amounted to was that he wrote a simple melody on lyrics, about American life, for a libretto largely about American life. They were not very good lyrics, but he didn't write them. Although the style for American musical theatre had not been developed yet, his style was—for want of a better word—American. It certainly was not Viennese. Not very much music had been thought of as purely American. I think that Herbert just happened on to this form and gradually it grew away from his operettas and feelings. Then, Jerome Kern took it over. It was he who began talking about integration of music, dance, and acting. Jerome Kern did the experimenting and, he influenced the young Richard Rodgers and George Gershwin. Gershwin was the one to carry it much, much farther.

So America developed a form which has never been taken as far in any other country. Very few English shows can be said to be in the same class. The Germans have tried it; the Russians tried it; the French have tried it. No go! It's ours. It's a simplification of plot, lyrics, melody, dance, acting, ALL these things. I don't know how we did it, but we did.

Our best things are really universal. More universal than the great operettas of Johann Strauss and Franz Lehar. I used to think FIDDLER ON THE ROOF was about Jews in Russia in 1900; the minute I read that FIDDLER was a great success in Tokyo, I realized that in Japan, as in the play FIDDLER, the generation gap is terribly important. And that's what lure of the music in Japan was about.

The style of musical theatre composers in the United States has a common denominator. Oh, each is a little different from everybody else; George Gershwin had his unique style; so did Jerome Kern; Richard Rodgers; and Arthur Schwarz, Harold Rome, Stephen Sondheim, the works. But the point is they are all really American. I'm not trying to wave a flag, but they are not like any composers anywhere else in the world, and when you hear them you know this is the American musical style.

Q. I'm responding to your answer, Lehman, to the first question: you said very significantly, ". . . the tune is slow or fast, it goes."

Engel: Yes, it moves . . . and another thing about the American musical is that it projects emotions so well.

We know how to do it by opposites. For example, Adelaide's lament in GUYS AND DOLLS, or "I'm Just a Gal That Can't Say No," in OKLAHOMA; both are sad, sad songs, but they make us laugh!

In the opposite manner, if we want an audience to cry, we will be optimistic against a sad background; for example, "You Will Never Walk Alone" from the musical CAROUSEL, Billy Bigelow has just died, but the heroine sings a very 'up' song about it. Even if we didn't understand the power of opposites in the '20s and '30s, we do understand them now.

In SWEENEY TODD, Stephen Sondheim wrote a duet called "Beautiful Women," which is light and airy. Sweeney sings it as he is shaving the man who is his arch enemy, whose throat he is going to slit. The twelve beautiful women of the song have nothing to do with that situation except that the mood of the song is exactly right for that moment.

Q. What are the elements of a musical?

Engel: I've learned through long experience that composers want the music performed exactly as they've written it: the notes, the rhythm, . . . everything. If you change the rhythms around which is what so-called pop artists do, the composer goes absolutely wild. On Broadway as musical director, it was my job to insist that the cast give the same performance they gave opening night. They may want to sort of play around with it, but they can't do that on Broadway. The elements of Broadway style of the rhythm, the melody, the whole feeling exactly as the composer wrote it. There is no other way! No interpretation! No self expression. Frequently, cafe singers and foreign singers "interpret" the material and turn a funny song into a charming, terribly unfunny song. That is not acceptable in the theatre. Another element of an American musical is vitality. The Paris production of HAIR, for instance, didn't have that American energy and drive we expect. The performers in American musicals really have to become the characters who are, in general, very simple people. They are not baronesses or counts of early operettas. They are simple and very direct. The libretto of an American musical show is brief; including text, lyrics, and stage directions. It is never more than about 90 pages. A play is about 140 pages. Musical theatre has less time to say things, and we have to be direct all the time.

Q. As musical director, do you have to guide the singers in the interpretation of their roles?

Engel: No, I think that is largely the job of the writer. Let us take Judd's song in OKLAHOMA, "Lonely Room." Anyone who sings these lyrics by Oscar Hammerstein II, reveals Judd wants only one thing, and that is love; and he's furious because he hasn't got it. Well, it's anybody who is furious and thwarted because he hasn't got love. It's not only Judd in OKLAHOMA.

Another example from OKLAHOMA "I'm Just a Girl Who Can't Say No!" I've heard thousands of girls ruin

Ado Annie's song because they sing it as a cutesy-pie affair. It's not that at all. In her mind she feels, "I have an incurable disease in the final stage. Why is it when a boy kisses me, I want to kiss him back?" She's desperate, and that's funny. If you do it cutesy-pie, it's not funny. If a song has been written properly, you just sing it. The character comes from the words, I don't attempt to do much in the way of help with characterization.

Q. I gather that you have a deep conviction that it's necessary for the singer to get the words out. Does the music also communicate character, situation, and plot development?

Engel: Music can convey nothing except mood and that mood would be very different to an Oriental from what it would be to a Westerner. Words are the only ways of being specific. Words should be said in such a way that they are appropriate to the music, but basically you need the words to tell you what it's really, specifically, all about.

Q. Even though you didn't speak Japanese, you probably felt quite secure with the Japanese cast of GONE WITH THE WIND in Tokyo because you could keep them on beam insofar as the music was concerned.

Engel: Yes, as long as I felt that the words were being chiseled out; they could communicate something American, while being Japanese.

The songs say it all. It's up to the stage director to place the actors so that these things are accentuated. And for the translator, if there is one, to understand his function.

In Turkey, I was musical director for a production PORGY AND BESS at the Turkish State Opera. A charming, talented lady, there, adapts into Turkish all the American musicals and also English and American plays. I said to her one day, "Tell me, how did you translate the "Rain In Spain" from MY FAIR LADY? She replied,

"That's a speech exercise, isn't it?" I said, "yes." "Well," she said, "I threw out the original lyrics; and I took a Turkish speech exercise which had nothing to do with Spain but of which all Turkish people knew and based my lyrics on that exercise."

Here was one human being who understood the art of translation, because the point of "The Rain In Spain Falls Mainly In The Plains" is that it is an exercise in the sound 'ain,' and any good translation must make that point.

One of the main things in musical theatre is to tell the actors that they mustn't relate to other characters onstage nearly as much as they should to the audience. It was Bert Lahr, I think, who said that he acted with Ethel Merman for 25 years and had never seen the front of her face. Another aspect of training for musical theatre concerns vocal style. The other day, one of my students in Workshop brought me a 30-minute opera he had written, based on an O'Henry short story. He wanted me and the class to hear it and comment.

Well, the worst thing about it was the performance, because the singers thought they were opera singers, and so they were full of 'grandeur;' it was all absolutely terrible.

When it was all over, I said, "Well, first of all, I'd go out and kill the singers because they are mispronouncing the English language. They have no sense of style." "But," the composer said, "This is an opera!" I replied, "If I were you, I'd get some Broadway-type singers. You'd have to work very hard to teach them these notes, which are complicated. But in the end, you'll get a performance that will have an American sound. It was terrible the way they were mispronouncing words. I can't stand people singing "Thees is my beloved." It's this, "This is my beloved." We don't say, "Thees" unless we're fugitives from Italy."

Q. Is a knowledge of the manners of the period important in a musical?

Engel: I think it's very important. If the character is a lady wearing a hoopskirt, she should be dressed underneath it as fully as did people in times past because the modern body doesn't stand like those bodies stood. So she has to wear the appropriate corsets and all the rest. In the same way, she's not going to be able to just plop down in a chair with her hands in her lap. She'll have to be aware that the skirt is way out to here. So her hands are going to be resting out there or together in front. She has to be aware of a way of sitting, of standing, of walking, of speech.

Q. How important to a production is authenticity?

Engel: Let me quote some experts on that subject. The designer Robert Edmond Jones used to say, "Take a motif from the authentic and then go out and create." Our choreographer here, Pat Birch, has said, "Nothing can kill dancers quicker than to be slavishly authentic about footwear." I think it was Agnes De Mille who choreographed, OKLAHOMA who said, "Folk dancers are the biggest bore in the world. They are created for the people performing them, not for audiences to watch."

Q. For the musical director, how important is the knowledge of the physical form of the theatre for which the work was written?

Engel: Well, I must say I've been reared on the proscenium stage, and I rather like it. I think there's a certain magic in having a front curtain. The history of musical theatre has been on the proscenium stage with everything inside that stage. I prefer it that way. But if somebody can show me something magical would happen without the prosceniums then I'm certainly open-minded.

PATRICIA BIRCH choreographed the Broadway shows GREASE and CANDIDE, winning the Drama Desk Award for both, and a Tony nomination for GREASE. Her other hits include A LITTLE NIGHT MUSIC (New

York and London), and OVER HERE! (for which she won the Outer Critics Circle Award and another Tony nomination). She received still another Tony nomination for PACIFIC OVERTURES. She worked with Stuart Astrow's Musical Theatre Lab at the Kennedy Center on the production, HOT GROG, and choreographed and staged the musical numbers for George Abbott's MUSIC IS, based on 12TH NIGHT. Her choreography for the film, GREASE, was a high point of 1978.

GERALD FREEDMAN has directed for the stage, musical theatre, opera and television. His productions include MRS. WARREN'S PROFESSION, with Ruth Gordon and Lynn Redgrave; THE AU PAIR MAN, with Julie Harris and Charles Dumig; HAMLET, with Stacy Keach, James Earl Jones and Colleen Dewhurst; COLETTE, with Zoe Caldwell; and THE TAMING OF THE SHREW, (for which he won an Obie) at the New York Shakespeare Festival, of which he was formerly Artistic Director. He directed Bach's ST. MATTHEW'S PASSION for the San Francisco Opera, and productions of CORNATION OF POPPEA and BEATRIX CENCI for the New York City Opera. For Public Television he has directed ANTIGONE with Stacy Keach and BEVERLY with Beverly Sills. He also directed the original Broadway production of HAIR. He was co-artistic director with John Houseman of the Acting Company which produced THE ROBBER BRIDEGROOM on Broadway. And in 1979 he was artistic director of the Shakespeare Festival in Stratford, Connecticut, where he directed THE TEMPEST, JULIUS CAESAR, and TWELFTH NIGHT.

INTERVIEW WITH PATRICIA BIRCH AND GERALD FREEDMAN

Q. As I've listened to each of you at IASTA'S Musical Theatre Studio in Dallas, and Actor's Ladder in New York, you've touched upon questions of theatre practice which had also been addressed to master artists around the world. Let's talk about choosing and defining the style for a production.

Birch: I read the text first as slowly and carefully as possible. I listen to the score, if it is already in existence. If it's something I'm creating with someone, obviously, the method is different.

Q. As I remember, you said that at first you resisted getting involved in the musical GREASE, and that later you had to do a lot of homework to find your way into that period.

Birch: Oh, yes, it was a question of being slowly attracted to the material. GREASE was really my first move into musical theatre, so I think my hesitancy had as much to do with that as anything else. But once one has agreed to work on a piece, well, I work in so many different styles. I do as much research as I can stand. Then I turn the research off, and go to work.

Q. You've worked in musical comedy on stage and in films. Is there a style one can characterize as typically American?

Birch: I think there are several styles running along concurrently at the moment. There is what people think of as "musical comedy style" in terms of some kind of a hat, whether it be straw, or top hat, or derby and a cane. It has its roots in jazz dance; it has its roots way back in Africa in tap, in clogging. As we spread out in our discussion we have to differentiate between the musical theatre and musical comedy. They're two totally different things. They meet sometimes; they use the same symbols sometimes. But one is full of divertissements of a kind, and one is somewhere between traditional musical comedy and opera.

Q. Jerry, we're trying to come to terms with an elusive thing, style. What have you to say about musical theatre?

Freedman: I see classical theatre and its structure as being akin to musical theatre—the American musical theatre. The presentational style utilizing both the aside and the soliloquy, demands acknowledgement of the audience that's a part of both classical theatre and musical theatre. The kind of energy—performing energy—that is needed for classical theatre and musical theatre, is the same. The use of verse in the classics and the high concentration of language within the lyrics of a song are similar. Likewise, for each the actor needs to have a strong, well-trained physique for dance, fencing, acrobatics.

I look for musical performers when I am directing Shakespeare. I consider a musical theatre background a plus rather than a hindrance. In American musicals the performer may go from dialogue into a song and often into dance. This has a lot to do with how he plays a scene. The director has to get a scene to the point where the performer can go naturally into dance or go naturally into song. This not only means that scenes have to be written in a certain way, they also have to be played in a certain way. I use the word "elevation" because it makes me immediately think of the rib cage expanded, the leading with the chest and, in general, having the kind of physical position that will enable the actor or actress to go into the heightened areas of song and dance easily. That has something to do with style.

Q. If an actor has been playing a scene, shared with other actors, how does the director move the actor into a long speech or even a soliloquy?

Freedman: In the musical THE GRAND TOUR, Joel Gray had a song that was a fantasy about loving a certain lady. First, we had the lyrics to work with. Then we went back from the lyrics into what was the subject, acting out his fantasies. Finally, this exploration included dance. Originally, it had been all singing. We had to discover the heightened reality that would make the singing words have truth.

Q. Pat, you performed in WEST SIDE STORY. Would you characterize that as musical theatre?

Birch: I sure would. That's no musical comedy.

37

Q. In what direction is the musical SWEENEY TODD going?

Birch: It's lyric theatre, more than what we tend to think of as a musical or opera. The marriage of all three is particularly what we do best in America, when we're not scared to reach out and try new ways. Sometimes little dialogue; sometimes a lot of dialogue, sometimes almost a concert form; a collage piece such as THE ME NOBODY KNOWS. A CHORUS LINE is an event which turns into a piece of musical theatre.

PACIFIC OVERTURES wasn't a musical comedy; CANDIDE was somewhere in the middle. If you laugh a lot, is it a musical comedy? I don't know. If we're doing anything important in this field it's that we're breaking down the barriers.

Q. Is one of your motivations to try and push out and find new forms?

Birch: Oh, yes, new ways of doing it. That doesn't mean that you're not using all the old tools, the old shtick. I'm looking for stuff right now that's not necessarily about show business. That's so easy because there is always a performance; there is always a rehearsal; there's always a girl dreaming of her future.

But, some of the very early pieces were audacious. CAROUSEL was an audacious piece. GYPSY had its own form. It may be the most perfect example in a lot of ways. They are "theatre" pieces.

We, Americans, are awfully good at handling the joining of music, dance and dialogue. In justifying it, it doesn't always have to be integrated, either. I just don't know if there are any rules. People are always making them, and then somebody comes along to break them and find something else. I think the only rule that we've discovered is that of logic. It does not necessarily have to be plot logic. But, you do have to set ground rules at the top of the evening or people get a little insane.

Q. What would you characterize as the elements of style in musical theatre?

Birch: The good musical is so written that it needs to be sung rather than spoken. If a text can be spoken, if any moment can be performed spoken equally well, then why sing or dance it? The energy has got to be lifted to the point where it needs singing and dancing. How you do it depends, of course, upon the material.

Freedman: I agree. Style is a result of content; the writing dictates the style. If one goes at relationships in an honest way, the writing and the structure of the work create style, rather than a director's imposing style from the outside or from some idea. As I see it, the truth, the light, the energy of a piece of material is imprisoned in the writing; its Americanness, its Englishness, its Frenchness. So if one goes at the text honestly, and if it has been written honestly, the style emerges.

When I read a script I get impressions. They're often visual impressions: pictures, colors, or musical phrases that I'm reminded of as I read through something. I try to note them down, at my first read-through. Many times I'm puzzled by relationships in a script, and I just make a note that I'm puzzled by such-and-such. I don't know what the answer is. Sometimes when I'm lucky, I am moved by a passage. I just write down my impressions: this makes me think of such-and-such; or, why do I feel anger when I read this?

I think that is the beginning of the discovery of a work's style. Finally I have to find a way of expressing what I think is the author's intent.

Q. What do you consider the elements of style?

Freedman: I believe there is an American style, and when we do each

39

others' theatre, a difference in national styles emerges. The French language simply creates a different kind of rhythm. The tirade, the long speech, is the play. It's just not the content; there is something about the fall of language and the rhythm of the language which creates a driving force in the French play that we Americans can't get; the English language doesn't lend itself to that propulsion, and our kind of experience doesn't dictate that.

HAIR, in German, is certainly different from an American production; not totally different, but an explicitly definable difference. Japanese, dressed in jeans dancing to rock music; superficially their appearance makes the Japanese indistinguishable from the French, the German or the American actor, and perhaps he isn't different at any one given moment. But there's the context, and in the context of the whole there is a difference. Maybe the difference is as simple as the compactness of the Japanese physique as opposed to a more rangy quality of the American physique. This silhouette lends a different color to the same movement in acting or dancing.

Q. You spoke earlier of the amount and kind of energy that we bring to American musical theatre. To audiences abroad, this is one of the facets of a theatrical style that they recognize as being American.

Freedman: Yes, on the surface. But I keep thinking of the Japanese theatre in this connection, too, because I always feel tremendous energy there. Often an energy that's more contained, more compressed. And I feel a tremendous power that comes from a lid on the energy. Our energy, it seems to me, is much more explosive. But both are alike in content.

Q. Excellent as a German or a foreign production of an American musical might be, an American often senses something lacking.

Freedman: I've faced that problem when directing American musicals in London, using Englishmen. I did THE BELLS ARE RINGING and WEST SIDE STORY there. This energy quality was the hardest thing to communicate: the intensity at which we Americans go at movement. And that was aside from trying to communicate the strong physical techniques that American dance has imposed on dancers and on all other musical performers. You know the riddle: Which came first, the chicken or the egg? I think that the intensity of American musicals demanded a kind of movement and then that movement began to dictate the kind of musical theatre that now demands a new kind of energy.

Q. What is required to project this American quality in our musical theatre?

Birch: What we Americans demand is that the singing be believable. We're not totally hung up on just sound. We're not isolated in each area, as it were. Our best performers can handle it all: they can act; can sing; and although they may not be trained dancers they move very well. This is what American musical theatre is all about. Ethel Merman got it across; her voice was not a pretty sound, but it certainly got the moment across, the meaning across, and the excitement. American musical theatre has a lot of excitement.

Q. Is energy in our theatre an overworked cliche?

Birch: It's a "given" which is necessary; it's a gift of ours. We are an energetic country.

Freedman: I am thinking of a more genial time, the musicals of the '20s, with tap dancing and the rhythmical complexities that Gershwin or Cole Porter put into their music. Even though their musicals are jaunty and genial, again what is evident is their energy quotient. I never thought I'd be say-

41

ing this, but, it's a cultural thing, this success drive we have in the theatre. Our tradition of theatre has something to do with competition. There is a lot of competition built into a musical, in getting jobs, in choices of material, even how that material is developed on stage. We have to go for a "smashing" number, and that's even become a musical expression.

Q. Does each musical have its own correct style?

Birch: Oh, yes. I assume each musical piece has its own style. There are directors and choreographers who go in, leave their imprint of some kind, and they're very busy doing just that. I don't believe in doing that. I believe whatever is written must be illuminated; otherwise you're not servicing a piece, you're servicing yourself.

If it is a good, strong piece, I think it almost dictates its own style. You can go in and decide what it surrounds; you can decide different ways of presenting it; you can say, "Oh, yes, all the world's a roller skating rink. Let's do this as if." Or, "Life is a soup bowl; we are all the noodles." You can do any number of things in mounting a show. A lot of directors simply get in the way of its style by doing this. People are forever making that kind of analogy. They'll take something and say, "Well, we'll do this in the image of . . ." Sometimes that gets in the way, but sometimes it's a nice frame.

Q. You like to go into the piece and find what's there and bring it out?

Birch: Yes, and then frame it.

Freedman: I'm sure there must be a correct style. Yet, I don't know, for a great play can probably be done many ways. However, rather than trying to find a "new way" for the classics, just find what's there on the page and give that its voice. That's the hardest thing to do.

42

I don't believe that any work is really locked into one specific time or place, given the imagination of the gifted person.

However, I find that when someone has really reached to try to make a statement, he has often gone too far away from the basic tone. I characterize each work as having a tone, more than a style. There is a tone in the words, in the rhythms, in the construction of the work which should guide the director into a certain area. Within any given period in history, there are variations; lots of variables in architecture and in clothing. A director and his designer are not stuck with the same look.

Q. Are plays about particular people at a certain time and a certain relationship?

Freedman: There may be other directors who work from that point of departure more than I do. I can't see that. Mostly that makes me think of the visual and outer elements. I think of myself as an interpretive artist. My own personal feelings toward the material are expressed in the way I react to violence, or love. And I'm trying to communicate that to an audience by whatever theatrical means I can.

Q. How do you clarify for an audience the historical pressures which dictate behavior and relationships?

Freedman: First, costume does a lot of it. What the director and designer dress people in dictates how they behave as well as their use of objects. Costumes also determine how one uses objects. An actor, wearing a cuff of lace, picks up a bowl of cream differently from one who is wearing a short-sleeved shirt. For example, if you're a milkmaid, you pick up a bowl of cream differently from the Countess in her salon picking up a bowl of cream. Period dictates class distinctions which dictate behavior which result in style.

You have to do a lot of research into behavior to

43

understand how to use objects: canes, for instance. Research comes from paintings, from reading, and hopefully, from authorities who have made a study of different periods.

Q. Difficult as it may be in the commercial theatre, is it helpful to have vestiges of the costumes for rehearsals, especially in a period piece?

Freedman: Hopefully, from the beginning of rehearsal. I use visual elements as much as possible. Shoes are terribly important. What the pitch of the heel will do to a character's walk!

Birch: Exactly. That's why, not always, but eight times out of ten, designers make mistakes unless they understand what clothes have to do on stage. Shoes are the "funniest" ones of all because the designers are always wanting authentic shoes for the period on the stage. Do you know what that does to dancers? They're hobbling around, breaking ankles; designers and directors have to give up on certain things.

Freedman: The construction of undergarments or the lack of them has a lot to do with movement. You really get into bad relationship patterns if you rehearse a corseted period in blue jeans. It's not the same thing.

Birch: Singers can't sing in the tightest corsets. The musical really is a theatre of compromise, in the best sense of the word. I can give you authentic social dancing of any period and bore you to death with it. Whereas, when adapted to the stage, making it a little less authentic, can make it exciting. All musicals are bastard cases; creative compromise is the name of the game.

Freedman: I remember one wonderful experience of working on RICHARD III and doing it as its period of medieval dress. I kept reminding the actors that they would have voluminous trains and they couldn't get nearly as physical as they were rehearsing. Well, of course, when they put on the costumes, the actor playing Richard had to stand about three feet back from Anne; he couldn't embrace her, he couldn't hug her, and all the things they had been rehearsing. Their carrying-on's had been strictly actor's indulgences and had nothing to do with the problems in performance that we really had to cope with.

Birch: For the opening of PACIFIC OVERTURES, I tried to get the feeling of the whole tiny island of Japan. I made a little wedge of people, thrusting forward slowly. It seemed to work, and it gave a feeling of a tight little island of people. One can do that; but what's on the page is essentially what's there. One can only make generalities of staging in sociological terms.

In both film and theatre one can make moments between people and suggest tensions. If they're not there, you are hard put to invent them and dump them on top of the script. I'd rather go back and ask for a rewrite.

Q. You choreographed the musical GREASE for the proscenium-type stage of Broadway; was it different choreographing GREASE for the film?

Birch: Totally different. For film, you immediately nullify the proscenium. The camera dictates where you want people to look. On stage, you're in a middle-range shot the whole night. You never get up closer; you never get farther away, so the director has to do all that for the audience. In film, the camera does it for you. So you choreograph for it.

Q. A great deal of energy can build up on stage in a theatre, an enclosed area. For the film GREASE, did you have to counteract loss of impact, loss of enery when the scenes were shot outdoors?

Birch: That's just camera work, playing a game of coming out long, and then going in so the audience really relates personally to whoever or whatever the focus is, and then coming back out for design elements. You choreograph a camera right with the people.

Q. The stage directors in Communist countries sometimes strive to give Shakespeare, operas, classical ballets, a Marxist interpretation.

Birch: Sometimes change can make a script better; sometimes you find things in a work that the writer didn't even know were there. But, to go running around finding political implications in things is usually dangerous or is something that happens after the fact. I prefer to work specifically. If the implication is there, then maybe I can take it a little bit further with an image here or there. But to take that decision before production is really dangerous; then you're taking whatever the work is and fitting it into an arbitrary mold.

Q. Which is more important for you, a knowledge of the manners of a period or the knowledge of the social structure of a period?

Birch: I think the social structure, in a funny way, is probably more important; you know what you are relating to. Actually, they interrelate; it's very hard to take it all apart. But the social structure dictates the manners.

Freedman: I probably would say they are equally important. I think social structures are harder for actor and director to understand and comprehend. Whereas the manners are more easily dealt with. They're physical rather than psychological. I'm not sure that in American theatre we ever properly get an English master-servant relationship. It has not been a part of our American culture. We don't understand that kind of pure social stratification; an unquestioned acceptance of one's social station. It results in differences in how we approach the same material, even though our language is the same. English productions of English plays differ from American productions of the same plays.

Q. How important to a production is authenticity of dress?

Birch: I don't think it's important at all, if you decide what you are doing from the beginning. How many productions have you seen that were marvels in practice clothes and, then lost it all by bad costuming. Authenticity won't save a bloody thing. It will help it along. It can also take the eye away from what's happening, if you are not careful. You can either be authentic or you can make a statement about not being authentic. Again, I think it's a directional decision that you have to make very early, and it even has something to do with the writing. We approached GREASE as if it were a documentary. Everything was authentic, except the behavior was slightly "hyped." I'm not as much for authenticity as I am for the clothes working for the way you want to focus the production. There are ugly periods that you need to adjust to make them palatable. I don't care about looking at a lot of authentic costumes, if the essence of them is there. If you're doing a museum piece, you want everything authentic. Otherwise, I don't care.

Q. One has to think of what one's goals are?

Birch: Exactly. Why are you doing the piece in the first place. Everybody has to adapt to that, or it doesn't matter how beautiful the elements are.

Freedman: I think dress conditions behavior which says something about style. I don't approve of gimmicky productions which change the clothes, say, just for the sake of a decorative look or for anachronistic gimmicks. For instance, it's inconceivable to put WEST SIDE STORY into Civil War dress. One physically couldn't and shouldn't do it. Now that I think of it, the American musical perhaps may be more fixed; e.g. than Shakespeare. It may be absolutely important to put each musical into its proper period; ON THE TOWN has to be set in the '40s because that experience didn't exist earlier nor in any other time since. I think one has to be sure that one is trying to communicate some of the author's truth in a clearer way. Not as a director's conceit.

Q. How important is the knowledge of the physical form of the theatre for which the play or musical was written?

Birch: Oh, I think very important. Unless you know why and how it was done, you're left with a lot of things that don't make sense. If you want to switch it to the theatre in the round, or, a thrust stage, you ought to know what it was like originally. If it's in print it was fairly successful as it was done.

Freedman: In Shakespeare the needs of the play are best satisfied by a thrust stage. Many of the 19th century operas, the Verdi's, and 20th century operas, Puccini, need, I think, a proscenium arch. They need a background of visual reinforcement. There's just nothing to be gained by putting them on a different stage; they work best in the theatre they were designed for.

Q. It would seem to have shaped the playwright in a certain way?

Freedman: Absolutely. You know, I think of how the rediscovery of the thrust stage has freed the playwright to write differently. Or maybe the writer's awareness of film makes him want to create that same speed of transitions on stage that we experience in film. Film must have influenced writing and directing techniques and finally style. The stage production of COLETTE that I did was definitely cinematic, it had fades, dissolves, and closeups. It has been my experience to relate to Shakespeare on an Elizabethan stage, but many of the Elizabethan plays read like movie scenarios, as opposed to the naturalistic plays of the '30s and '40s. During the '70s we had many two-character, one-set plays. So the economics of the theatre also helps determine the style.

Q. Has style been a concern of theatres in the past or is it a modern concern?

Freedman: I think it's modern. A French director has said, "French actors think that the only way anybody would ever act is the way he acts." But French theatre has been changing, too. Our search for diverse styles is partly American and partly a sign of the times.

Author's note: Patricia Birch and Gerald Freedman were interviewed on separate occasions.

49

AMERICAN MUSICAL THEATRE

SELECTED BIBLIOGRAPHY

Abbott, George. *"Mister Abbott"*. New York: Random House, 1963.

Eells, George. *The Life That Late He Led: A Biography of Cole Porter.* New York: G.P. Putnam's Sons, 1967.

Engel, Lehman. *Their Words Are Music.* New York: Crown Publishers, Inc., 1975.

Engel, Lehman. *Getting Started in the Theatre.* New York: Macmillan Publishing Co., Inc., 1973.

Engel, Lehman. *Words with Music.* New York: Macmillan Company, 1972.

Harburg, E. Y. *At This Point In Rhyme.* New York: Crown Publishers, Inc., 1976.

Reed, Joseph Verner. *The Curtain Falls.* New York: Harcourt, Brace and Company, 1935.

Wilk, Max. *Every Day's a Matinee.* New York: W.W. Norton & Company, Inc., 1975.

MATERIALS AND BACKGROUND

Bordman, Gerald. *American Musical Theatre: A Chronicle.* New York: Oxford U. Press, 1978.

Gorer, Geoffrey. *The American People: A Study in National Character.* New York: W.W. Norton & Company, Inc., 1948.

Mitchell, J. D. "Contemporary American Theatre . . . a psychologic sounding board." *Natya, Theatre Arts Journal,* New Delhi: Spring, 1960.

MUSIC

The American Musical Theatre. Columbia Records 32-B5-004. With book by Lehman Engel and Introduction by Brooks Atkinson.

An Evening with Johnny Mercer, Allan Jay Lerner, Sheldon Harnick. Laureate Records LL-601   LL-602   LL-603.

PEKING OPERA

"the virtuoso actor as theatre"

L.T.M.

Peking Opera entered China from Central Asia during the Yüan period and flourished during the Ming period, 1350-1644.* Both music and texts were passed down orally within the lifetime of living performers; operas were not, until recently, written down or printed. Allowing for evolutionary changes due to an oral tradition, one may say that the melodies of even the modern revolutionary operas are centuries old. Originally, Peking Opera numbered from 500 to 1,000; now, only 100 are performed.

The orchestra is composed of two different groups; strings and percussion. There is a minimum of five musicians, one playing a two-stringed violin *(hu qin)* and four playing gongs and drums. The drum player at times functions as conductor for the orchestra which is located downstage, audience right. This locating of the orchestra onstage was neither accidental nor arbitrary. The closest of relationships exists between musicians and performers; in comparison to the West, the singer has more freedom to determine the pacing of the performance. Since there is neither a stage director nor a conductor as we know them, every sound onstage is musical. With the single exception of the clown, the actors' singing, talking, sighing, laughing, and crying are all music. Every movement is a form of dance.

Peking opera singing is not like singing in the West, with tenors, sopranos, baritones, basses and contraltos. In Chinese operas, singing is all on the same level, the same pitch, though singing and acting techniques of contrasting characters differ. Duets are very rare and consist of only one or two words, though two characters may alternate singing short lines of an aria. There is never a singing chorus.

All notes in the musical scale are used, as in the West, although *fa* and *ti* are rare and generally are used to express sadness. In contrast to Western music, certain tempos, especially the slower ones, may vary at the performer's whim or with his stage acumen; e.g. when the singer wants to end an aria, he or she prolongs the last phrase or work in such a way that the violin accompanist knows and cues the other musicians.

Music known as *pai zi* accompanies movement and swordplay. (Of

---

*Today's Peking Opera or capital drama "evolved about the middle of the nineteenth century." Scott, A.C. *The Classical Theatre of China.* London: Allen & Unwin Ltd. (1957)

approximately 500 *pai zi* only about 100 are known to professional musicians today.) Each *pai zi* has a specific characteristic and is used in a specific dramatic situation.

The Chinese character for *ban* means board or beat; it originated in early times, (it is believed), when accompaniment was primitive and a board was used to beat out the rhythm and accompany the tune. Despite its literal translation, *ban* is best understood as both beat and tune. There are seven most frequently used beats, always in combination with one of four basic keys or modes. Generally a connoisseur may spot a certain *ban* readily, yet he has to listen to the lyrics to tell which opera the aria is from. Though a literal translation of the Chinese characters for some of these designations provide little clue to their meaning, they do have precise meaning for musicians and actors. Each has its own fixed tune, structure, mode, rhythm and tempo. In rehearsing and performing, the actors dictate tempo and sometimes key. Singing and instrumental melody vary at times, but they are always harmonious. The melody for the singer is of course simpler, for just as in Western music, the accompaniment is much more complicated than the vocal line.

An aria has a stanza of four or six sentences, each contains approximately ten syllables, and the last syllables of all lines rhyme.

The cabaletta, that final section of an elaborate nineteenth-century aria of Western opera, made expressly so that each singer can best display his peculiar capabilities, does not exist in Peking opera. The Asian counterpart of cabaletta is in the movement: following a scene of stage fighting, the singer who has triumphed twirls a spear or baton with such virtuosity that it brings down the house.

There are signals that the actor or actress gives the key drummer and vice versa, and these are traditional. The player of the Chinese violin, on the other hand, has freedom to improvise to a considerable extent. Even today, the notes for this violin accompanist are usually not written down. It is still possible for a professional musician who knows the basic repertory to accompany a performer in a traditional opera he's never heard or played before. All that is needed is for the leading performer to tell the accompanist in rehearsal which beat and tune *(ban)* to use and where.

The actor is central in Chinese theatre. The color and richness of fabric of the costumes enhance the actor, his gestures, and his movements. The costumes serve a fundamentally theatrical purpose, and they are not necessarily accurate historically. The costumes have evolved in relation to the character and the demands of the acting, singing, and acrobatics of the role.

Roles are far less diverse than in Western theatre, and are easily identified on the Peking opera stage. Just as the Chinese audience for Peking opera is not concerned with the plot but rather with the expertise of the acting; so, too, it is not interested in the subtlety of naturalistic, individual characterization. The characters are stereotypes. This does not disturb the Chinese audience: it actually contributes to the immediate recognition of the role that the actor is playing in the story.

There are four main categories of roles; genteel male characters, female characters, exuberant male characters, and clown characters. A distinct characteristic of this last category is the cloverleaf, a white patch of makeup around the actor's eyes and nose. The makeup produces a comic effect and the character may, in that respect, play a part resembling the clown roles of plays in the West, but he may also be a central character in a play, and even a villain.

The clowns are more likely to be cracking jokes than singing. They (clowns) also are likely to use the colloquial Peking dialect (whereas actors playing other categories may use other dialects) and make direct reference from time to time to the audience. The vocabulary of stylish gesture is lengthy, highly developed, and elaborate; by comparison it suggests the vocabulary of Western classical ballet.

Plays written before 1911 are known as traditional plays. They follow most austerely the conventions of the old teahouse stage where the audience sat on three sides of a platform that was smaller than Shakespeare's thrust stage, but not dissimilar. (Almost nothing except the actor appeared on the stage.) At the rear of the platform was a richly embroidered hanging; a vertical slit to the audience's left provided for entrances, and a vertical slit to the right provided for exits.

A table and two chairs made up the basic stage furniture. Each was draped with an embroidered cloth. The simple combination of table and chairs could be used as furniture, or as a city wall, a mountain or a throne.

No curtain existed in the traditional Chinese playhouse; the property man, dressed in a long, dark gown, would rearrange the furniture in view of the audience.

The dialogue of the entering actors, the rearranged properties, or perhaps an appropriate banner, told the audience immediately of the change of scene. The stage lighting for traditional plays was unchanging; it was simply the brightest amount of light available for lighting the actors onstage.

When hand props, such as whips or swords, were needed, the proper man arrived onstage and handed them to the actors, even in the midst of a battle. Few hand properties were used other than knives, daggers, spears, swords, banners, whips, or batons. The horse whip was an important hand property. A baton with tufts of fringe indicated that the actor carrying it was riding a horse. Mime was used instead of most hand props, and the traditional Chinese actor was a master of mime.

After 1911, new plays were written although the stories were derived from myths and classic novels. The style of singing, the costuming, and the categories of characters remained the same, but backdrops began to be used as scenery.

Traditionally, there are no stars in Chinese theatre. Instead of using dressing rooms, the troupe dresses communally in an area onstage behind the acting area backdrop. Actors assist each other as needed, irrespective of seniority or prominence within the company.

*   *   *

We wish to acknowledge and express thanks to David R. Godine, Publisher, for allowing us to quote from the authors' "The Staging of Peking Opera" from THE RED PEAR GARDEN, copyright 1973, by David R. Godine, Publisher, 306 Dartmouth Street, Boston, Massachusetts, 02116; as well as to OPERA NEWS for allowing quotes from the authors' "Two Faces of China," copyright 1974, by the Metropolitan Opera Guild, Inc., 1865, Broadway, New York, New York, 10023.

The first interview is with Peking Opera actress Hu Hung-yen, who is in her forties. She and her brother Hu Yung-fang were brought to this country in 1961 by the Institute for Advanced Studies in the Theatre Arts

(IASTA) to direct BUTTERFLY DREAM *(Hu Die Meng)*. On December 17, 1973, at Carnegie Recital Hall, she gave a solo performance under the auspices of the Carnegie Hall Corporation and the Performing Arts Program of the Asia Society.

Miss Chiang Chu-hua, who is in her twenties, was interviewed in Taiwan shortly before the tour of the United States by the Peking Opera troupe from Taiwan in 1970. Among the roles she performed during the tour of the United States was the role of Blue Snake in the play WHITE SNAKE *(Bai She Zhuan)*. Miss Chiang is considered today's best Peking opera actress, and her acrobatic skill is especially prized.

It is appropriate to point out that the theatre known to the West as Peking Opera is more accurately translated as capital drama.

INTERVIEW WITH HU HUNG-YEN *

Q. In the West today *style* is of interest in all the arts. Would you describe the *style* of Peking opera?

Hu: Its style is lucidity and lack of ambiguity. Whenever an actor, as a character, walks onstage, the audience at a performance of Peking opera knows immediately the category or *emploi* of the actor and whether, as a character, he is a good person or a villain. For example, the moment a *san hua lian* comes on stage, because of the painted patterns on his face, the audience knows immediately that he is a *chou* or clown. Now if a *da hua lian* comes on stage, he is likely to be a hero or a villain, and it is from the color or colors and the elaborate patterns painted on the face that the audience can know at once whether he is good or bad. For example, white denotes a sinister, red a heroic character.

A Chinese audience is relieved of the burden of trying to figure out his character and his social status, and it can concentrate fully on each actor's skill in performing.

Chinese actors' voices can be divided into three different types. I should like to elaborate on this, for the audience focuses its attention on the quality and contrasting styles of singing. The *xiao sheng* with a "little" voice; the "little" voice or, more literally, "small throat" produces a high-pitched sound and is used to sing a young male role. Singing falsetto is a convention for the scholarly young man role. This seems very difficult for a non-Chinese audience to accept, non-Chinese ask, "Why does a male sing with a female voice?" Actually, to us it is not a female voice; in Chinese we say, "The *xiao sheng* is singing with his own natural voice or 'big' voice blended with a 'little voice'." It is the two voices blended, thus creating a falsetto voice. The blending of voices is difficult; therefore the training of a *xiao sheng* is arduous. The actor portraying a *lao sheng* character will always wear a long beard and use "full" voice or, more literally, "open throat." The voices of actors playing *hua lian* roles will be very loud, booming and orotund. It is a unique quality of voice not to be found outside Peking opera.

Q. Why do the Chinese go to the same Peking operas repeatedly?

Hu: The Chinese say that they go *to hear* Peking opera, so one may say they go to savor the style of singing. It takes a lifetime of training and hard work for an actor to perfect himself in the singing, as well as in the movement, gestures, acrobatics, sword-play.

But before an actor learns to sing, he is first trained in acrobatic skills. Thus not only will an actor on stage have a clear and a good voice, but every movement of his hands, head, and body will be full of charm. Only then will the audience be enchanted. For this to occur, the audience must see not only the actor's performance but they must sense the thoroughness of his training.

You see, a Chinese audience understands Peking opera when they go to see one—I should say, "hear one."

They are not performers themselves, but they are equipped to tell good performances from bad. I believe that even a non-Chinese, when he sees a Peking opera, can tell the difference. True, a Chinese audience which is steeped in its traditional culture sees more. But, (I say again), even a person without the Chinese cultural background can still judge an actor's singing, his movements, and his acrobatic and martial skills.

Q. How would you compare Peking opera to Western opera?

Hu: When I first came to the States, I did not know anything about Western opera, but I was impressed by the voices. It came to me, however, during the performance, that the actors' sole concern was their singing.

In Peking opera a *hua dan,* for example, has to excel in acrobatics as well as in singing. The demands of *hua dan's* arias are comparable to those of Western opera. I think I may say that the dancing and the mime of the role are as challenging for her as for her counterpart in Western ballet. Each Chinese performer has to train for singing, as if it were Western opera, and for movement, as if it were for Western ballet.

Q. An American impression is that Chinese are a very ceremonious people. Relationships are complex, requiring different courtesies, multiple forms of address: in short, an elaborate etiquette. When you were studying to be a Peking opera actress were you required to master and to distinguish between the period manners dictated by social relationships for different roles? For example, when a court minister presents himself to an emperor, or when a daughter greets her parents, or when a wife addresses her husband, is there a special etiquette to perform and does it differ from play to play?

Hu: Yes, to each question. Every play is likely to have a different etiquette, and there are different courtesies to be learned. For example, the period of the play FOURTH SON VISITS HIS MOTHER is the Qing Dynasty; therefore, the costumes differ from those of plays set in earlier dynasties. Then, when the hero of the play sees his wife, he performs one type of salutation; when he sees his mother, he performs a different type of salutation.

For the *qing yi* part, the courtesies performed differ; when she is greeting a peer, she flips her sleeves (the long "water sleeves"); when she greets someone who is above her socially, she abases herself bows, or kowtows.

Q. Did the manners, movements and gestures of the characters in the plays really occur in daily life? For example, in the Qing Dynasty, did the people really twirl their sleeves, lift their robes, as we see the actors do while impersonating Peking opera characters on stage?

Hu: Yes, they have been made more theatrical. The gesture called "water sleeves" has been put on stage purely for theatrical effect, to give aesthetic pleasure.

Q. Almost all gestures then are part of a tradition?

Hu: Yes, but today the actor usually makes himself up to individualize or to be more appropriate to the age of the character. (For example, nowadays if an actress is playing an elderly queen, she uses less powder in her depiction.)

Q. Is each specific movement and gesture taught for each play?

Hu: Yes. In my time when we had finished learning one play and had performed it on stage to the teacher's satisfaction, we started learning the next play. (Let me elaborate.) We never used scripts. When I was a student, thirty years ago, no plays were written out or printed. The teacher would sit; all students stood around him. The teacher would say a line; we students would repeat the line. Every line, every movement was memorized, never to be forgotten. This was very difficult because one not only had to remember one's own lines in the play, one had to remember everyone else's; we learned the complete play. This method had distinct advantages. Anything learned in childhood is retained throughout the rest of one's life; it enables me now to direct a repertory of one hundred Peking operas. The disadvantage is that, as we studied without scripts, we never learned to read well; we were so busy learning the performing arts that we neglected the literary arts.

Q. Where did you start your theatrical training?

Hu: I come from the Hung Ch'un Academy, which was located in the city of Nanking. We devoted our days and nights there to learning Peking opera. Everything we learned concerned the stage. But today, the authorities want all students to be educated, so half the time in Peking opera academies is devoted to academic studies. This has its advantages, and it has its disadvantages.

Q. How did your teachers guide and eventually place the students?

Hu: During our first year in the school, after we had completed the primary training, we played extras in the performances, such as maids, guards, attendants. This was to enable us to conquer our fears and know where to be on stage. We were constantly being tried out in contrasting parts. As time passed, through observations, the teachers would come to know for which type of category one would be best suited. If one proved good enough, one would ultimately be prepared for leading roles. If one was not even good enough for them, then one was destined to play servants, guards, bannermen, etc. If the teachers decided that the student should not perform on stage, he was trained to be a musician. Though not acting, he would still be important to the performance of Peking opera.

Peking opera is a difficult art to appreciate. The audience must understand every gesture and every line that is sung.

Generally, Peking operas can be divided into two categories: the old and new plays. True, the old dramas are long, but one can cut the number of plays performed in an evening's bill. Usually managers put on two or three such plays in one evening. That is a mistake.

The so-called new plays were quite popular in the old Shanghai. They introduced scenery. WHITE SNAKE is a new play, using some backdrops, stage lighting, and many costume changes.

In the old Shanghai there was a public which preferred traditional plays, but there was also a public which wanted new plays. Some theatres played only traditional; others only new plays. The veteran audiences, those that liked traditional plays, were the connoisseurs who knew the plays by heart. These Peking opera "buffs" would even hum and sing along with the performers (and not always quietly). So if an actor were to make any changes in lines or scenes of these traditional plays, the spectators would object noisily and violently. By contrast, one can make a new play out of any story.

INTERVIEW WITH CHIANG CHU-HUA *

Q. Miss Chiang, how many students applied for your class?

Chiang: There were between twenty and thirty applicants. Twenty students were taken, but only fourteen were graduated.

D.C.

Q. How long is the training period?

Chiang: Altogether it's six years. When a student first enters the school, no decision is reached as to the type of character for which he or she is to be trained. Everybody begins with physical exercises and basic acrobatics. All do the same thing. After the first year, the children are separated into the four different major categories, and they will be trained for the different types of characters.

All the students, no matter what types they will become, do basic acrobatics early in the morning. At nine we breakfast; at ten each goes to his individual training area or classroom. That means, the acrobatic students go to practice movement and martial arts, and the singing students practice singing. At noon we break for lunch and for a two hour rest. (One of the teachers was my godfather, so before the two o'clock period, during the rest break, he gave me special instruction.) At two o'clock all the students again resume the practice of acrobatics and the use of weapons; swords (of wood), staves, spears. The evening is reserved for academic studies; Chinese language, mathematics, etc. Since the oldest among us were no more than twelve years old, all the courses were elementary school courses. As we grew older, English came to be a required course. After the dinner hour, if there is no show to put on, we have additional lessons. Since the children are very young, they need additional lessons whenever they can be fitted into the evening hours.

I must admit that at night we students were all very tired and did not have the inclination or energy to give much heed to academic work. For the first four or five years it went on like this. After six years we were graduated.

For a year following the training period we "serve", that is to say, we undergo a kind of internship by performing.

This is compensation for the training we have had. So altogether it is a commitment of seven years.

Q. During the time you were in school, which aspect of the training was most difficult?

Chiang: I feel that the basic movements, taught when a student first enters the school, are the most difficult. I was only seven years old when I first went into the school. Such basic movements as a complete backbend until the upper part of your body completely touches the ground, or splitting the legs to a full horizontal, were very difficult for me. I was as supple as a child of seven could be, but for a child of twelve, the age of some of my classmates, these were excruciating.

Q. How is it possible for you to have achieved success in both acrobatics and singing?

Chiang: At school I was assigned to concentrate on acrobatic skills. I never received a great deal of training in singing, nor was I trained in any particular singing role by the Academy, although even when we are performing in martial or *wu* plays we still have to sing a few lines. After I graduated, my mother, who is a performer in Peking opera, told me, "When you get older, your skill in acrobatics and martial arts will diminish." So after I had fulfilled my duty of internship to the Academy and its troupe, I went back home to live with my mother and she taught me all her singing roles. My uncle was also recruited to help with my development as a singer.

Q. How is it decided what category a child should go into?

Chiang: During the first year of basic training the teachers observe with keen eyes and listen with sharp ears to determine which students have the bigger voice or better singing quality and which students have good physical dexterity.

(The teachers know which students have good physical dexterity. So, by the end of the first year the teachers know which student should be trained for the type he will play for a lifetime.)

Q. While you were in school, to which category were you assigned?

Chiang: I was assigned to play the *wu dan* category. This is a subdivision in the *dan* category, a female role requiring acrobatic and martial skills. That's the meaning of the two words: *wu* is martial and *dan* means maiden.

Q. How many years did you stay with the Ta P'eng Academy?

Chiang: I stayed with my school and its troupe for eleven years in all. After that I was with a troupe called *Lian Qin* for two years.

Q. How do you feel about the three-and-a-half years that you have been with the Qi Lin Company?

Chiang: I think that I have gained a lot of experience by singing two shows a day. An actor needs to perform continuously. Then he will feel that all parts come easily, even the singing goes along more smoothly. My teacher once said to me, "To rehearse a hundred times is not as good as to perform once on stage. An audience watching you demands the ultimate in concentration. Experience is performing on stage."

Q. Personally, do you prefer to perform in the old plays or the new ones?

Chiang: I like the old ones better. They demand more technique in singing, in movement, gesture, mime, and I have to concentrate much more. Classic plays have more of a backbone (that is to say, more structure), and then the kind of instruction that I had under gifted teachers was for the traditional Peking opera repertory. For a traditional play, the director gives everything in detail. As for new plays, one just "plays it by ear."

Q. Is it true that traditional plays are no longer popular? Or is it simply easier to do contemporary plays.

Chiang: It is not that traditional plays are no longer popular, but that audiences today are different. Audiences of old knew the sources of the stories and they knew the plots. Today's audiences may not know the old novels, histories and romances. A spectator new to traditional Peking opera does not know the tale and loses interest.

Q. I noticed that recently there's a trend toward happy endings for the plays.

Chiang: Yes, now when I sing PEACH BLOSSOMED FACE I use the happy ending version instead of the traditional tragic one. It seems that most spectators now want happy endings.

---

*These interviews appeared in Educational Theatre Journal, May 1974; they appear here with the permission of the Journal and Donald Chang and Roger Yeu, Dr. Mitchell's co-authors.

After the Cultural Revolution ended in China and the Gang of Four had been put under house arrest, the theatrical arts began to reassert themselves. Today there are companies in the major cities performing Peking Opera. Performers of Peking Opera who had been put into prison or had been sent out to farms on communes doing humble work are back brushing up on their skills and are performing. The troupes have even toured the United States and other parts of the world.

The Western inspired theatre of China has made a return. We were told that about 100 plays are produced or published in a year now. A major company in China is the Peking Theatrical Troupe which has 100 actors in the troupe. They are able, with this large troupe, to produce from three to four plays simultaneously. The play TEA HOUSE by the revered playwright and author Lau Shih (who reputedly committed suicide as a result of his persecution during the Cultural Revolution) is a large play. It required from 30-40 actors. There were many sets.

A theatre like the Peking Theatrical Troupe will give about 300 performances in a year and 100 performances on tour. The subsidy for the troupe may run as high as a half million yuan. Their major theatre has 1,382 seats. At the height of the season, we were told, they are likely to have eight plays in repertory. A new play will be performed for about a month.

As for the distribution of tickets, it is poorly organized and tickets are distributed, largely, through channels. (This may account for difficulties for the tourists in getting tickets to plays that are very popular with the Chinese public.) Tickets through channels may go to factory workers. He is encouraged to go because the amount of time that he spends going to the theatre is sometimes considered as working time!

We were told that the goal of the contemporary theatre, now, is to find good plays to open up fields of creation, to introduce foreign plays, to produce modern Western plays.

If a hospital worker is able to demonstrate that he has the motivation and the talent for writing plays, he may acquire 'creative leave.' This subsidizing of an emerging playwright should enable them to catch up, they hope, and get new plays reflecting the aspirations of the new People's Republic of China.

How are plays selected? We were told that the threatres are likely to have five persons who read plays. These could be plays and manuscripts or they could be plays which have been published in magazines. There are magazines which serve as an outlet for the plays being written and these plays are read by theatre staff as well. The regional or provincial theatres get their plays from various sources. They read carefully the plays that achieve publication. They also may produce plays which are recommended by the big urban theatres; e.g. The Peking Theatres.

There are, again, several academies for training people for the theatre. These are academies where the style of theatre is for contemporary theatre. This is obviously the theatre that was inspired by the theatre of the West early in the 1920s. This theatre movement flourished greatly in Shanghai.

67

The following is an interview held in 1978, with Dan Ni, director of the Shanghai Dramatic Theatre, and with Theatrical Theatre, Wang Syau Ping, former actress, now a teacher of acting, at the Peace Hotel, Shanghai, Peoples Republic of China.

INTERVIEW WITH DAN NI AND SYAU PING

Q. How large is a Shanghai troup?

A. A troupe may number 350 actors. They play at least 3 plays simultaneously.

Q. Where are the tickets obtained?

A. Factories get group tickets for their workers. However, individuals go to the box office and purchase tickets also. The demand for entertainment exceeds the supply.

Q. What do tickets generally cost?

A. There are three prices for tickets: 60¢ seats; 40¢ seats; and 20¢ seats.

Q. At what age do actors start training for Peking Opera?

A. There has been no change. Training in depth for Peking opera still begins at a very early age, as it was before the revolution. Today, children are chosen at 10 years of age; they live at the school.

　　As in training for realistic acting, the Peking opera students get their academic training along with performance training. However, emphasis is on their life's work, that of performing. Peking opera students are still trained for specific types of roles; the clown *(chou)*, the painted face *(hua lian)*, the coquette *(hua dan)*, etc. There's been no change in type casting.

Q. How can a company of 350 actors *all* perform?

A. The troupe of the Shanghai Theatrical Theatre does number 350, but that number of actors makes it possible for the troupe to perform in 3 theatres at the same time (different casts). At the moment, two casts are performing and a third is in rehearsal.

Q. How does one qualify to be an actor?

A. Students have to qualify for study of acting or directing. Since there is great need throughout China for actors, directors, and writers, when they are graduated, all find employment. We often go in search of unusual talent. We audition youngsters around the country, on farms, in factories, in the army, and, if as a result of auditions and a process of elimination we find some who are exceptional, we train them for acting, directing or writing. Our search for talent never stops.

Q. Are there stars?

A. There are no stars. The star system is not encouraged.

Q. Is there a search for talent for Peking opera?

A. We frequently go to the Children's Palace in search of talent, picking 100 children. Through a process of elimination, eventually we decide on the few who will go on to professional training for the stage and Peking opera.

Q. Since Shanghai is the largest city in the world, how many theatres are there?

A. There are 12 theatres in Shanghai and 65 cinemas.

PEKING OPERA

FILM

"Aspects of Peking Opera"

"Martial Arts of Peking Opera": both obtainable, for rental and purchase, through the Institute for Advanced Studies in the Theatre Arts (IASTA), P.O. Box 1106, Radio City Station, New York, NY 10101 or Gil Forman, 310 W. 56th St., #1B, New York, NY 10019.

SELECTED BIBLIOGRAPHY

Chang, D. and Mitchell, J. D. *Wild Boar Forest*. Midland: Northwood Institute Press, 1976.

Chang, Pe-chin. *Chinese Opera and Painted Face*. Taipei: Mei-ya Publications, 1969.

De Bary, Wm. T. *Sources of the Chinese Tradition*. New York: Columbia U. Press, 1960.

Dolby, William. *Eight Chinese Plays*. New York: Columbia U. Press, 1978.

Hung, J. H. *Classical Chinese Plays*. Taipei: Mei-ya Publications, 1971.

Ming, Kao. *The Lute (P'ip'a chi)* (Translated by Jean Mulligan.) New York: Columbia U. Press, 1980.

Mitchell, J. D. *The Red Pear Garden*. Boston: Godine, 1973.

Scott, A. C. *The Classical Theatre of China*. London: George Allen & Unwin Ltd., 1957.

Scott, A. C. *Mei Lan-Fang*. Oxford: Oxford U. Press, 1959.

Scott, A. C. *Introduction to Chinese Theatre*. New York: Theatre Arts Books, 1959.

Scott, A. C. *Traditional Chinese Plays, Vols. I & II*. Madison: U. of Wisconsin Press, 1967, 1969.

Scott, A. C. "The Butterfly Dream". *Drama Survey*. Minn: Drama Survey, 1962.

Zung, Cecilia S. L. *Secrets of the Chinese Drama*. New York: Benjamin Blom, Inc., 1937.

MATERIALS AND BACKGROUND

Chen, Tzu-Shih and Shaw, Emil. *Paper Sculptures of Chinese Opera*. Taipei: Great China Book Company, 1969.

Crump, J. I. *Chinese Theatre in the Days of Kublai Khan*. Tucson: U. of Arizona Press, 1980.

Hajek, Lubor. *Chinese Art*. London: Spring Books (N.D.)

Hsu, Francis L. K. *Americans and Chinese*. New York: Doubleday, 1970.

Jsu, Francis L. K. and others. *China: Day by Day*. New Haven: Yale U. Press, 1974.

Mitchell, John D. and Chang, Donald and Yeu, Roger. "Two Faces of China". *Opera News*. New York: April, 1974.

Mitchell, John D. and Schwartz, E. K. "A Psychosocial Approach to the Peking Opera". *Pergamon Press*. Oxford: 1974.

Scott, A. C. *Chinese Costume in Transition*. Singapore: Donald Moore, 1958.

Snow, Lois Wheeler. *China On Stage*. New York: Random House, 1972.

MUSIC

Beating the Dragon Robe, Folkways Records FW883.

Professor Liang Tsai-Ping and his group. China's Instrumental Heritage. Lyrichord LL 92.

SHAKESPEARE: MACBETH

"the universal"

JOHN BLATCHLEY was a director at the Royal Shakespeare Theatre (Stratford-on-Avon) and formerly assistant director of the Royal Court Theatre. Mr. Blatchley has been directing plays since 1955; prior to that he was an actor and, during this period, was a member of John Gielgud's Haymarket Company, the Old Vic, and the Michael Redgrave production of MACBETH. As an actor he has appeared in 31 of Shakespeare's plays.

Mr. Blatchley has directed many of Shakespeare's plays, including JULIUS CAESAR and MEASURE FOR MEASURE for the Royal Shakespeare Company. He has also directed Shakespeare in French and has lectured on the playwright at the Sorbonne. In addition, Mr. Blatchley has directed plays in France and England, including Genet's The MAIDS, Miller's DEATH OF A SALESMAN, Schnitzler's LA RONDE, Wilder's OUR TOWN, Chekhov's PLATONOV with Rex Harrison, and Brecht's THE CAUCASIAN CIRCLE OF CHALK. The Paris drama critics awarded Blatchley's production of the Brecht play the PRIX MOLIÈRE as the "best presentation of the year."

Mr. Blatchley is also one of the leading directors of opera in England and is a Director of Productions of the English Opera Company. He has staged Janacek's THE MAKROPOULOS SECRET, Mozart's MARRIAGE OF FIGARO, and the world premiere of Richard Rodney Bennett's opera, tentatively titled THE TRAVELERS. His direction of Wagner's RING in English has been recorded.

Mr. Blatchley came to the United States for the first time in 1964 to direct MACBETH in observance of the Quadricentennial of the birth of William Shakespeare. In recognition of this visit the late William Inge, Pulitzer Prize playwright and Trustee of the Institute for Advanced Studies in the Theatre Arts, wrote: "We do not honor Shakespeare so much as we honor ourselves, on the anniversary of his birth, probably the greatest man produced by Western civilization. We honor ourselves that such greatness has lived with us these four hundred years, providing new light and beauty for each generation that finds life anew in these fathomless plays that seem to emcompass all our existence."

TWELFTH NIGHT, a comedy and seemingly smaller in scale than the tragedies, had been proposed. Mr. Blatchley countered with MACBETH. Later, as rehearsals of MACBETH progressed, it became evident that Mr.

D.C.

Blatchley had been deeply shocked by the assasination of President Kennedy; the nation's loss had stiffened his resolve to stage MACBETH.

For the April 23rd birthday performance the illustrious cast performed in the Library of Congress, Washington, D.C. The interview with Mr. Blatchley took place in London.

"Shakespeare is the most marvelous way of growing as an actor. It presents you with all sorts of difficulties which—if you can solve them—will help you as a performer.

"People told me that American actors could never speak the poetry. No one can pretend that it is not just as difficult to speak the text of Arthur Miller or the text of William Shakespeare. It is just as difficult. It is just as varied; the tempo patterns are just as rich. It happens to be in a slightly different form, that's all. If an American actor can get through something like AFTER THE FALL or WHO'S AFRAID OF VIRGINIA WOOLF, then he can certainly get through a Shakespearean text.

"It seems to me that anyone with a standard American accent is perfectly suitable in any play of Shakespeare's. Of course, it does require a certain kind of discipline over one's laziness. It is not the fact that one *can't* speak it in this country; it is more that one does not get enough chances to speak it. Consequently, Americans do not get used to the disciplines which are required.

"If this performance of MACBETH can show that actors are not only able to grasp the essential truths of the particular 'world' of MACBETH, but what is more important still, are able to communicate those truths, then we shall have achieved a double victory. There can be no question that the content of MACBETH is well within the range of anyone who is aware of the violence of our contemporary world. We, all of us, have to make decisions concerning this violence and the evil or good implicit in the choices that our politicians make for us. So the action of the play not only concerns Elizabethan Englishmen, nor even Englishmen of the 20th Century, but men everywhere. It occurred to me also that the language form of the play contains less of those conceits with cliches Shakespeare is so often associated with, and it seemed to me to be a good choice by which to try to gain the elusive victory which I have described above."

JOHN BLATCHLEY

INTERVIEW WITH JOHN BLATCHLEY

Q. How do you choose and define the style for a play of Shakespeare?

Blatchley: By style I suppose they mean wearing tights and all that. Well, I think it is ridiculous to say that there is a Shakespearean style. Shakespeare wrote some 36 plays and there are 36 different styles within these plays. I do not see any essential style in Shakespeare. I would define style as the particular world of the play.

The classic style for Shakespeare is not the traditional style—one must go back and strip off the accretions. To play Shakespeare, I would advise actors to seek to see what the speech is all about. The speech is not the reason for the scene, however. The dramatic side is equally important as the poetic side. One mustn't impose upon the play a certain kind of mad activity which sometimes is very inventive, very funny, very dramatic, which leads further and further away from the heart of the matter. Structure and dramatic concept must not be ignored because of desire to find reality. The verse must be spoken as written; it can't be interpreted by physical action. An actor cannot ignore what Shakespeare makes clear in his speeches, but the actor should never add a lot of extraneous action.

Q. Do you feel that there is a tangible national theatre style?

Blatchley: Ah, the English tradition; the tradition that goes way back. The fact is that that is not the real Shakespearean tradition, but the false Eighteenth and Nineteenth Century acting traditions that grew up; the English poetic tragic style.

Q. Does each play have its own "correct" style?

Blatchley: I don't know whether the word should be "correct"—but every good play (and I'm going on the assumption that we are only discussing good plays, whether serious or not in

77

content) presents to an audience its own particular and complete world. Each play shows a reality which the audience is invited to share, and in order to do this each spectator is required to make the act of faith of "suspending his disbelief." According to his willingness to do this, so will his pleasure, understanding and appreciation of the play, be enhanced or reduced. All plays present their own inevitable logic (even though the activities within a play may appear to be illogical, yet all its actions are governed by its own particular rules and regulations), and it is this logic which the designer, director and actors must strive to render acceptable to their public. But the logic by which one play is ruled is not necessarily applicable to another, even when two plays may be written by the same author.

People speak of a Molière style, or a Shakespearean style, but they have probably never had to come to grips with actually animating two such disparate plays as MACBETH and ANTHONY AND CLEOPATRA (both tragedies) or LOVE'S LABOURS LOST and AS YOU LIKE IT (both comedies) or, for example, TARTUFFE and LE BOURGOIS GENTILHOMME. What could be more foolish than trying to perform in THE CITIES JUNGLE and GALILEO in the same manner? Even in the matter of plays by authors like Chekhov, there is not in my opinion an overall, generalized, reality—but each of these four great works, THE SEAGULL, UNCLE VANYA, THE CHERRY ORCHARD, and THE THREE SISTERS, has its own personal truth, its own special vision of the world—and it is this that we must attempt to capture.

Q. Are plays about particular people at a certain time and in a certain relationship?

Blatchley: I personally don't believe that any great play is about a certain time, although naturally considerations as to the actual time for which plays were written must be taken into consideration when presenting them. I do, however, believe that all great plays are connected with the idea of relationships and it is vital that actors and directors do communicate the essence of a series of relationships in a way that can be clearly understood, within the frame and context of the play itself. If, as in the case with great plays, this rapport between human beings can also present truths which are outside the framework of the given performance, as well, so much the better. For me, (this is a very personal thing, of course) the greatest satisfaction in theatre is when I come away from a performance with this kind of experience.

Q. How does one clarify for an audience the historical social pressures which dictate behavior and relationships?

Blatchley: I would have thought that in most great plays these kinds of pressures are implicit in the actual happening that the audience sees. I know that very often this information is obscured because the director and actors don't seek to render the events clearly, through playing the acting of the scenes, and the super-objective of the characters, but I can't off hand think of an outstanding play in which this kind of information is not contained within either the dialogue, the story, or the activities, or motivations of the characters. In MACBETH, for example, it seems to me pointless to try to "do" particular things with the witches in order to make them dramatic or to justify Macbeth's reactions to them. It is quite implicit in the play what the attitude of the people of this world is towards witchcraft, evil, superstition, etc., and we should not need, because modern audiences are—shall we say—more skeptical, to explain or justify these attitudes. The conception of honor for example that animates much of the behavior of characters in plays by Lope de Vega, or the religious fervor that justifies many of Calderon's heroes and heroines,

79

which may be totally foreign as conceptions of life to us to-day (alas!), are contained so firmly in the play that a pro-gram note only becomes necessary when the acting and direction have obscured the sense of these motivations. If, when the rehearsals of a particular work have nearly reached a stage of presentation to a public, and the par-ticipants still feel that essential information for the understanding of the play is lacking, and if they can solemnly acknowledge that there is nothing that they can do about it in their playing, then by means of re-rehearsing, each director will find his own solution. This may in the long run lie in the use of making an-nouncements between or during the scenes, introducing symbols which are self-explanatory, projections of texts, or pictures, even music, and I think that all and any of these mechanisms are viable and justifiable in any play, no matter what period or style it belongs to. Our aim must surely above everything else be concerned with com-municating the truth of the play in all its depth and com-plication.

Q.   How important is a knowledge of the etiquette, the man-ners of the period?

Blatchley: I personally don't believe that a knowledge of the manners of a period is of much use to a general audience. I think that if the style has been found by all concerned, the behavior that the public sees will be convincing however strange and remote it may appear to us as compared with our own behavior patterns. I don't think that an audience will ever laugh, for instance, or have doubts, about what is going on on the stage if the group has achieved this primary magic of suspending the audience's disbelief. Anyone who opens the first page of "Alice in Wonderland" say, and who mutters "rubbish" when the rabbit takes out his watch and speaks, had better put the book away; for what follows will only serve to irritate him—but the reader who says "that really is not possible, but I will accept for the space of four seconds and a half that on a summers day, in a field by a river, in England, in eighteen hundred and something, that it *could* happen," this reader will only find more and more joy as he reads on. I believe that most of the information about manner comes again from the text. In a play by Congreve, for example, it is from the way that the actors think, speak and act, and by knowing something of the way in which their characters dressed (so that they know exactly the freedom or encumberance of the ordinary every-day clothes of these peoples), that we shall know how they actually moved, how they actually behaved in terms of manner. No amount of snuff taking and waggling of fans will convince me that the performers have understood the manner of a particular time if their understanding of the basic premise, both in form and content, of the play is inferior, or lacking altogether.

Q. Is knowledge of the social structure of the period important?

Blatchley: I believe that some idea of the social structure of the world of a play, whether it take place in another age or our own, is important, and I would do everything I could to make this clear, first in playing and general presentation, and by all the other means that I have already suggested, and if these failed, I suppose I would finally use a program note —although I think this last means is not very effective— better, in my opinion, to interrupt the flow of the play with announcements. But again I would come back to my argument that it is what the audience sees and hears that counts. If directors and actors continue to perform authors, for example, Labiche, with such a total and overwhelming misunderstanding of the style, then, of course, these questions that you ask are fundamental ones. But if Labiche is played without that "fay" otherworldly quality, and if he is performed with that immediate, forthright, tough, virile reality which is proper to him, then I think that many of these problems about form, manners, social structure, are resolved in front of the audience's eyes at the performance.

Q. How important to a production of a classic is authenticity of dress?

Blatchley: Although we may with a certain amount of money recapture exactly the external conditions of a particular play— costumes, settings, furniture, properties, and even the theatrical architecture of the period—we can never re-create the main element of the theatrical experience; i.e. the audience, and so our primary aim has to be to present the play in a manner that will reach our own time.

Q. What decision did you make as to costumes for MACBETH?

Blatchley: The costumes of MACBETH should be blue denims, trousers and tops, preferably ex-army issue. These should be bought from a surplus store then treated. The treatment consists first of washing them, then soaking them in water for about a week, then leaving them to dry, then putting them on the floor where everybody can tread on them, trample on them, throw dust on them. Then they should be washed with hard soap and left to dry, and then they should have glue, mud, cement, paint, wood shavings, etc., stuck on to them. By this time they look like CLOTHES and not costumes, that have been WORN, rained on, sunned on, winded on, hailed on, fogged on, sweated in, blooded on, etc. If various colors are available, so much the better—khaki, grey and blue would be splendid.

The shoes would be ex-army boots, heavy woolen dark socks, with one or two pairs of basketball shoes for the lighter characters like Malcolm, young Banquo, Fleance, Donalbain, etc.

The appearance of MACBETH has got to come away from Druids with grey beards, or kilts, or Stone Age men. The trousers should be tightened at the ankle, so that they HUG the leg, almost like tights, but without the smooth soft look that tights can give. On the top part, in some cases, we attach pieces of gas capes (army issue again) which give an appearance of cloaks for the stronger and firmer characters. NO WIGS. NO MAKE-UP. Hard white light and black, black shadows. NO HATS. If people want to *grow* beards, that's fine, or cut their hair to nothing, that's fine too. THIS WILL NOT LOOK LIKE A MODERN DRESS PERFORMANCE—but will be reminiscent of a human silhouette that we've seen SOMEWHERE.

Very little tailoring; no expensive materials. Clothes don't need to FIT like a glove; they fit just as soldiers' clothes do fit—in all the necessary places. Have the costumes for the last three weeks of rehearsal, and since they are the kind of clothes we wear ordinarily, there would be none of that "phoney" style movement that so many of the bard's plays have to put up with.

The basic costume for the female characters—the witches part—is long dark colored woolen skirt—to floor level—long sleeved woolen jumper/sweater/blouse for the top part—close fitting—dark colored. The shoes must be flat and light, probably ballet shoes. Lady Macbeth's basic costume is a gas mask cape of a different color and jewel studded when she becomes a queen. A big woolen scarf is worn.

Lady Macduff is exactly the same as Lady Macbeth—no second cloak. Gentlewoman has a basic skirt with a rough hession or sack blouse and a woolen scarf.

The witches must look like those old creatures that you suddenly encounter on a country road—you wonder at first whether they are scarecrows standing in a field and only when you approach them do you see that they are human beings. The materials should be of sacking, bits of various colored cloth—the witches MUST NOT IN ANY WAY APPEAR SUPERNATURAL; they must look slightly "odd." If you have a Negress in the group it would be good if she could play one of the witches. No wigs, no horns, no wings. They should look like piles of muck and rubble—like alcoholics or drug addicts that one finds sleeping in a doorway on a very cold and rainly night in December. They huddle—they are "closed in."

Since the play has to be cut for this production, some of the "interesting" smaller parts find their roles very much mangled. Duncan has a whole scene cut. The Porter may have half his scene cut. Banquo has his death scene cut. The Witches have the big cauldron scene cut. If I find that we are playing very swiftly, AND WE MUST, I may be able to restore some of these shorter scenes, but I can't promise.

Q.   How important is a knowledge of the physical form of the theatre for which the play was written?

Blatchley: I think it is very important to realize that Shakespeare wrote as he did because of the conditions he was in. The same way that Edward Albee, for example, knows that if he writes a play that has four characters, he has much more chance of getting it put on Broadway than if he writes a play that has 54 characters. Now this doesn't mean that he is a hypocritical man who compromises. This consideration has to be somewhere in the back of his brain. And in the same way, these considerations that were imposed on Shakespeare—the kind of platform he

had, the kind of stage he had where these plays were performed, the fact that women were played by men—all
these things he took into account, but what is marvelous
in him is that these aren't kind of brakes to his talent, they
seem to inspire him. Do you see what I mean? So I don't
think that there is any compromise in it or rather, if there
is, he makes out of the compromise rather than losing
because of it.

Q. You are an actor, teacher, and stage director, How do
you direct?

Blatchley: The most unhappy memories I have are really of first
readings. Actors know what the set up is. They get asked
to play a part because they are the right size or shape,
because they're a star or because nobody knows them or
because somebody knows them. Then an actor comes
along and he sits at a table and the director then talks for
an hour and tells actors what the play is all about, tells
them what he thinks about the play. Then actors sit and
read it. Some of the actors don't know each other; others
do know each other. An actor shouldn't want to know
what I think about MACBETH; I want to know what my
actors think of MACBETH. I think it's terribly important
that the actors and I discover a play together. So I prefer
not to work the usual way. I prefer simply to talk through
the play with everybody reading different kinds of things.
Nobody necessarily reading the role of Macbeth or Lady
Macbeth, but everybody reading a bit of this and a bit of
that and a bit of the other. And, most important of all,
stopping all the time. I think an actor should stop
whenever there is anything he does not understand. This
requires, of course, a tremendous kind of humility,
because to put your hand up and say "what does 'If it
were done when 'tis done then twere well . . .' mean?"
one has to be tremendously humble to do that, I think.

But I think that unless one does do it, one never digs this play; one will only get a kind of general feeling about it.

Oh, yes! MACBETH is a play about ambition. This is what people tell us. I don't think it is about ambition at all. I don't know what it is about myself, really. I have some ideas and I think actors probably do have some ideas. So, there's a copy of MACBETH. I put it down there and I think the actors and I should now kick it about a bit. I want actors to tell me, please, (I presume they have all read MACBETH) tell me about MACBETH, tell me what they think is good about it; what is exciting about it; what is terrible about it; what is boring about it; what they don't understand about it; what they think our problems are going to be in terms of doing it. Rehearsal is not a classroom, understand; it is not students and teachers and that sort of feeling about it at all. It's only that I think I'll be able to talk a bit if the actors ask questions. And what I say may be somewhat interesting, simply because they've asked that question. I think it works better than if I simply sat around spieling away for hours on end.

I think each character has a function. For example, if you take the English doctor, which is nearly always cut, and which, in fact, when I started on the play I said, "We've got to make some cuts in order to keep it in its proper duration. One of the first things that will go will be that English doctor." This was because I thought I knew the play. Then I read it again. And I started to question. Why the hell is there an English doctor here; what is he here for? And, of course, once you ask that question, the answer is that that, in fact, is the turning point of the play. Because the imagery of that particular instant in the play goes from devils, evil, blood, to grace, God, and all that section of imagery. So that suddenly you find in this chaotic kind of nightmare of a world, a resolution in terms of goodness which happens between Malcolm and Macduff because an English doctor comes on and talks about the great God-given healing power of King Edward or whatever his name is. So that one begins to see how important that is and I feel that it is the same with every single character in the play. I think that if you look at a play like PERICLES or RICHARD III, there are very often people who simply serve the function of pushing the plot line forward. But I think in this play this is not the case, which is why I think it is one of the most difficult plays to cut. Anything you cut, you cut a somehow minor perfection. Minor, maybe, but a perfection nevertheless. And I think we shall find as we go through this that your doubts about the incompleteness of people will be soon dispersed. I think also what we must be terribly careful about (and I think that this is a danger in approaching Shakespeare) is that too many of us have the tendency to think of the plays in terms of characters. We tend to forget that a play like MACBETH is a poem. It is a dramatic poem. It is as complete as any kind of symphonic work, or any kind of set of variations by a composer like Bach. It also happens to have people in it. Very interesting people, very interesting characters, but I think that one must always be terribly careful in approaching a Shakespearean play not to judge it from the point of view of characters, but to try to judge it first of all from the point of view of what it is, which is a poem put on the stage. Then, of course, the problem is to find how these characters are people. This is what is so marvelous with Shakespeare; that he is able to express his poem in terms of people.

Q. You have been directing opera for some years now. Is directing opera very different from directing plays?

Blatchley: Music is only *one* component of opera. What people say, think, believe and communicate; their relationship and their *inner* life is what it is all about. Those notes and silences are only one of the ways of communicating this. Anything that I've said here represents also my general attitude to opera.

SHAKESPEARE

FILM

"Shakespeare's Theatre and Macbeth": obtainable, for rental and purchase, through the Institute for Advanced Studies in the Theatre Arts (IASTA), P.O. Box 1106, Radio City Station, New York, NY 10101 or Gil Forman, 310 W. 56th St., #1B, New York, NY 10019.

SELECTED BIBLIOGRAPHY

Abbott, E. A. *A Shakespearean Grammar.* New York: Dover Publications, Inc., 1966.

Baldwin, Thomas Whitfield. *The Organization and Personnel of the Shakespearean Company.* Princeton: Princeton U. Press, 1927.

Bradbrook, M. C. *The Rise of the Common Player.* Cambridge: Harvard U. Press, 1962

Brooke, C. F. Tucker and Paradise, Nathaniel Burton. *English Drama 1580-1642.* New York: D.C. Heath and Company, 1933.

MATERIALS AND BACKGROUND

Harbage, Alfred. *Shakespeare's Audience.* New York: Columbia U. Press, 1941.

Levin, Harry. *Shakespeare and the Revolution of the Times.* New York: Oxford U. Press, 1976.

Palmer, John. *Political Characters of Shakespeare.* London: Macmillan and Co., Limited, 1945.

Tillyard, E. M. W. *The Elizabethan World Picture.* New York: Macmillan Company, 1944.

MUSIC

Byrd, William. Madrigals; Motels; Anthems. Saltire Singers (4-66) Lyr. 7156.

Dowland, John. First Booke of Songes 1597. Rooley, Consort of Musicke. 2-Oiseau DSLO-508/9.

Holborne, Antony. Pauens, Galliards, Almans, and other short AEirs. Bruggen Consort Tel. 641074.

KABUKI

"theatre as beauty of form"

L.T.M.

Kabuki and Noh Theatre are uniquely Japanese, but the two National theatre styles differ greatly, Kabuki being more passionate, complex, ornate, immature, and extroverted. Kabuki tends to permit greater activity, and greater participation on the part of actors and audience. The audience for Kabuki comes away from a performance entertained and catharted. It has rid itself of something rather than having acquired something. It has been like a dream in which one awakens refreshed and recuperated, ready to face life's less acceptable reality.

Kabuki developed in the 16th century during the Yedo era, (during which much of the development of Kabuki took place), when distinctions between the warrior class and the commoners was more rigidly observed than at any other time in Japan's history. Kabuki was patronized mainly by the merchants (of those days), who had become increasingly powerful economically, but had to remain socially inferior as they belonged to the commoner class. For them, Kabuki was significant as an artistic means by which to sublimate their emotions. Thus, fundamental themes of Kabuki plays are conflicts within a feudalistic system.

The Kabuki auditorium is long and shallow and contains two balconies. The total seating capacity is usually just under 2,000.

The distance from the proscenium to the rear row of seats is 55 feet. The width of the stage is approximately 90 feet. Visibility and audibility are excellent throughout the auditorium. A significant and characteristic feature of the Kabuki Theatre is the runway known as the "hanamichi."

By means of this runway, which is equipped with its own footlights on either side, Kabuki actors may make theatrical exits or entrances out through the auditorium. At a position approximately seven-tenths of the length of the runway from the rear of the auditorium, there is an electric elevator in the runway which is customarily reserved for the entrance and exits of demons or supernatural characters.

All Kabuki performances have a morning program running from approximately 10:30 to 5 in the afternoon; the evening program is from 5:30 until 10 at night. The typical program consists of a number of scenes from different plays of the extensive Kabuki repertory.

There are numerous intermissions, ranging from 10 to 30 minutes, allowing for elaborate costume and scene changes. During this time refreshments or luncheon or dinner may be taken in one of several restaurants within the theatre. Though not as flourishing as it once was, the Kabuki theatre is still a popular theatre and draws large audiences.

Mastery of the style or patterns *(kata)* of Kabuki acting begins in Japan at the age of five and requires an apprenticeship which may last forty years. The challenge to both Kabuki director and his American actors was to capture something of the spirit and aesthetics of the 400-year-old tradition. What took the audiences by storm was not only a remarkable demonstration of American actors' mastery of a fantastic technique of acting, but also the assault on the unconscious by both the Kabuki style and the content of the particular play, NARUKAMI.

*   *   *

Onoe Baiko VII, famed *onnagata* and actor-dancer of classic roles in the Kabuki theatre, is the eldest son of the late Onoe Kikugoro VI. Baiko made his stage debut in 1920 at the age of five. In addition to his Kabuki training, he received a University education. In 1935, he was given the name of Kikunosuke II and began to build a reputation for himself as an *onnagata* actor (one who plays female roles). He also distinguished himself in young hero roles and as a solo dancer. He succeeded to the distinguished title Baiko in 1947 and became a leader in the Kikugoro Troupe in 1949. He has been designated by the Emperor and government of Japan as a national monument and treasure.

Onoe Baiko VII left his native land for the first time when he came to IASTA in 1960 to direct THUNDER GOD (NARUKAMI).

INTERVIEW WITH ONOE BAIKO VII

Q. How do you define the style for a production of a Kabuki play like THUNDER GOD (NARUKAMI)?

Baiko: When I talk of the style of Kabuki I enter into the beauty of form, *yoshikibi,** from my own heart. In Kabuki it is im-

---

*The Japanese *Kanji* or Chinese characters were adopted by the Japanese more than a thousand years ago. Read as Chinese, it means "energy holding or maintaining."

portant to make the false look true and you have to do it in a beautiful way. *Kata* can be translated as form (individual traditional stage business). When Princess Taema is pouring sake for Priest Narukami, there is a traditional *kata* or pattern of movement executed by Taema. Just to pour sake from the over-sized cup with the wrists is contrary to the totality of dance movement *(kata)* of Kabuki: the kneeling *onnagata* enacting Taema starts the movement of pouring from the soles of the feet, the movement is carried through the torso to the wrists which tip the cup to pour. The maturing, talented *onnagata* may have achieved the traditional *kata* to perfection, but if it lacks *kimochi*, it is empty. The *kimochi*, the feeling true to character and action, must fill the vessel that is *kata*.

Some may say *kata* or style(s) of Kabuki evolved out of the early actors' motivation to display the elaborate, richly colored and embroidered kimonos. One cannot deny it. Kabuki, as well, is dance. Taema's simple act of pouring sake involves the whole body, as does all acting in Kabuki.

When we speak of *kata*, however, we do not speak of style alone. *Kata* includes handprops, costumes, stage settings, music, and the script.

Q. What are some of the elements of Kabuki style?

Baiko: Spectacular beauty, *yoshikibi*, constitutes a fundamental characteristic of Kabuki. In fact, sets, costumes and the makeup in Kabuki are recognized to be the most lavish and extravagant in the world. The wonderful spectacle of superb color, as sets unfold, dazzle the eyes even when the spectator is not convinced of the validity of the story.

Music is an integral part of the art of Kabuki. The percussive effects, the sounding of wooden clappers at the opening and closing of the play, are among Kabuki's most unique elements. With rhythmical, staccato measures, the wooden clappers underscore the actions during the

94

course of the performance. The most distinguishing feature of Kabuki as a theatrical art is that all elements place primary emphasis upon the actor. At the heart of Kabuki acting is classical Japanese dance; so that 80% of the training is physical and 20% is vocal. Even in a realistic Kabuki play, the most trivial gestures are frequently more closely related to dance than to acting. Nearly every gesture is accompanied by music. There are scenes where symbolic actions have been carried to a level of abstraction, and the resulting formalized actions of the character are no longer relevant, but directly conflict with a rational interpretation of the role.

Kabuki acting may be considered to be a series of close-ups, as in film, and during these closeups attention should be focused on the principal actor. Part of the beauty of Kabuki is in vocal delivery, closely akin to singing.

There is another element not to be overlooked. A Kabuki performance has distilled every element of realism and sentiment from the moment, so that all that is left is a crystalized, formalized statement. The actors on stage do not live it, but express it, leaving the audience free to feel and to cry.

The costume is very important in Kabuki because the actor must be able to make the costume dance with him. Working with the costumes makes the actors realize how important a costume is to their acting. It is important to be totally in control of the costume when a Kabuki actor momentarily freezes (mie)* in a dance.

Kabuki actors learn that behind the style there is reason; it isn't arbitrary dance movement. A natural movement has been made theatrical, polished and improved by succeeding generations of actors. Kabuki actors do not de-

---

*Read as Chinese, the character means "to perceive and obtain."

L.T.M.

pend upon physical attractiveness; they depend upon their art.

The basic dance posture is to squat slightly, bending forward from the hip (basic Japanese dance posture). Kabuki utilizes a "sitting in the saddle" position. All Kabuki actors watch the lead in a play; they have to breathe with him, know his acting, his way of thinking. The actors are never supposed to turn their faces fully away from the audience.

Q. What is the *mie* and its function?

Baiko: The *mie* and final pose of the play are very important in establishing the status of the characters. Hands and arms of the actor lead the turning of his body; never does another part of the body lead. The actor, standing on one foot and holding his arm before him in a set position, turns his head abruptly, jerking it to a full stop. Crossing his eyes, it is a *mie*. Simultaneously, a stage assistant at the side of the stage strikes blocks of wood on the floor to punctuate the pose. The use of wood blocks, for percussive effect, is an incredibly stimulating sound to an audience; it builds suspense and emotion.

Q. As an actor, what are some of the aspects of the acting of an *onnagata**?

Baiko: The position of the thumb is very significant: a female character's thumb should never show. The hand should look smaller than it really is, with the fingers closed together and curved and the thumb hidden. A man's hands are held wide apart to look larger and stronger. An actor needs tremendous coordination of body, suppleness, ability to adjust from one position to another, and he must have perfect balance.

---

*Read as Chinese, the Chinese characters mean "female shape."

Q. Would you characterize voice quality and style of delivery used by the Kabuki actors?

Baiko: Even in the realistic, domestic plays, speaking is not that of daily life, but is an idealized elocution. Long monologues, in particular, have fascinating cadences half way between singing and conversion. This is especially evident when dialogue and monologues are delivered to the accompaniment of music. Too much inflection in the voice indicates a lower social status; a character such as Princess Taema in NARUKAMI is limited to one tone of voice, compared to the vocal freedom and range allowed Narukami, the hero priest. Vocal and physical discipline, economy and pin-pointing of emotions, and magnification of reality are all necessary in Kabuki. Expressiveness and beauty of stylized movement make for a theatre of color, glamour, excitement and the extraordinary. A change of personality of character can be represented by the taking off of one sleeve of the outer kimono (a *kata*); it represents a sudden change of atmosphere. The fan is to the dancer what the sword is to the warrior. With the fan, many things can be symbolized: a mountain, a flowing stream, a water fall, a parasol, a hat, a bottle for drinking, a cup, the writing of a letter, and so on.

Q. How do you prepare for a role?

Baiko: I read the script and analyze the character I am going to play. I begin to study the character. The interpretation of a character is different from one actor to another. A part means something different to each actor*.

---

*With permission for reprinting from Educational Theatre Journal and Professor Leiter.

Q. Suppose, for instance, the part that you are to play is that of a jealous woman. Is there a set Kabuki way for expressing jealousy, or does the actor find his own way for expressing the emotion?

Baiko: Both. If I can use a traditional form to portray an emotion, I do so. If the traditional form in a certain scene does not suit my style, I think it over and proceed to perform as I see fit, even if it means a change from the conventional manner. *

Q. Then would you say that the actor in Kabuki begins by learning basic externals, while the experienced actor gives new life to the old forms—or finds new forms for himself?

Baiko: I would say so. The forms, you know, have come to be only because of an interior psychological need to express meanings. Even the *mie* have each a meaning. The "stone throwing" *mie* was developed because in a certain play at a certain point, a stone had to be thrown.

Q. Do you try to forget yourself in the very exaggerated Kabuki roles?

Baiko: I try to. Though the world of Kabuki plays is far away from the present day, the actor should try to enter the heart of the character.

Q. Is it possible that discussions during the rehearsal may result in a performance style different from the play's conventional style

Baiko There is rarely a change in the style of acting a piece from the classical repertoire. The forms there are too fixed. However, I may occasionally want to act in a new form in these plays, and when I do, there is a noticeable change.

---

* Ibid.

A reciprocal influence then becomes apparent in the acting. The actors, of course, will have agreed on the new forms beforehand.

Q. Is it important to preserve a traditional Kabuki?

Baiko: Traditions on stage have to be kept. But not necessarily the offstage traditions; some dressing room *(gakuya)* traditions have to be changed; and bad traditions are to be discarded one by one. It is not that all traditions or customs are feudalistic, but some are bad. An example of a bad custom would be what we call *shumei*, a name-giving ceremony. In a broad sense it would be comparable to a Western actor giving his autograph to every person in the audience before the performance.

Traditions of training actors, staging classics, must and will be preserved. The acting levels of Kabuki, playing full front to the audience, became fixed by the stage and theatre of the 18th century. The *hanamichi*, for certain plays the double *hanamichi*, brought the actors into the midst of the spectators. Old prints (wood block) show spectators crowded into areas of the stage proper. In that much smaller Kabuki theatre (today's Kabuki theatres have a proscenium 90 feet wide), the use of candles for stage lighting necessitated proximity of audience to the actors; for the same reason some early troupes discovered that the conventionalized dead-white makeup *(kesho)* on the actors faces heightened visibility of the actors' faces. The turntable stage, the *mawari butai,* of Kabuki may very well be the first turntable stage in use in a theatre. Western theatre influence in the 19th century modified the stage which retreated behind the proscenium. We are, now, used to the present shape of the Kabuki theatre.

Q. What is the system of training of the Kabuki actor?

Baiko: The training of a Kabuki actor starts with dance, because in Kabuki everything must be expressed beautifully. To achieve this, dance is at the very basis of training for acting. This will not change. After this the child actor is taught the *samisen*, the *tsusumi*, small hand drums. Each help develop the actor's use of rhythm. This system will continue, for at the National Theatre, there is the school for training actors in Kabuki.

Q. Why does a spectator return to see the same performance repeated by the same performer?

Baiko: A Kabuki buff or scholar is interested in seeing differences in an actor's interpretation, seeing how he has grown since the last performance.

As supporting actors change from performance to performance, these actors surrounding the leading actor may change and improve from performance to performance. The serious spectator perceives reactions of the leading actor as casts change.

Q. Do actors, as in the traditional Kabuki family, rear their children to be actors?

Baiko: In my case, I have given my children their freedom. However, actors' children accompany their parents to the theatre; they quite naturally and spontaneously develop an interest in the theatre, wanting to be like their parents. But if my children were to say that they did not want to become actors, I would not make them become actors.

Q. What is the public attitude today towards actors?

Baiko: From the public's viewpoint, we actors are practicing old things; therefore, we are away from reality, but, being away from reality only happens on stage; once offstage we are just like other people.

We are not discriminated against. We look at the recent popularity of Kabuki with pleasant surprise, and we hope more people will come to like Kabuki.

Q. How does a master actor teach young actors to be proud of being an actor?

Baiko: A master teacher first teaches his pupils how to become great actors. He gives advice, not only in acting, but also in daily living so that he will not be less an actor than any other actor. Ultimately, an actor's goal may be to outshine all other actors, but certainly he would not wish to put to shame his fellow actors nor his master, but he'd want to live up to the expectations of the troupe.

Q. What method of direction did you use with American actors?

Baiko: Truth is the same among artists anywhere; in this instance, I think, my method was the same as that of any other director: to search for truth within the actor. But, we worked from the outside in. The actor first learned from me the exterior movement, and then filled it in with meaning. I went, of necessity, into immediate blocking. There was no time for deep probing of character. With my assistant, Miyoko Watanabe, I set the movements and line readings. My American actors told me there was always a great feeling of tradition in rehearsals; they did not question my direction. They felt, they said, the need and desire to become part of a tradition. Trained in Kabuki, I took a sharp interest in details, and as I had been trained from childhood, I asked them to copy my form. I learned that aside from dance training, this was an unusual procedure for American actors, but I was convinced it was necessary and was enjoyable for the actors. I knew exactly what I wanted in space, and I moulded the actors into the patterns of the play. There is no room for improvision in this style. I worked for visual perfection and a filling out of the emotions, but in my staging of NARUKAMI, I left the creative process up to the actor—outside rehearsal. I wanted and demanded great precision of movement.

Most of the early rehearsals were done in front of mirrors, with my kneeling in front of the actor, perfecting every detail. I would hint politely, relying on the individual actor's creative ability. Beyond Kabuki movement and physical placement, I was satisfied to prod the actor a bit and then sit back and guide his development, interjecting only on the broader corrections. This, I think, is a much more satisfying way of working for the actor who is trying to "stretch," as they say.

Q. How did the American actor respond to this kind of style work?

Baiko: They learned by doing. They learned how to wed thought, action and speech; to make the action suit the word. Because of the tightness of form, they learned, I believe, how to be specific without fear or a feeling of rigidity. They became more deeply aware of the need for discipline and craftsmanship. Compassion and understanding are keynotes to good acting, and they only come with a greater "look-see" into lives other than our own. They told me that they learned concentration, endurance and control. I think they realize more strongly than ever, the technique of clarity of gesture and movement to illuminate meaning. With my assistant and interpreter, a bicultural American, I strove to give them help in the areas of vocal and physical discipline through emphasizing the values of economy, pin-pointing emotions, and magnification of reality.

Q. Can American actors learn Kabuki style?

Baiko: Those who had a strong desire to learn, have learned. These Americans were better than Japanese actors who have been exposed to Kabuki all their lives. It is better to do it once than to see it a thousand times!

KABUKI

FILM

"Aspects of the Kabuki Theatre": obtainable, for rental and purchase, through the Institute for Advanced Studies in the Theatre Arts (IASTA), P.O. Box 1106, Radio City Station, New York, NY 10019.

SELECTED BIBLIOGRAPHY

Bowers, Faubion. *Japanese Theatre*. New York: Hermitage House, 1952.

Brandon, James R. *Kabuki, Five Classic Plays*. Cambridge: Harvard U. Press, 1975.

Dunn, C. J. and Bunzo Torigoe. *The Actors Analects*. New York: Columbia U. Press, 1969.

Ernst, Earle. *The Kabuki Theatre*. New York: Oxford U. Press, 1956.

Ernst, Earle. *Three Japanese Plays*. New York: Oxford U. Press, 1959.

Gunji, Masakatsu. *Kabuki*. Tokyo & Palo Alto: Kodansha Ltd., 1969.

Haar, Francis. *Japanese Theatre in Highlight*. Tokyo: Charles E. Tuttle, 1952.

Halford, A. S. and G. M. *The Kabuki Handbook*. Rutland, VT: Tuttle, 1956.

Keene, Donald. *Chushingura*. New York: Columbia U. Press, 1971.

Kincaid, Zoe. *Kabuki*. New York: Benjamin Blom, Inc., 1966.

Motofuji, F. T. *The Love of Izayoe and Seishin*. Tokyo: Charles E. Tuttle, 1966.

Pronko, Leonard. *Theatre, East and West*. L.A.: U. of California, 1967.

Scott, A. C. *Kabuki Costume*. Tokyo: Charles E. Tuttle, 1966.

Shaver, R. M. *Kabuki Costume*. Tokyo: Charles E. Tuttle, 1966.

Toita, Y. *Kabuki, The Popular Theatre*. New York: Walker/Weatherhill, 1970.

Yonezo, Hamamura and others. *Kabuki*. Tokyo: Kankysha Ltd., 1956.

Yoshida, C. *Kabuki*. Tokyo: Japan Times Ltd., 1977.

MATERIALS AND BACKGROUND

Albery, Nobuko. *Balloon Top*. New York: Pantheon, 1978.

Benedict, Ruth. *The Chrysanthemum and the Sword*. Rutland, VT: Tuttle, 1959.

Debary, Wm. T. *Japanese Tradition.* New York: Columbia U. Press, 1972.

Hearn, LaFadio. *Japan, An Attempt at Interpretation.* Rutland, VT: Tuttle, 1955.

Kawasaki, Ichiro. *Japan Unmasked.* Palo Alto: Kodansha, 1966.

Keyes, Roger S. and Mizushima, Keiko. *The Theatrical World of Osaka Prints.* Boston: David R. Godin, 1973.

Mitchell, John D. and Schwartz, E. K. "A Psychoanalytic Approach to Kabuki: A Study in Personality and Culture". *The Journal of Psychology.* New York: 1961.

Mitchell, J. D. and Drew, G. "Ein Besuch Im Neuen Kabuki-Theater in Osaka," *Buhnentechnische Rundschau.* Berlin: June, 1960.

Rudolfsky, Bernard. *The Kimono Mind.* New York: Doubleday, 1965.

MUSIC BOOKS

Malm, W. P. *Nagauta, Heart of Kabuki Music.* Tokyo: Charles E. Tuttle, 1963.

Malm, W. P. *Japanese Music.* Tokyo: Charles E. Tuttle, 1959.

MUSIC

Geza Music from the Kabuki (Phonodisc) Nonesuch Records H-72012 77-288326.

Kabuki Nagauta Music (Phonodisc) Lyricord LLST 7134 24-99533.

The Azuma Kabuki Musicians. Columbia ML 4925.

JACOBEAN: DUCHESS OF MALFI

"death and rhetoric as theatre"

J.D.M.

That Webster "was much obsessed by death" is well known. So, of course, were all the Jacobean dramatists, and their plays depict societies bloated with corruption and guilt, bent on self-destruction. Broadly, we can trace this preoccupation to the decline of Christian certainty, to the growing awareness that science was uncovering more mysteries than it could resolve, and to the political and religious turmoil of the time. By the beginning of the 17th Century, if not earlier, the Copernican displacement of man and his world from the center of a universe that was presumed to be benevolently cared for by a loving God-Father was throwing into question men's belief that human life was of spiritual significance and value. "We are merely the Starres tennys-balls (stroke and banded/Which way please them)."

All the major tragedies of this period were written by men who stood aghast before the discovery that the whole process of living may be no more than a huge cosmic joke. "The new philosophy throws all in doubt." It hardly needs to be said that the experience of doubt and meaninglessness on a cosmic scale is not alien to our own time. Camus has described that "weariness tinged with amazement" follows upon the discovery of the unreasonable silence of the world. Perhaps for men like Shakespeare and Webster it was an even profounder shock than it has been for ourselves, because they lived in a world which was still to some extent governed by ideas of order and value, both social and religious, which we have never known. The tension between the two ways of experiencing the world is certainly most clear in Shakespeare, who seems to have fought his way through to a personal security which could accept chaos and order, death and life. Webster does not seem to have effected this reconciliation; with him we are more aware that the experience of living was corrupted at the source: that whatever positive values might flourish for a time, their existence would always be threatened and finally uprooted by the incoherence and destructiveness of the surrounding chaos.

> "Oh this gloomy world,
> In what a shadow, or deepe pit of darkness,
> Doth (womanish, and fearfull) mankind live!"

The individual may justify his actions as best he can, but he will in the end come only to "a little point, a kind of nothing." The best that he can do is to die well.

Against his weary knowledge of the injustice and corruption of the world, Webster sets the positive affirmation of the Duchess, who at least decides what she is, and what she wants to do, and enjoys her freedom of action. In this exercise of freedom, her life acquires a permanent value. In the end, the pressures of the social order she has rejected must crush the Duchess, but in killing her that society also kills itself and leaves no more behind it "than should one/Fall in a frost, and leave this print in snow/As soon as the sun shines, it ever melts,/Both forme and matter." Incidentally, the story of the DUCHESS OF MALFI is a true one.

DESMOND O'DONOVAN

DESMOND O'DONOVAN, IASTA's visiting director from London, began directing plays at Oxford, where he was a student of English Literature under Professor Nevill Coghill. His professional career started with productions of OTHELLO, THE GLASS MENAGERIE and ALL MY SONS at the Salisbury Playhouse. Subsequently, Mr. O'Donovan directed Wedekind's SPRING AWAKENING and Peter Gill's THE SLEEPER'S DEN for the Royal Court Theatre. He has also directed at the London Arts Theatre and the Hampstead Theatre Club.

When the National Theatre was formed in 1963, Mr. O'Donovan joined as an assistant director and worked as Sir Laurence Olivier's assistant for the inaugural production of HAMLET. He was co-director, with John Dexter, of the original production of THE ROYAL HUT OF THE SUN. Mr. O'Donovan was guest director of TRELAWNEY OF THE 'WELLS' and THE CLANDESTINE MARRIAGE at the Chichester Festival before becoming Staff Director at the National Theatre.

THE DUCHESS OF MALFI was presented at the IASTA Theatre, New York, on April 6, 1966. The interview was in London, 1967.

INTERVIEW WITH DESMOND O'DONOVAN

Q. How do you define style?

109

O'Donovan: Style is a very French word that we all find ourselves using. It seems to be a pre-supposition about how things should be done. A style is not something one can consciously impose or really worry about. Style comes from one's sense of knowing what one's doing. The truth of the play is the truth of the various situations in which the dramatist has put the actors, depicting the characters. Doing the play the right way, one should find the right style for doing it.

The difficulty of these plays is that they're written in verse and this tends to betray actors and directors into a kind of false and poetic style. This accounts for the fact that recently is has become a fashion or practice to say, "Don't bother about the verse." That is only true to some extent. If you can develop a good ear for verse structure, you can develop an ear for the kind of music which is a sense music and not a word music. But it is music. I think you will find that that is a discipline, a direction.

Q. Could you give specific examples?

O'Donovan: For example, simple things like not breaking the line, observing the punctuation, observing the stress. All of these things.

In fact they are the material of the actor's characterization. We do a certain amount of work on the language— the phrasing. In the minutiae we often find what the dramatists thinks of the character. This is not only a problem in verse plays written several hundred years ago; it's in all plays.

Because of Stanislavski, the method, etc. . . . the danger is that the text becomes peripheral. Particularly when it is a text that one does not deeply understand or deeply sympathize with. I mean in a sense that it is not a vernacular text. Actually it wasn't a vernacular text for the Elizabethans. They didn't speak in blank verse, although their prose rhythms are very often more like blank verse

110

than ours. For the Elizabethans blank verse was more like spoken language than ours is.

The value of the play is to establish the primacy of the word: to make the imagery of the verse do the work for the actors. It is the verse that thinks. The thinking and feeling are not something to go on past words. It is the verse that thinks for you. The triple process of: think, feel and then say. The technique is that these should be *one*. That's very important.

We are so insensitive to the rhythm of the verse. One breaks the line sometimes because the language is unfamiliar and the actor realizes it's unfamiliar to the audience and sometimes he becomes very heavy. On the other hand the danger of this is that one begins to chant. One can get into a kind of musical pattern and get carried along with the beauty of the words and it doesn't mean very much.

We're concerned with finding the truth, and if we find the truth we will have found the style.

Q. Do you feel there is a national, English, style?

O'Donovan: There is no "English" way of doing Webster. There is no English style. Since the time of Garrick, English acting has been renowned (which has sometimes shocked the French) for its kind of realism.

Q. Does each play have its own correct style?

O'Donovan: I'll answer it this way. The truth is being faithful to the conception of the author. Our guide is simply the text and what he has made clear of his intention in that text.

The most useful thing we can do with this play is to find out what Webster is doing. That is, to go through a process of imaginative indentification with his picture of the world. Let the play speak for itself through the actors.

D.C.

Q. How does one clarify for an audience pressures which dictate behavior and relationships?

O'Donovan: Jacobean writing occurred at a time when the theatre had the function—occasionally this happened in other cultures—of being the central expression of the feeling of the age. And the theatre is an extrovert art.

THE DUCHESS OF MALFI is not a fantasy. It is based on a true-life story, just as if it had appeared in a newspaper. This is important for the actors to remember at all times.

The real imaginative effort one has to make, in a play like this, is about death; for the Elizabethans and the Jacobeans it was right at the front. It's not the first time nor will it be the last that this obsession with death has occurred. It tends to happen at a point when religious faith (in the case of Christianity and the real positive achievement of Christianity) has tended to have expended itself. What was left in this case was an afterglow of the Christian world view.

This obsession included an almost morbid sense of the decay of the flesh. It certainly is an element that has to be taken strongly into account by us in this play, and in almost any play written at this time. It's something which is peculiarly disturbing to us because it is something we don't want to think about particularly. But a great deal of the imaginative life of the play does depend upon this sense, the degree in which one can think oneself into that particular obsession: death and decay.

With the character of the Duchess, Webster does choose to present something much more positive. All the characters of the play sniff the air for death at every opportunity, but in the love affair of Antonio and the Duchess one gets a sense of a real live, mature, sexual experience which arms the Duchess against the coming of death. Nobody's been particularly armed or impervious to death, but Webster achieves through this love relationship, a sense of the Duchess being the thing which death cannot touch.

Q.   What is your approach to the actor in rehearsal and to the text?

O'Donovan: The question is, not what do actors want from me but how shall we, together, discover the author's intention.

I choose an edition that had the original punctuation as it came down from Webster. My view of the original punctuation is that it is like a musical notation coming from the author.

To explore and see how far we can go, exploring the rhythms, to work on the verse in a certain way (not necessarily that this is the way for actors to work on their parts), but it is an approach to the way the text is laid out.

It can be useful because I get the feeling when I read this play that Webster's (and Shakespeare's) actors probably spoke a lot faster than we do. We've gotten in the habit of acting in between the gaps, as if the acting was one line and the words on another. While acting I noticed that on the pauses actors tend to put in the "ah's" and "hums" and little laughs here and there—British actors do it too—to give a kind of lift. In beginning of speeches it particularly happens, as if the actor were climbing on to the speech and getting off.

I'm sure that the Elizabethan actors were much more mobile, that they used words much more sexually than we do. I cannot teach an Elizabethan style of verse speaking, but looking at the text, one will see that the rhythm of it is so important. It will do a lot of the work for the actor. He can chew into it a bit.

One must always remember that one is speaking a text (unless one is specifically improvising) and that the author, if he knows his job, has usually got a better instinct about how it should be acted. This Elizabethan playwright,

Webster,would seemed to have used parentheses as we would today use commas.

Webster's audiences must have responded much more deeply than we do to the words and the images; since they had nothing else on the stage, they communicated by language much more than we. They had a much more sensual response to words. The actor should try to work with all the images—this play's packed with image—to find an equivalent sensation in himself. For example, the word 'Screech Owl,' he doesn't have to demonstrate it, but if it is a word for him that is colored, that color will communicate and the actor will have to spend time on it. He has to spend a lot of time on certain words. Actors sit on certain words. I want to get the actor to be *carried* by the speech. There's also a danger that he'll just get carried away!

What I feel reading over the text is that the colon is more like a 'flick' to carry the actor on rather than a 'stop.' I think that the comma was less important to Webster or Shakespeare than it is to us. It's more a reading thing. Yes, I think the comma is not something emphasized in the speaking, but I think the colon is a 'flick of the wrist' and the full stop, the period, is for them a *full stop*. Of course, they may tend to use a colon where we would use a full stop, but if the actor recognizes the colon as a 'flick of the wrist,' he'll find that he's speaking the verse more quickly.

The other thing that he should look for is the length of the sentences: units ending in colons are like sub-units leading up to the full stop. Note, there are not many full stops. Also, I want the actor to notice the length of the words that Webster uses. The actor suddenly gets a series of monosyllables; "Actor, sensitize yourself to that sort of thing which will then give you a difference in pace." There is such a variety of pace and intonation with the use of long vowels and then short, quick accentuated words. My, it must have been colossal, it must have been like piano playing.

I do not try to do a pseudo-Elizabethan production, but I try to find the life of the play. To speak it with speed and to act it with speed is the way in which it was done and was intended to be done by the author. It moves fast and in a theatre of Elizabethan size the actor can get away with it, but it does involve speaking very well and having a very flexible palate.

I get the sensation of having to speak in a certain time. One might almost be able to conduct the DUCHESS OF MALFI. It's not that one wants to be musical, but a sense of having to say a line to a beat and to vary the beat somehow gives one much greater freedom. Actors play one moment and then at that moment there is the word the actor sort of wants to color. Listening to verse is sort of like being hit from time to time with balloons. I find that sort of tension rather like skiing, rather exciting. One has to approach a play from all sorts of directions. This approach through the verse is one method of attack. There is something syncopated about it. It's a more direct way to an audience emotionally.

We must be aware of where characters share a line, the balance of a line of verse can be picked up by the other characters but the units of a line have to be observed. *A line is a unit that has five beats.* The pulsation, even in a broken line, has to be kept to the five beats of the iambic pentameter.

Q. Would you summarize some of these acting tips?

O'Donovan: Be conscious of when the text goes into shorter words. Think in long sections: full stop to full stop. Not every colon means the same thing. It's good to try to say it within a certain time sequence. You need more breath to take a long section. You can speed along when it's more factual. When you come to a passage going into an image or images (open vowels in sequence as well) slow down. Get a sense of space there. Variety and color of the words are to be observed. Staccato can be good, but not at the expense of the wider songs. Don't jump on a word just because you suddenly realize you're going "chop-chop." "Ski!" One has to change direction, as in skiing. Use the image of skiing. The actors usually cope with language like this verse by underlining very heavily certain words. However, pace and punctuation tend to give the unity of the speech. Caution: one tends to lose the meaning, and only remember words. The actor must be like quicksilver. Express fear—yes, but express it in three beats! Though the emotional pattern is always very structured, THE DUCHESS OF MALFI is not as rhythmical as PHÈDRE is within a very much more regular and definite rhythm. DUCHESS is much more haphazard, not as much emotional pressure (as in PHÈDRE) going all the time. It's almost impossible not to get a rather fast beat. What is more difficult is finding the parts to slow down and open up. Find a common way of doing: what one means by style.

Be able to take up where the other actor has left off. Get the flow between characters. Try to find the rise and fall, taking the stage at certain points. There is nothing mysterious about the use of the long line, the short line.

In general, do not break a speech to get oneself off to a new thought. Go lightly from "one note to another" without necessarily having to stop and rethink. It's all directed toward making the thought go into the text, not somewhere beside it.

Each of the words should be given their kind of sensual value, e.g. "Cut my throat with diamonds . . .," a sharper sound, a sharper thought, than "To be smothered with

117

cassia . . .," or "Shot to death with pearls." These three different ways to die; you must find the central image for yourself. Each image should be expressed very sharply as different. Not three different thoughts; three different experiences; central ways of concern about dying; central experience for you behind the image. The sensations you have experienced, have stored up, give the real color to it. In speaking a text, to convey the color of it, explore your own vocal resources. If the images are not an experience for you, it won't be for the audience hearing it. If you don't have the sensation of having your "throat cut with diamonds, etc." then the speech would be rather meaningless. You have to do a double thing: experience it, and then communicate it.

Use of rhyme: a couplet at the end of a scene. One tends to think of it as a dying fall; in the middle of a scene, it tends to mean that the idea is stronger. If you observe the structure of the scene, then it is much easier to find the emotion. We must trust absolutely in the text. This can be carried too far, can become external, e.g. just with the stress—no emotion. This is a preliminary to work; rather than a method of work. We want to get behind it. One instrument is the words: the other is oneself. There is a pressure in the text, a pressure on the actor, a time pressure. Emotion is being expressed, not at any kind of length one chooses but through, for example, five and a half lines.

Compare learning to playing the piano; you can't express emotion of feeling if you can't play the notes. (You have to observe the time the composer has set—always within the context as to how it is written.) Emotion has to be experienced in time. Today we tend to value emotion almost for itself. We're not as sensitive to words as were the Elizabethans. For them words assumed the importance that scenery, costumes, lighting, etc., have assumed for us. We have to be aware of the difficulty, of reinstating the primacy of the word over motivaton of characters. We must know the nature of Jacobean times.

In the current English theater, many have rejected John Gielgud's approach to reading blank verse. Laurence Olivier found a way, an exciting way, of delivering blank verse, but he has and did bring to it an enormous technical skill. One thing that Olivier presents is *a sense of being controlled*.

Q. For a classic, how important are authentic costumes?

O'Donovan: I saw a production of Webster's THE WHITE DEVIL in New York's Greenwich Village. The absence of authentic costumes did not harm nor did it aid the production. It had vitality. However, if the actors had had more experience in verse drama, they would have come closer to Webster's intention.

Q. How important is a knowledge of the physical form of the theatre for which the play was written?

O'Donovan: The National Theatre at the Old Vic remodeled the proscenium opening to achieve a thrust stage. It seemed important for Shakespeare's verse plays. These plays do seem to work best in the round, on largely bare platforms. But as I've been saying, the physical environment for the play is not the primary consideration.

JACOBEAN

SELECTED BIBLIOGRAPHY

Bentley, Gerald Eades. *The Jacobean and Caroline Stage, Volumes I and II*. Oxford: Clarendon Press, 1941.

Moore, Don D. "John Webster in the Modern Theatre." *Educational Theatre Journal*. Washington, D.C.: American Educational Theatre Association, December, 1965.

Webster, John. *The Duchess of Malfi*. London: Chatto & Windus, 1958.

Wells, Henry W. *Elizabethan and Jacobean Playwrights*. New York: Columbia U. Press, 1939.

MATERIALS AND BACKGROUND

Nagles, A. M. *Sources of Theatrical History*. New York: Theatre Annual, Inc., 1952.

MUSIC

Court Music 16th Century   None. 71012.

Festive Music from 18th Century (2-68) Turn. 34216.

SPANISH GOLDEN AGE:
LOPE DE VEGA: CALDERON

"theatre as 'cape and sword' "

*capa y spada

"Spain had an extraordinary Golden Age; three playwrights alone, Tirso de Molina, Lope de Vega, Calderon; they should be performed constantly. Calderon has written so many comedies, so many beautiful plays, and even *autos sacramentales*. Of the latter, at least forty or fifty are totally unknown; and so for Lope, there are hundreds of works which are not known. We simply do not know them! There are always just two or three which we perform all the time, and no tradition for doing them. The two columns, the two pillars, the two legs upon which the Spanish theatre rests are Lope de Vega (1562-1635) and Calderon de la Barca (1600-1681). Lope created the theatrical art of Spain—before him there was only babbling—and Calderon perfected it. Calderon is known for his work in two genres: he brought the *autos sacramentales*, a form of play in one act in which the themes are religious and the characters are symbols of vices and virtues, to a stage of refinement previously unknown. And he created the Zarzuela, a verse play interspersed with musical compositions (e.g. *El Laurel de Apolo*). In Calderon, the Spanish theatre reached complete maturity. We find his characters contemplating life, death, the brevity of youth, as well as attempting to deal with philosophical and moral problems."

—JOSÉ LUIS ALONSO

The fact that Lope de Vega wrote well over 500 plays does not in itself establish him as a great dramatist; but when we come to see that his immense output was itself an aspect of his nature—inexhaustible, creative, impassioned, adaptable, amused, devout, patriotic—it is apparent that the quantity enriched rather than diminished the quality. From 1620 to his death in 1635, the masterpieces became increasingly frequent, though he wrote plays of the first order as early as 1608. Some are vast frescoes from Spanish history (he went back as far as the Visigoths for subjects); some are dramatizations of crimes which had recently engrossed the public; some, like THE SHEPHERD'S WELL, are powerful blows for social justice; some have rare poetic tenderness (his is the best telling of the story that Maeterlinck wrote as SOEUR BEATRICE and that Reinhardt staged as THE MIRACLE); some, like THE GARDENER'S DOG, are high comedy of the finest silver pen; many are light-hearted dramas of love and honor and loyalty.

It is not the fault of many great dramatists that their works are not easily assimilable by us today; other gulfs than time separate us from Euripides and Terence, Racine and Goldini, the Japanese Noh and Goethe. Many of the conventions that govern Spanish drama of the Golden Age seem artificial to us, as ours would be to that audience. *El Caballero de Olmedo*, however, meets us more than half way. Lope wrote many times the figure of the old woman who inserts herself into homes as a go-between among lovers, but never with a sharp relish that he here brings to Fabia. It is a mark of his range that in this same play he can give us also a scene that leaves an ache about the heart—in which the hero on his lone night-ride hears a voice in the distance singing a ballad which is a premonition of his death.

THORTON WILDER

Don José Tamayo, head of the Teatro Bellas Artes de Madrid and the Compania Lope de Vega, and founder and director of the Compania Lírica "Amadeo Vives", is one of the foremost stage directors in Spain today. In addition to his fame as an interpreter of the plays of Lope de Vega, Sr. Tamayo directed numerous operas, musical comedies and zarzuelas. He is also acclaimed for his productions of contemporary American works.

The Institute for Advanced Studies in the Theatre Arts' production of THE KNIGHT FROM OLMEDO was performed on the 400th birthday of Lope de Vega, October 25, 1962, in the Coolidge Auditorium, Library of Congress, Washington, D.C. Its first New York performance was on November 15, 1962, at the IASTA Theatre.

The interviews with the three directors, José Tamayo, José Luis Alonso, and Miguel Narros, were conducted in Spanish in Madrid in the early 1970s.

Miguel Narros was born in Madrid and studied in Paris with Jean Vilar at the Théâtre Nationale Populaire (T.N.P.), and with the Comédie-Française.

Returning to Spain, Sr. Narros founded the Piccolo Teatro in Barcelona. In 1964, he became Director of Productions and Cultural Events at the Spanish Pavilion of the New York World's Fair.

In 1966, Sr. Narros was named Director of the Teatro Nacional Español de Madrid where he made his debut with a production of NUMANCIA by Cervantes.

José Luis Alonso is head of the Teatro Nacional Maria Guerrero. He has been the recipient of many Spanish honors and awards, among them the First Award from the Spanish Government for the best director in 1959 for TAMING OF THE SHREW, and again in 1964 for EXIT THE KING.

PRIMER ACTO, the leading theatre magazine of Spain, awarded to Senor Alonso and his Teatro Nacional the First Prize for the best overall theatre produced in Spain during the season 1963-64.

INTERVIEWS WITH JOSÉ TAMAYO JOSÉ LUIS ALONSO, MIGUEL NARROS

Q. Sr. Tamayo, what are elements of style for Lope de Vega's THE KNIGHT FROM OLMEDO?

Tamayo: THE KNIGHT FROM OLMEDO was based upon a real event—the death of Don Juan de Vivero on his return to Olmedo after attending the bull fights in Medina del Campo. This episode inspired Lope de Vega to write his *Baile Famoso de El Caballero de Olmedo*, a form of pantomime-poem, which some years later, about 1622, with his genius at its fullest maturity, he developed into a play which has since become a classic. The outstanding characteristic of THE KNIGHT FROM OLMEDO is its skillful combination of realistic, poetic, natural and super-natural elements. The action begins as a comedy of manners, love and intrigue; later, with the introduction of other elements—omens, predictions, dreams—it turns toward the symbolic and allegoric. Lope de Vega, with his unique talent, managed to interweave the happy mood of the play's beginning with its tragic third act.

Q. Sr. Narros, what is your definition of style?

Narros: Style is personality. Why not say that's how it can be defined.

Q. What is the style for THE KNIGHT FROM OLMEDO?

Narros: It is difficult. THE KNIGHT FROM OLMEDO is a pre-Romantic play. Yet Lope accomplished something essentially poetic and romantic. The style of his comedies was entanglement, comedies of 'cape and sword.' In reality, Lope de Vega grounds the play in a love-death motif, within a style conceived by the playwright.

Alonso: Style is a subtle word in Spanish, you know.

Q. It is a very difficult word in English, also, but what is style?

Tamayo: In setting, the style for THE KNIGHT FROM OLMEDO is one of great simplicity and fidelity to history. The costumes must be of an historical character, but very much of today in inspiration. The style one gives to a work ought to be the style the production requires; for example, the Spanish *autos sacramentales*, which are uniquely plays of the Spanish theatre, can require a completely simple, or a baroque production; they permit two interpretations. For the development of Lope de Vega's widely varied themes, he also necessitates an acccommodation to various and diverse styles.

Narros: There is a sense of tremendous premonition in THE KNIGHT FROM OLMEDO, the destiny which the knight pursues is fascinating.

Q. As preparation for your production of THE KNIGHT FROM OLMEDO, Sr. Tamayo, did you use music and dance of the period to prepare the actors?

Tamayo: Yes, in New York. It was not necessary in Spain.

Q. How did the actors create the sense of feudal relationships which existed in Spain during the 16th century?

Tamayo: The role of the King is clearly defined by his commanding presence, elaborate dress, cultivated voice, and or-

126

namented speech, as compared to his subjects. The relationship between the comic servant, the *gracioso*, and his knight is more complete. Although as a servant he is humble, he is a party to his hero's secrets and adventures. There is a kind of unity of values and of thoughts between master and servant. He is a comic figure but also a man of enterprise capable of shuffling things with real art and craft.

Q. I am reminded of Velasquez's famous painting of the actor in the Prado Museum in Madrid.

Alonso: Ah, yes, the jester, Pablo de Valladolid, posed for a long monologue. Only an actor with a great voice, great talent and the industry to work hard can carry off the tirades. In the Spanish tirade the actor is talking aloud about what he is thinking in such a way that the public feels it is participating in what he is thinking. This is achieved in a way that doesn't sunder the ecstatic distance between actor and spectator. It is spontaneous. The words are those a person would use when alone.

Q. Is there such a thing as national theatre style?

Alonso: A national style of interpretation? Well, I believe it did exist when there were many great actors and actresses, great plays. As in the whole world, there is need for a theatre ensemble. In Spain in the last twenty years, more than the actors, it has been stage directors who have advanced the theatre in Spain.

In the Golden Age of Theatre, works had been written in verse. Then, the actors were familiar with the style of epic and poetic theatre, for it was their contemporary theatre; they knew the style. Centuries passed and a tradition for playing classic works in Spain was not maintained, as in France. Spanish actors hated the classical theatre.

Q. How is the situation changed?

L.T.M.

Alonso: The modern actor has come to appreciate the fact that Calderon and Lope de Vega anticipated by centuries some of the techniques, methods and styles of so much of what we associate with contemporary, musical theatre.

When directing the PHANTOM LADY, I tried to instill in the staging that amorphous air of light comedy, that vertiginous rhythm which Calderon demands, while keeping in mind that the interpretation and overall unity must rest upon the harmony of a classical base. Without achieving a complete reproduction of a 17th century performance, I tried to overlay the course of the action with authentic details most characteristic of those performances. Thus the play begins with a *loa*, a short composition in which the old companies used to introduce themselves to the public (so feared for its aggressiveness) and to beg its attention and favor. Other typical aspects of plays of the period which are utilized are guitar music, songs, scene-changers and the *zarabanda*, a dance in which the entire company takes part to conclude the performance. I staged the production in the manner of the *corrales* theatre, without any scenery. We began the play with young actors dashing in through the theatre while the audience was entering and taking their seats, reproducing the feeling of a courtyard theatre of the 16th century.

Q. How did you, Sr. Tamayo, analyze the characters in THE KNIGHT FROM OLMEDO?

Tamayo: The strong, or principal characters in THE KNIGHT FROM OLMEDO are those of Don Alonso, Fabia, Tello, and to a certain extent Ines.

Alonso is the prototype of the Spanish man; religious, strong personality, great passion. Alonso considers love the strongest and most powerful force in life. He lives, fights, or dies for love, facing everything spontaneously and without premeditation. He does all naturally, and when he has to prove himself fully, he does. Neither does he hesitate to fight nor do what he feels is his duty. Duty dictates that he depart from the woman he passionately loves and for whom he would give all. A devoted son, he travels to see his aged parents; everything seems to contribute to his death. The sense of duty is natural to him, and as such it is related to the fate which will cause his death.

I've been asked if the death of Alonso is caused by Fabia's Machiavellian contacts with Satan, her witchcraft. Definitely not. Fabia exploits the diabolic, as do many characters in Spanish literature. The Spanish people, besides being truly religious, do have other older beliefs in spirits and reappearances of the dead. All are part of Fabia; but she doesn't determine the course of the play. Fabia, another Celestina, acts naturally, firmly believing in her petty magic. She is truly interested in receiving a golden chain, a few coins to help buy the necessities to survive, and she sincerely finds joy in helping young lovers. Fabia had had a gay life and had once been a very beautiful woman. She identifies with young couples and helps them, all the while getting herself into trouble by trying to solve their problems. Fabia doesn't act out of selfish interest or as a procurer; she aids youth for her own enjoyment.

Q. Is it important, Sr. Narros, for the stage director to know about people's emotions and movements at a given time?

Narros: Yes, I believe it is necessary for the director to know a good deal about these historical matters. What the education of the 17th century man was, for instance, what problems he faced, his government, church, society, the painters of the period and, in addition, the director should know a lot about the fashion and dress of the period.

In the 17th century a woman with a girdle, a corset

made of wood, to keep her figure long, moved in a specific way, completely different from the way women today move without the restriction of old-fashioned undergarments.

Q. Do you include as part of style the dance, music, furniture and the costumes of the period?

Alonso: For the production of THE PHANTOM LADY, the costumes were brought from Spain. All the wigs of the period were designed after the wigs one sees in the paintings of Velasquez.

Q. Do you include . . .

Alonso: . . . The music and the furniture, yes. The atmosphere even includes a chair of the period; it gives off something, it collaborates, in creating an atmosphere for the performance.

Q. Does the use of the correct music, costumes and dance of the period help foreign actors identify with the characters of the play?

Alonso Yes, it shapes the actors, influences them, because in those full skirts the actresses have to walk like Spanish girls. The skirts obliged them to walk in a certain manner, to seat themselves in a certain way. Slippers without a heel conditioned a way of walking and moving, they may not have wanted to walk that way, but the shoes brought it about. In those immense wigs, as in the painting of Velasquez, the actresses couldn't move their heads quickly, or easily. They had to walk with the neck very straight; and everything through this adaptation became logical and contributed to the style of the 17th century characters of the play. The way of moving derives from the costumes, the dance forms, just as the way of sitting is derived from the intentionally low chairs.

Q. What of the manner of the use of gloves and fans in a Spanish play?

Alonso: Fans are a completely Spanish thing; they are very much a part of the Spanish woman. American women and foriegn women don't use fans as do Spanish women. It's curious, isn't it? Fans are not to cool oneself; they are used for emphasis, punctuation in polite, animated conversation.

Q. Is it possible to mount a production of THE KNIGHT FROM OLMEDO in modern dress?

Narros: I don't know. In THE KNIGHT FROM OLMEDO there is something that is contemporary, true for all times; a man struggles, debates between his instincts and the established powers, right? The conflict with an establishment could be treated as modern; that conflict is today still with us. I think to give a classical work to today's world, it is necessary that there be a point of contact; the anxieties and the passions of modern man are to be made evident.

Tamayo: The theatre of Lope de Vega is close to the clothes, manners and style of this epoch. The descriptive indications given by Lope de Vega are explicit; I wouldn't have the courage, as does Sr. Narros, to try to put it on in modern dress.

Q. Is the poetry of the text important?

Tamayo: The text is very important, and since the text is poetry, the poetry is very important. I remember that for the production in New York the critics praised the fine translation that had been made from the Spanish text into English because it kept the sense of the poetry and the charm of the verses of Lope de Vega.

Q. Is there a difference in style between Lope de Vega and Calderon?

132

Narros: Yes, of course, Lope de Vega created a theatre close to the people, for the people, from the people; he created a living theatre, a theatre he intended to be critical, a theatre to speak to humble folk, people of the lower classes.

Calderon, on the other hand—a man who was completely closed in on himself—lived a very austere life, without worldly experience prior to taking up a religious life; there, Calderon is much more philosophical, more concentrated, more scholarly.

Q. What is the challenge, if any, in directing a classical play for a modern audience?

Tamayo: The most difficult part is the text. Lope de Vega's language has to be made to seem real since it is written in an old Spanish. Otherwise, there is no problem.

Q. Sr. Alonso, we were talking about the *corral de comedias* or courtyard theatre of Spain's Golden Age of Theatre. Does the form of that theatre shape the play?

Alonso: Yes. The *corrales* theatre was something peculiar to Spain. Theatre in a courtyard, between houses, made neighbors, or innkeepers, the first impresarios. They rented space for theatrical production. Later religious confraternities took over the *corrales* and gave plays for charity.

Q. Is it important to recreate the environment and the manners of an era?

Narros: If it is done in a critical manner, yes. If it is just for the sake of recreating dead history, then I don't think it is of any interest. I'm going to use one of Bertolt Brecht's phrases: "You cannot truly copy a classical painting: you may find a skilled copyist of classical painting, but what he copies is dust."

Q. Is it important to know the politics of the century of the play?

Narros: Yes, it is important, and the class relationships among the characters are also important to know.

Q. How effective is the American actor in a classical Spanish play?

Tamayo: I haven't found specific difficulties. On the contrary I've found in the American actor a great vocation, which I wish I had found in other professional actors in other countries. Good preparation. They know one of the principle things an actor must know; e.g. voice. This impressed me greatly. What is more, they showed technique, and in this way they achieved what otherwise actors would get through intuition and temperament. I have seen quite good work from my American actors.

Q. Sr. Tamayo, what would you say are the aims of the theatre in Spain?

Tamayo: For each of us, the theatre has a different aim. Spain is not a country in which we directors sit down and discuss what should be done. Each theatre entrepreneur has his own ideas. One of the fundamental characteristics of Spanish theatre lies in its diversity of styles, plays, costumes, props, manners of each period, even in the so-called Spanish Golden Age. Authors then directed their own works. With perspective one comes to understand that each author has a chosen style and demonstrates his own personality. But in general, the Spanish theatre always faced the public and for two reasons: first, we have an authentic theatrical tradition; second, it is the public which sustains the theatre. Are these not two good reasons?

Author's Note: Each of the three directors was interviewed on a separate occasion.

SPANISH GOLDEN AGE

FILM

"The Spanish Golden Age of Theatre": obtainable, for rental and purchase, through the Institute for Advanced Studies in the Theatre Arts (IASTA), P.O. Box 1106, Radio City Station, New York, NY 10101 or Gil Forman, 310 W. 57th St., #1B, New York, NY 10019.

SELECTED BIBLIOGRAPHY

Calderon, de la Barca. *Calderon de la Barca* (Four Plays). (Translated by Edwin Honig.) New York: Hill and Wang, 1961.

Crawford, J. P. Wickersham. *Spanish Drama Before Lope de Vega*. Phila: U. of Pennsylvania Press, 1937.

Fitzgerald, Edward. *Eight Dramas of Calderon*. New York: Macmillan Company, 1906.

Flores, A. *Spanish Drama*. New York: Bantam Books, 1962.

Garcia, Enrique Ruiz, *25 Anos de Teatro en Espana* (José Tamayo, Director).

Gonzalez Pedroso, Eduardo. *Autos Sacramentales*. Madrid: Biblioteca de Autores Espanoles, 1952.

Green, Otis H. *Spain and the Western Tradition* (Vol 1). Madison: U. of Wisconsin Press, 1963.

Holt, Marion. *Modern Spanish Stage* (Four Plays). New York: Hill and Wang, 1970.

Rennert, Hugo Albert. *The Spanish Stage in the Time of Lope de Vega*. New York: Dover Publications, Inc., 1963.

Vega, Lope de. *Lope de Vega* (Five Plays). (Translated by Jill Booty.) New York: Hill and Wang, 1961.

Underhill, John Garrett. *Four Plays by Lope de Vega*. London: Charles Scribner's Sons Ltd., 1936.

MATERIALS AND BACKGROUND

Bottineau, Yves. *The Wonders of Spain: 164 Photogravure Plates*. New York: Viking Press, 1962.

Brown, Dale and the Editors of Time-Life Books. *The World of Velazquez 1599-1660*. New York: Time, Inc., 1969.

Cable, Mary and the Editors of the Newsweek Book Division. *El Escorial*. New York: Newsweek, 1971.

Pritchett, V. S. *The Spanish Temper*. New York: Norton, 1976.

Wethey, Harold E. *El Greco and His School* (Vol. I & II). Princeton: Princeton U. Press, 1962.

Prado Madrid. New York: Newsweek/Great Museums of the World, 1968.

MUSIC

Juan Cabanilles. En Los Organos de Daroca y Toledo. Coproduction Hispavox-Erato HHS 9.

Music of the Spanish Theatre in the Golden Age. Decca Records DL79436.

Musica Espanola Figueras, Van Mees, Ens. Tel. 642-156.

Spanish Music of the Golden Age Lyr. 7296.

COMMEDIA DELL'ARTE

"words turned into a sort of music"

L.T.M.

Commedia dell'arte is a form of witty, often bawdy popular comedy that, starting about 1500, flourished for some three hundred years in Italy and France and that created a distinctive style combining mime, ballet, acrobatics, the use of masks, and a convention of verbal improvisation by actors working from a scanty scenario.

In the sixteenth century, the phrase commedia dell'arte meant "of the profession," and indicated that the actors of a touring company were true professionals, capable of improvising comic dialogue at will. Written comedy of the same epoch was called *commedia erudita*, or "learned comedy."

In the Mystery Plays of the Middle Ages, some of the devils were close to commedia dell'arte characters. Masked actors reappeared during the Renaissance in a different form. These were the Zannis, Giovanni (Giovanni-Gianni-Zanni), hungry fellows in search of work, who usually ended up by carrying coal and exercising a less tiring profession, that of a go-between.

The sixteenth century Zannis were realistic looking, in their ragged clothes with variegated patches, and they walked with a wobbly gait. The Zannis of the seventeenth century became stylized mask-characters. The patches assumed a regular lozenge shape, and the gait had a dance-like rhythm. The Zanni is now Arlecchino.

This change of appellation stems from the return to Italy of the famous Zan Ganassa, under the name of Arlequin, which the Parisians had pinned upon him in memory of a traditional agile red devil.

In the eighteenth century, Arlecchino was raised by Goldoni to a higher level; he was allowed to take off his mask and fall in love. In so doing, however, he lost his original identity and became a person like any other.

Opposing Goldoni's reform was Carlo Gozzi, a nobly born Venetian journalist and writer. The defense of the commedia dell'arte and its flights of fancy were the theme of Gozzi's plays. Mask-actors and the traditional imaginary background returned to the stage.

A mask-character from the commedia dell'arte of Gozzi is Tartagliona and Tartaglia, the successor to the boastful Captain, a tender-hearted, stammering braggart, who brays like a donkey when he is moved to tearful emotion. Another of Gozzi's themes is the magical wonder of the Orient.

Some of his works, among them TURANDOT and I PITOCCHI FOR-
TUNATI, take place in the Middle East. Gozzi created a new mask-
character, Muzzefer (Mustapher), a comically ferocious Oriental military
man.

Among the characters descended from *commedia dell'arte* are Harle-
quin and Columbine, Punch, of Punch and Judy, Molière's unscrupulous
Scapin, Beaumarchais' Figaro, and all circus clowns.

Contemporary clowns are different in appearance, but their essential
nature is that of the mask-characters. Masks and stylized costumes make
their voices and gestures abstract. On the basis of these expressive modes,
clowns may be said to constitute the commedia dell'arte of modern times.

GIOVANNI POLI

GIOVANNI POLI, a Venetian, was the leading authority in Italy on
commedia dell'arte. Mr. Poli had adapted and translated into modern
Italian many of the commedia scenarios originally outlined in dialect, and
published books and articles on commedia. In addition, Mr. Poli gained
fame in his country as a director of plays by international playwrights. His
company, Teatro Ca'Foscari of Venice toured Europe and South
America. In 1960 at the Festival of the Nations in Paris, Mr. Poli won the
grand prize for his direction of "LA COMMEDIA DEGLI ZANNI," and he
has been awarded the highest honors by the Academy of Italian Drama.
Mr. Poli was the founder of the Teatro L'Avogaria in Venice. THE GREEN
BIRD by Carlo Gozzi was staged for IASTA in 1962

The interview took place in November, 1971.

Q. What are the elements of the Italian style?

Poli: You speak of the Italian style, the right Italian style. For
me there is only one Italian style and that is the style of the
commedia dell'arte. As a style it is special, and difficult for
me to explain because it is my own style. I don't say that it
is *the* Italian style because it is mine. Giorgio Strehler of
the Piccolo Teatro Di Milano follows the same style. Style
is three things: the staging; the interpretation; the

characterizations. Moreover, this style is a vision of theatre, and it is not naturalistic. This style is contrary to other movement of *verismo* (realism) of the 19th century, after Goldoni. The naturalistic style of Pirandello and others does not satisfy the public today. It can no longer satisfy the demands and needs of audiences because the theatre has new ideals.

The commedia dell'arte is related to the anti-naturalistic, in which the interpretation of the actor is not an expression of reality nor an imitation of daily reality, but is an abstraction of daily reality. In contrast, television and film give an exact interpretation and representation of reality. The actor, in commedia, doesn't speak, but going in the direction of music, he sings. His voice becomes a musical instrument to communicate his feelings better, as does music. Since the goal of the actor is not to imitate reality, the body, arms, head, legs, move as in dancing. As a caution, in commedia dell'arte, I think the voice shouldn't go too far in the direction of music, through the extensions of the musical scale. The tone of the voice should be narrative to permit recounting or telling of things which are not in fact music. Commedia dell'arte is halfway in the direction of dance. The two elements, music and mime, dominate the style of commedia.

Q. Do you feel Italy's national theatre style is the commedia dell'arte?

Poli: I think commedia dell'arte is the most important thing that Italy gave to world theatre, and this is shown by the great interest in it that the audiences in all the capitols of the world have demonstrated. The roots of much European theatre are in these Italian characters of the commedia dell'arte who are similar to those found in the theatre of Molière and Marivaux. There is influence of commedia in Shakespeare's comedies. Feste in TWELFTH NIGHT

shows evidence of commedia. Certainly, Shakespeare's
COMEDY OF ERRORS shows influence of Italian theatre
and commedia, as it is derived from a comedy of Plautus.
It is possible that the Elizabethan actors made tours in
Europe and might have seen Italian actors perform. It's
possible, too, that Italian actors performed in London at
the time of Shakespeare.

Q. Does each play have its own correct style?

Poli: THE GREEN BIRD was written by Gozzi in 1764. I
arrived at the style for it, not through scripts, but through
careful examination of the documents which exist about
the whole history of the commedia and the characters
developed through two centuries. In order to truly understand the plays of Goldoni and Gozzi, it is necessary to
understand the characters from the moment they were
born, and to understand how they developed until they
appeared in these plays. The style comes from *my* inter
pretation of these documents. The rhythms of the words
of the text can suggest the gestures (acting) and the vocal
patterns. I did not intellectualize about the style for commedia from study of these documents, but I arrived at this
reconstruction through my emotional response to these
texts. In short, it came out of my knowledge and love for
these literary documents. The style was not found easily.
It is not possible to find a style that does not exist anymore
and has been lost. There are no films, no exact represen-
tations of what commedia was like at the hands of the
original actors. It is not to be found alone by study and
loving the texts; it was possible through inspiration to rediscover what commedia was originally. I came to grasp
how a role was interpreted by studying the music of the
words. For example, Pantalone does not speak, but he
"sings" his lines in a special way, and the word-music
serves as a guide to gestures. I learned from commedia

that there is a rapport, a connection between the words and rhythmical gestures.

Q. Are the texts for commedia important?

Poli: Yes, yes, yes. They are important, especially the texts of Gozzi. Gozzi's art is not a pure interpretation of the indigenous commedia because there is infiltration from oriental tales; for example, THE THOUSAND AND ONE NIGHTS. He was, however, a profound interpreter of the characters of the commedia. For instance, he was the only one to enable us to come to know the characters Tartaglia and Tartagliona. They are not found in the plays of Goldoni. Gozzi's Pantalone is much more alive and quicker than the Pantalone of Goldoni.

The commedia of Goldoni is much lighter. Goldoni characters became more refined, human, similar to realistic characters of today, and Goldoni's characters lose their energy, their leaping and their vitality.

Gozzi conserves that energy in the characters of Truffaldino, Brighella and Pantalone because he generally doesn't write out a text, but makes a *canavaccio*, an abstract scenario of an action. From documents on Brighella, Pantalone and Truffaldino, it is possible to reconstruct the text of the roles which had never been written out.

Q. Are the characters like people of the eighteenth century with a particular social relationship. Or, is it only fantasy?

Poli: It's not fantasy. For example, the Arlecchino was a servant and belonged to a very low social class. They were people who had to serve and who didn't have enough food. Arlecchino in Goldoni is always hungry. Gozzi's Truffaldino (Arlecchino) was depicted as always hungry. These servant characters do not have the possibility of satisfying their hunger; they are of the particular world of the proletariat of their time. The traditional Truffaldino or Arlecchino costume with all its patches indicates a suit made of bits and pieces of rags. The higher class in commedia is the bourgeoisie—Venetian bourgeoisie. For example, the character of Pantalone is a masked character of the merchant class; he has made a great deal of money from the Orient. He sells spices and fabrics of the Orient throughout Europe. It is said the name Pantalone derives from the fact that he, as a merchant, planted in foreign soils the lion symbol, the flags and banners of Venice.

In Goldoni one finds a character who represents the culture of Venice, an erudite culture. The character of Il Dottore has studied much, has read many books, but in the end knows nothing because he is not intelligent. He symbolizes the negative aspect of Venetian culture. Erudition which is not culture is only memorized learning. Il Dottore had divided his mind into many drawers where he's put the things that he has memorized. This personage of the world of commedia is very comical.

Q. With regard to your production of Goldoni's SQUABBLES OF CHIOGGIA in Montreal, you said that it is not a satirical play, but simply a view of the life of the town of Chioggia and the city life of Venice. Would you expound?

Poli: In Goldini's THE SQUABBLES OF CHIOGGIA, the characters of the commedia have been transformed into real people, fishermen of the suburb of Venice, Chioggia. It is no longer possible to say that this play belongs to the world of commedia. Goldoni had already made drastic reformations of commedia into realistic theatre. He left behind the characters of the commedia. Not only do the characters Arlecchino, Pantalone, etc., not exist in the play, but the conflicts of the commedia do not exist in the play, either. There are other conflicts. For the first time, Goldoni brought on stage real fishermen rather than the upper class bourgeoisie. Without his knowing it, Goldoni started the theatre on the path to realism and a theatre of ideas. He set in motion a new movement in theatre. He was a man of the 18th century with his eyes open; he saw a need for important social reform. Even though he didn't subscribe to the new Humanism of the French, he did anticipate change and the French Revolution. He left behind the commedia. and after his last two comedies, he left Italy for Paris.

The connection between Gozzi, commedia dell'arte and Goldoni is complex and cannot be explained in a few words.

Q. Is it necessary to try to duplicate an historical period through costumes, manners, etc.?

Poli: Historical costumes, properties, furniture, scenery and the way of life of a period cannot be changed. I see this as an eternal problem in the theatre. To duplicate history, I think that is possible. However, it would be beautiful to get away from externals like costumes, properties, etc., and to find the humanity of the characters, the reality of the characters. That is something very difficult, and I am still searching how to do just that, to find a living relationship between the commedia and our problems today. I cannot say that I have found it.

Q. In view of what you have said, do you think it would be possible to do a modern dress production of THE GREEN BIRD?

Poli: It would be possible to have a production today without the costumes of the 18th century, but very difficult. I saw a Polish production of THE SERVANT OF TWO MASTERS without traditional costumes. It was not convincing. However, the actors were very capable. In my opinion there was too much symbolism: the costumes tried to express the essence of the characters. There was a maladjustment, a lack of balance. On the other hand, to costume the characters as they would have been costumed in their own day is a thing also that we're not able to accept. Productions of Shakespeare in modern dress or out of period are frequent. His plays are always acceptable in any place and time. But as for Goldoni and Gozzi, it's a bit difficult because they lived in one special place, Venice, and in one special time alone. It's difficult to judge, to discover the essence or the center of what makes a person or a character universal. There has been a production of Goldoni's GLI INNAMORATI (THE LOVERS) in modern dress, but the language of Goldoni is not the language of today. So the costumes and the language clashed. I do not know if this happens to Shakespeare's plays in English; I assume it doesn't happen. Shakespeare is timeless; what he said in *his* language of *his* time could be said today.

Q. Must your actors know the social relations, the political climate of the time of the plays of Goldoni and Gozzi?

Poli: It is the task of the director that the actors know as much as possible about the politics, the arts, the social relationships and the religious movements of the time.

Q. Did the commedia dell'arte theatre of the 18th century have a proscenium?

Poli: Our thinking today is that for the commedia the shape of the physical theatre of the 18th century in Italy is not important. Commedia can be produced or played anywhere—in the street, on a platform in a room, in a theatre: anywhere! The physical theatre of the 18th century was the theatre of lyric opera. But this was not the theatre of commedia. Commedia had no need of a theatre; it was performed in a Piazza. There were neither the needs nor the problems of a theatre as we think of it today.

145

COMMEDIA DELL'ARTE

FILM

"Commedia dell'Arte"

Gozzi's "The Green Bird" (newly edited): both obtainable, for rental and purchase, through the Institute for Advanced Studies in the Theatre Arts (IASTA), P.O. Box 1106, Radio City Station, New York, NY 10101 or Gil Forman, 310 W. 56th St., #1B, New York, NY 10019.

SELECTED BIBLIOGRAPHY

Bentley, Eric. *The Genius of the Italian Theater*. New York: New American Library, 1964.

Bentley, Eric. *The Classic Theatre, Volume I* (Italian Plays). Doubleday Anchor, 1958.

Drake, W. A. *Memoirs of Carlo Goldoni*. New York: Alfred Knopf, 1926.

DuChartre, Pierre Louis. *The Italian Comedy*. New York: Dover Publications, Inc., 1966.

DuChartre, Pierre Louis. *La Commedia dell'Arte*. Paris: Librairie de France, 1925.

Goldoni, Carlo. *Dalle Maschere Alla Commedia*. Venice: Carlo Ferrari, 1957.

Rosi, Luigi. *I Comici Italiani*. Florence: Fracesco Lumachi, 1905.

Smith, Winifred. *Italian Actors of the Renaissance*. New York: Coward-McCann, Inc., 1930.

MATERIALS AND BACKGROUND

Barzini, L. "The Italians," New York: Athenium, 1977.

Mitchell, John D. "In Search of Commedia dell'Arte." *Players Magazine*. New York: January, 1963.

Poli, Giovanni. "Commedia dell'Arte—A Renewal of the Theatre". *Players Magazine*. New York: January, 1963.

Poli, Giovanni. "Commedia dell'Arte—Its Application Now". *Equity Magazine*. New York: Winter, 1963.

MUSIC

Fleetwood Singers Italian Music (12-58) Lyr. 775.

Goldoni. Commedia dell'Arte Melodramma. Stereoletteraria STI 26.

COMEDY OF MANNERS

"stand-up and talk as theatre"

L.T.M.

MOLIÈRE

The Comédie-Française is the oldest theatre in the world. Officially founded in 1680 by Louis XIV, its actual founding was in 1643, the year Molière created his troupe, the "Illustre Theatre." We are Molière's continuators and that is why the Comédie-Française is frequently referred to as the House of Molière. In spite of many revolutions, changes in regimes, changes in the people's attitudes, our theatre has continued to function without interruption. Because of the Comédie-Française's age, we actors have a certain esprit de corps, tradition, a solid foundation behind us. We live together, we work together. The "sociétaires" at the Comédie-Française sign a contract for a minimum of twenty years. A "sociétaire" is like a landlord and a "pensionnaire" is like a tenant. The "sociétaires" own the theatre, its walls, pictures, rugs, books, costumes, repertoire, everything. We cannot leave the Comédie-Française without the permission of the Administrative Committee which is made up of around six "sociétaires." We, therefore, form a type of community. We have our habits, our style of acting, our tempo, a love for beautiful texts, and an admiration for the home within whose walls our masters worked. It is like a torch which we hand down from generation to generation.

JACQUES CHARON

In 1960, the late Jacques Charon, *Doyen* of the Comédie-Française, directed Molière's "The Misanthrope" in New York for IASTA with professional American actors, among them Jessica Tandy. As a distinguished actor, as well as a director, M. Charon demonstrated the skill and knowledge of comedy acquired through many years of association with the Comédie-Française.

In the wake of M. Charon's work in New York, he directed Lord Laurence Olivier and the actors of the British National Theatre in a farce of Feydeau. Later, in Hollywood, he directed Rex Harrison in a screen treatment of the same Feydeau farce. While performing as an actor on the stage of the Comédie-Française, it was not uncommon for Jacques Charon to be staging, simultaneously, three boulevard comedies mornings and afternoons. M. Charon's autobiography is aptly titled: "*Moi, un comedien.*"

INTERVIEW WITH JACQUES CHARON

Q. How does one define the style of a production of Molière? What are the elements of this style?

Charon: If style can be defined, it must refer to the evocation of a time, a place, a kind of society. Much depends upon physical things: the way one sits, the way one moves, the way one handles objects. Actors should have some knowledge of the time of the play. Style is also the job of the director, because he brings the externals. Ultimately, of course, the style rests in the text itself, with Molière's rhythm of the verse. You cannot toy with plays of Molière by moving them out of France in the period of Louis XIV. The very fact that the premise of the play is based on the morals of that period makes the experience more real. The whole play is more "standing in place" than contemporary actors are used to. There is very little moving around just for movement's sake. Movement is rapid, as is the dialogue. This is "stand-up drama."

    The key to performing in this style is simplicity. Molière supplied it all in the texts: the director, ultimately, can only make pretty pictures. Costumes are equally important in the play. An actor has to be aware that he must act with his arm on a parallel with the floor; raise it higher, and his sleeve falls back, revealing his wrist, and this is a bad line. The actor must be constantly aware of looking attractive, while being relaxed and having absolute control over the tempo and music of the dialogue. Never substitute style for anything else: style expresses what is underneath the form.

Q. Do you believe that there is a tangible national theatre?

Charon: There are two kinds of theatre in France: classical; e.g. Comédie-Française, and popular, commercial plays performed in the Boulevard theatres. What a repertory the French actor has to husband. This most beautiful repertory of the French language, quite simply, is the flower of France. One feels an extraordinary well-being to take in one's mouth the words of certain authors, to polish them, to project them, quite clearly, roundly, sonorously, into the hall of the theatre.

Q. Does each play have its own style?

Charon: There is a great need to orchestrate vocal levels in THE MISANTHROPE, for instance. A pitch of voice at the end of a laugh of the marquis must pick up and continue into his speech. Each entire scene, essentially, is orchestrated. The improvisations of the first actors of Molière, their orchestration, has been passed on to our present Comédie-Française actors; it has become a part of our tradition. There is a formality about THE MISANTHROPE. The women must always move on a line verticle to the stage. Not a balletic or operatic pose, but an elegant, perpendicular line to the floor. There is never any sentimentality, only a conscious restraint. Molière's language is action; he uses words as an instrument to achieve a purpose (as are words in all verse plays). The actor needs to be aware of the full connotations of each word to convey that particular thought. This is an acting problem peculiar to Molière and verse plays. The mind must click with rapidity, and the actor must be absolutely clear in his mind as to exactly what he is doing every moment. There's no time to wait for inspiration for the right mood to come!

Q. How do you direct?

Charon: I have a definite procedure. First, after the play is cast, we read through the script together. Then, while sitting down, I give the *mise-en-scene*, the blocking, and the

150

actor writes it in his text. Next, we walk the blocking, making minor adjustments to the stage and the furniture. From then on, we do run-throughs to achieve individual performances, and to orchestrate each of the scenes in the play.

The *sense* of the lines must come first, the rhyme and rhythm after. Molière's writing is not realistic, but stylized. It is rhymed, therefore, it must be *played* bigger than life, but the playing must begin with the meaning of the text.

I take the men aside early in rehearsals and work with them at great length on bows, walks, physical stance, and the use of plumed hats and tall walking canes. Then, it is put immediately into the context of the staging.

For the style of Molière an actor needs constant voice and movement training. Very long speeches have to change in thought direction (afterthought, sub-thought): tempo, vocal pitch, have to be orchestrated. The actor needs to be aware of what he is doing, both in rehearsals and in his role, I never give a line reading. Oh, I show *how* a fop would talk, but never give a line reading. One can use modern images. For a fop's entrance I may suggest the image of people greeting each other in a theatre today. I use images with which today's actor can identify. Actors should come to rehearsal to enjoy themselves; to "perform" for me.

There is a specific key to each scene, both technical and subconscious. They must be orchestrated vocally.

Q. Not only are you a famous actor, but you teach as well. What is your approach to teaching young actors?

Charon: Ah, my credo for the student actor. The actor's instrument, poorly exercised, will not have become strong enough, supple enough, to enable him to express what he would wish. An actor is a prisoner: he has the spirit of a violinist, but he has no violin in his hands! The instrument of the actor is he, himself.

At the Conservatoire of the Comédie-Française courses are given in general culture, literature, history of theatre, and also courses having to do with physical expression, fencing, makeup, etc.

When Louis Jouvet was asked what he taught his students, he said, "I teach them to breathe." The classics have been written for vocal athletes. The words demand of actors the ability to hurl them, project them, to fifteen hundred spectators, The Conservatoire teaches actors the ability to project so that they are fully understood by everyone in the audience, including those in the last row of the farthest balcony.

On stage it is not necessary to cry to make the audience cry. To cry at will is a quirk of the lachrymal glands; you have it or you don't have it. It has nothing to do with the sensitivity of the actor, nor with success with the public. The big tears rolling down the cheeks are lost, except for the first row of the orchestra. The great weepers leave the audience stiff as marble. By contrast, when the whole theatre is crying its eyes out, a Madelaine Renaud is as dry as a desert. Edith Evans said to John Gielgud, after a performance of RICHARD II, "If you had cried less, the audience would have cried more." For laughter, it's the same thing; less is more.

To make one laugh is a gift, but also a technique. As for laughing by oneself on stage, it is not amusing! It has nothing to do with spontaneous joy. The great part of laughing on stage results from training in breathing. It starts with the diaphram: it's important to start on a low note and then to build, with diaphramatic support, up the scale of notes. Control of the diaphram is essential. With rigorous and sustained practice the conscious physical act evokes an emotional desire, a conditioned reflex, to laugh.

Q. How does one clarify for an audience the historical social pressures which dictate the behavior and relationships?

Charon: Through manners and movement; e.g. a man of Molière's time never showed the inside of his hat. There are elaborate *révérences* on entrances and exits, but an actor must never reveal the inside of his hat. The use of fans is not conventional; they are used for pointing and punctuation.

The character Eliante of THE MISANTHROPE describes social types, friends, and says that true love comes to everyone. She uses a fan to describe them while seated, facing full front to the audience.

In scenes of one or more characters, the actor does not play *to* the other actor so much as *at* him, while being aware of the audience out front. This is "playing through the back of the head," a perfectly valid way to act. We do it in real life all the time (standing at a window talking to someone behind you, although the visual focus is somewhere else). Arsinoé is too coy to play a love scene directly to Alceste; it is played by implication, angled downstage visually and emotionally. Likewise with Alceste and Célimène, because her mind wanders while he raves on. It works quite comically as both face the audience. Alceste talks and rants, and we enjoy seeing when Célimène is no longer "with him," when her attention strays.

Q. To what extent is authenticity, tradition, important in the production of a classical play?

Charon: The Comédie-Française is committed to preserving the traditions of style of acting as they have come down directly from Molière and his troupe. The Comédie is the "House of Molière."

Q. To what extent is authenticity of costumes, decor, props, important in the production of Molière?

Charon: Hats for Molière's characters are very important: they all wear them. Alceste and Philante do not wear swords because a salon is on the floor above the ground floor of the house, and they've probably left them below. The two marquesses have highly styled costumes because of the difference in their characterization; they *do* wear swords. They wear petticoat breeches and little bolero-type jackets, different from the long coats and ordinary breeches worn by the other characters. It is a tradition and it also establishes the type of character upon appearance.

In the "gossip" scene, most of the cast face front; they must have the space in which to move because they are all very alive. The elaborate dresses, with trains, the swords for the marquesses and the shoulder-high walking canes for the other male characters, necessitate room to make the simplest move.

Q. Of what importance is it to know the physical structure of the theatre for which Molière wrote?

Charon: Frankly, the present Comédie-Française is the familiar proscenium-type theatre of the 19th century. We find no fault with it. Molière's troupe played often before the King at Versaille, Fontainebleau, on temporary and improvised stages. The greater forestages of the Paris theatres of his time undoubtedly helped bring the actors closer to their public—too close in the case of the titled fops who placed themselves upon the forestage. But closeness was a necessity for the actors, playing as they did by candlelight. Molière's stage resulted in a presentational style of acting; we emulate that style today. And it works.

COMEDY OF MANNERS
(Jacques Charon)

FILM

"Molière and The Comédie-Française": obtainable, for rental or purchase, through the Institute for Advanced Studies in the Theatre Arts (IASTA), P.O. Box 1106, Radio City Station, New York, NY 10101 or Gil Forman, 310 W. 56th St., #1B, New York, NY 10019.

SELECTED BIBLIOGRAPHY

Bordonove, Georges. *Molière genial et familier.* Paris: Robert Laffont, 1967.

Dussane. *An Actor Named Molière* (translated by Lewis Galantiere). New York: Charles Scribner's Sons, 1937.

Fernandez, Ramon. *Molière, The Man Seen Through The Plays* (translated by Wilson Follett). New York: Hill and Wang, 1958.

Molière. *Tartuffe* (translated by Richard Wilbur). New York: Harcourt, Brace & World, Inc., 1961.

Rudin, Seymour. "Molière and the Misanthrope." *Educational Theatre Journal.* Washington, D.C.: American Educational Theatre Association, December, 1965.

MATERIALS AND BACKGROUND

Charon, Jacques. *Moi, Comedien.* Paris: Éditions Émile-Paul, 1967.

Gaxotte, Pierre. *Versailles que j'aime . . .* Paris: Aux Éditions Sun (N.D.)

MUSIC

Music of Lully Remy, Grande Écurie Turn. 34376.

Lully: Le Triomphe de L'Amour. Weissberg, Vienna Symphony. Audio Fi. 50079.

L.T.M.

CONGREVE

By an act of Parliament, the theatres in England were closed from 1642-60. However, this period of suppression was marked by continuous skirmishes as the hard-pressed companies attempted to provide theatrical activity to the drama-hungry Englishmen.

With the restoration of the monarchy, every effort was made to turn the clock back to the gay, carefree days of the 1630s. The arts flourished, clothes blossomed into ruffles and ribbons and there was ribaldry and excess. The court of Charles II brought French manners, styles and customs to England. The King was very fond of the theatre, and upon his return to England he not only attended court performances as he had in France, the Netherlands and Germany, but with his favorites he went to the public theatres where he had a royal box.

The greatest difference between the acting companies of the Restoration and those before the Commonwealth is that the new groups included women. This in itself allowed the acting traditions of Molière's company to enter more fully into the new English style.

Although the inspiration for the new comedies had come from France, they were imbued with a peculiarly native quality that made them the ultimate achievement in the comedy of manners.

George Devine, London born, was co-founder and Artistic Director of the English Stage Company, with its home at the Royal Court Theatre, Sloane Square, London. Under Mr. Devine's guidance, the English Stage Company has proved to be a most dynamic force in the English Theatre, presenting the works of new and classic playwrights both from England and abroad, with special emphasis on the contemporary British writer; several of their productions, including "Look Back in Anger" and "The Entertainer," have appeared on Broadway.

Irving Wardle, drama critic of the London Times, has written his biography, "The Theatre of George Devine."

Mr. Devine directed the professional actors of IASTA in Congreve's, "The Way of the World" in New York, 1960. The interview occurred during and after the production in New York.

INTERVIEW WITH GEORGE DEVINE

Q. How would you define the style for a production of THE WAY OF THE WORLD?

Devine: THE WAY OF THE WORLD was written in 1700, forty years after the restoration of the monarch and the re-opening of the theatres. It marks the peak of the complex and brilliant style known as Restoration. For Congreve, it represents perfection in characterization, sensibility, and complexity of plot and language. In addition, it contains elements new to Restoration Drama: by depicting real love between Millamant and Mirabell, and by omitting the customary bawdy tone, Congreve added depth to the Restoration style, and foreshadowed the approaching sentimentality of the 18th and 19th centuries. Congreve's masterly dialogue, of course, daunts all but the most skillful actors in England, where Restoration Comedy is more frequently performed. When we taught the 18th century theatre in the London Theatre School, the students used to learn it through the dance. All the dance movements are in the round, so there was air between the actor and the audience.

Congreve is almost like a musical score. Americans find it most difficult to speak fast enough to provide the necessary modulation that the text requires. Actors need to feel that the style and world of the play are not as strange, remote and extraordinary as it might appear. One can draw contemporary parallels—there is still such a thing as high society. Actors must attain the proper mood—you have to feel the way you feel when you feel real good—a feeling of excited elevation and animation.

Q. What are the elements of this style?

Devine: The dancing master's function in preparing Restoration and 18th century plays is comparable to that of a co-director. Preparation for such a production gathers specialists in each faction: music, historic play research, dance, decor and costumes.

First, it's important to create an atmosphere of the Restoration period. This requires dedicated work from all concerned. For movement, awareness of the dance and its place in the reconstruction of Restoration plays, it is important cast members are taught some of the dances of the period. They learn to feel the rhythm and music of the period, and thus learn the style and manner.

The text of THE WAY OF THE WORLD is like music and requires great virtuosity and vocal range. A lot of practice is needed to master the Restoration technique. It is extrovert in character, compared with the introvert conception of contemporary dramas. There is meter for these balanced sentences. There is need to be careful about stress and words that give meaning and rhythm, to avoid putting stress mistakenly on words which do not merit it. To be "hot" with words and "on top of the text" it is a necessity to have a well-trained voice; this particular style requires a sharp edge and a driving force in delivery of lines. On the other hand, we teach the actor not to underestimate the value of the lines themselves by over delivering them. By establishing the character first, the actor can carry scenes without super-human effort and bring greater response in the correct way. This points up the hair-line difference between high comedy and farce. If the first is established through character and vocal control, the lapses into the second will not bring the wrong reactions from the audience.

The ladies must be aware of keeping their knees together, because they were taught that they had the golden apple between their knees; and all men were out to snatch it. The use of the fan is with quiet dignity, like a lady of quality, not like a soubrette of the music halls.

Modern actors may seem overly self-conscious about showing the delicacies of good breeding as they seem to equate it with a lack of masculinity, probably a result of their over-exposure to the cliche of maleness of the current trend in theatre and movies. By the 18th century, jousting had been outlawed and gallants were forced to win their ladies and prove themselves through dancing to respond to these truths, and the minuet no longer seemed mincing exercise, but a distinction of finesse. Their spines elongated and their lines (physical) improved. Every actor should have a feeling of wit and beauty. Actors must keep this style while making it as easy as possible for the audience to understand the plot. Perfection of speech and movement are great advantages in doing any style. The sheer sensation of being in the presence of style in its very highest form is a very important thing.

Q.   Does each play have its own correct style? Are plays about particular people at a certain time in a certain relationship?

Devine: A gesture with a fan may be made by a silent character on one side of the stage, as a kind of unspoken aside, while a conversation is going on at the other side of the stage. I have the character Marwood do this. I am also very particular about the letter from Mistress Marwood. So, plays are about particular people at a certain time in a certain relationship. THE WAY OF THE WORLD does have its own correct style.

As for the movement, I do not leave the actors to find movement out of their emotions in a play like this. I give them the movement and have them in turn give it life. For movement is rooted in style; both of the play and of the players. There must be a necessary distinction in movement between the gauche, more impulsive servants, and the mannered, deceiving gentry. The entire show is played at minuet tempo, except at times when there is a

160

conversation without movement. The tempo for the last act must be more rapid because it is the wind up: I direct the actors to play it fast, not to give the audience too much time to think.

Q. How does one clarify for an audience the historical social pressures which dictate the behavior and relationships?

Devine: Within these overly civilized characters there must be a realization of the development of their character through word as well as action. The actor must attain a complete comprehension of the text, and search for those things which give the production a complete form. Costumes, fans, any prop becomes so much a part of the actor that we need only deal with the immediate problems of character and meaning.

Q. Do you believe that there is a tangible style in the National Theatre?

Devine: There are many styles: Shakespearean, Jacobean, Restoration, Edwardian, etc. THE WAY OF THE WORLD requires the Restoration style.

Q. How do you direct?

Devine: I impart an idea of the technique by example. But, you know, I'm an actor myself. I try to get the actors to feel the spirit of the play and also try to make them realize the specialized world in which the play takes place. For example, the position of the two feet in relation to each other; women's feet pointed outwards in opposite directions. Men's feet are pointed in the same direction more, with one of them behind the other. A balanced position for Millamant in the love scene: her left arm placed along the back of the sofa while her right arm falls indolently on the right arm of the sofa, wrists limp, hand holding fan; her left foot is drawn under and placed behind the right foot, which is set forward and out. The position of the arms for the woman is always above the waist, with the elbows bent, never hanging by their sides.

Q. To what extent is authenticity, tradition, important to a production of a classic?

Devine: I abominate the "traditional" approach to anything. I could not direct in a way that "traditional" implies to me. What I try to do is to get American actors to find the way to perform Restoration comedy, based on the style in which it is written, but with the same reality as they'd approach Tennessee Williams. As for costumes, the silhouette of the period costume will do nicely.

Q. To what extent is authenticity of costumes, sets, props, important to a production of a classic?

Devine: The mood and the text should be the real props; to be direct and simple with the text; use no gimmicks.

Q. Which is more important, a knowledge of the manners of the period or a knowledge of the social structure of the period?

Devine: One has to establish the practical circumstances of the play (how it was originally performed)—the relationship between the actors and audience was a special one; there was a kind of intimacy. Restoration comedy, therefore, requires a way of being toward an audience. This kind of play essentially has to be played out front, preferably far down on a deep apron stage, more in horizontal than perpendicular placing of the actors. They are ornamental figures against a painted background.

The dramatist is the source in the theatre, but not the only source. Theatrical experience can finally depend on a kind of chemical mixture of writer, designer, director and actor. But, the mixture could not take place if the dramatist is not there as a catalyst.

I am interested in all theatrical means of heightening or compressing expression of which song, dance, mime, acrobatics and heightened forms of speech are very much a part.

Phoney explorations into style are no better than no style at all. People can be inspired by seeing and experiencing different sorts of style in theatre, providing that they are done honestly and not in a gimmicky manner.

Q. How important is a knowledge of the physical form of the theatre for which the play was written?

Devine: The use of the planal areas of the stage to produce comedy is a very special technique, so knowledge of dance and the shape of the body help to produce the broader expression of the comic aspects of the words. The percussive gesticulation or change in the shape of the body, sinking from a high plane to a low plane on the stage, with a patter of distorted word accompaniment, punctuated by quick dynamic changes in body shape, is one of the examples of master craft for comedy. So, it's important to know the physical form of the theatre for which the play was written, but not so necessary to reproduce it. It's more important that the actors' physicality be reproduced.

COMEDY OF MANNERS
(George Devine)

FILM

"Aspects of 18th Century Comedy" (includes scenes from Congreve's "Way of the World"): obtainable, for rental or purchase, through the Institute for Advanced Studies in the Theatre Arts (IASTA), P.O. Box 1106, Radio City Station, New York, NY 10101 or Gil Forman, 310 W. 56th St., #1B, New York, NY 10019.

SELECTED BIBLIOGRAPHY

MacMillan, Dougald and Jones, Howard Mumford. *Plays of the Restoration and Eighteenth Century*. New York: Henry Holt and Company, Inc., 1931.

McAfee, Helen. *Pepys on the Restoration Stage*. New York: Benjamin Blom, Inc., 1952.

McCollum, Jr., John I. *The Restoration Stage*. Boston: Houghton Mifflin Company, 1961.

Nicoll, Allardyce. *A History of Restoration Drama 1660-1700*. Cambridge: Cambridge U. Press, 1923.

Summers, Montague. *The Playhouse of Pepys*. New York Macmillan Company, 1935.

Taylor, D. Crane. *William Congreve*. London: Oxford U. Press (N.D.).

MATERIALS AND BACKGROUND

Gilder, Rosamond. *Enter the Actress (The First Women in the Theatre)*. London: George G. Harrap & Co. Ltd. (N.D.)

Wilson, John Harold. *Mr. Goodman the Player*. Pittsburgh: U. of Pittsburgh Press, 1964.

Wardle, Irving. *The Theatres of George Devine*. London: Johnathan Cape, 1978.

MUSIC

Dioclesian: Masque and Instrumental Music   Sheppard Le Sage, Deller, Worthley, Todd, Bevan (Henry Purcell-Comp.) Van. HM-13

Harpsichord and Clavichord Music   Purcell   None. 7102

MARIVAUX

Pierre de Marivaux was forty-nine when LES FAUSSES CON-FIDENCES was staged in 1726. This was his last great three-act comedy. Many commentators consider this work, together with LE JEU DE L'AMOUR ET DU HASARD. Marivaux's masterpiece. In any case it differs essentially from the latter comedy, and this is partly due to the author's age. The characters are noticeably older, the tone is often more serious, the main characters (especially Araminte, but also Dorante) no longer have the youthful freshness of the lovers of LE JEU DE L'AMOUR ET DU HASARD or that of the other lovers and the other young widows who abound in Marivaux plays. They take life more seriously, and even if love remains their main interest, they have other preoccupations as well, for example, money. Lastly, one can say that the outer world makes insistent incursions into the comedy. We are no longer moving in the ideal world represented by the paintings of WATTEAU. Life intrudes with its material needs, and hearts are no longer *ideally* pure. To amuse, but at the same time, to touch and move his audience was Marivaux's aim in writing this masterwork. It has been *our* aim, in this production, to reveal the essence of the play in the same terms.

ROBERT MANUEL

Robert Manuel, Sociétaire emeritus of the Comédie Française, is a native of Paris. After winning a First Prize for Comedy at the National Conservatory of Dramatic Art, as well as the Critic's First Prize, which is an exceptional honor, M. Manuel was invited to join the Comédie-Française. He made his debut in Molière's "Less Fourberies de Scapin." M. Manuel has been a Sociétaire since 1948, and is a Knight of the Legion of Honor. A leading French director and actor, he has appeared in about 150 plays in the classic and modern repertoire and has directed 45 plays for the Comédie-Française and other theatres, including musical comedies and operettas. He has also directed at the Opéra and the Opéra-Comique and has written two ballets for the Opéra; "Fourberies" and "La Belle Hélène." He has appeared in over 40 motion pictures including, "Rififi" and "Candide." During his career, M. Manuel has played all of the male parts in Marivaux's "The False Confessions." He is Artistic Director of the Théâtre Marigny, Paris. M. Manuel directed the IASTA actors in Marivaux's "The

False Confessions" in New York, 1964. The interview, in French, took place at his home in Paris, in 1971. "Qu'Allais-Je Faire Dans Cette Galère" is the title of M. Robert Manuel's autobiography published in 1975.

INTERVIEW WITH ROBERT MANUEL

Q. How do you choose and define the style for a production? What are the elements of the style?

Manuel: For a production of a Marivaux play, it is important to achieve the style of Marivaux. It is very important to study the times, the 18th century, the manners, the mores, the dance, the music.

It seems to me that tradition is quite simply respect, fidelty, and tenderness for the author and for the work. It is total love, passionate (amour-passion) and reasoning (amour-raison).

Honesty means to want to put on a play exactly the way the author and his actors would have wanted it; with all that this entails as to the artistic autonomy; with scrupulous honesty—to avoid betrayals.

It irritates me, it displeases me to see an author betrayed and staged in a timeless manner. It is too easy to say that a play's theme is extraordinary, and its subjects are timeless: love, death, deep emotions. There are plays which are fixed in time. So then, when one is putting on Marivaux, it is necessary to surround oneself with all the precautions of knowing what the dress was like, how people danced in those days.

Obviously, we are not going to put on a play lighted by candles, we have our eyes and ears wide open to all the inventions modern theatre can provide, as instruments to help us hear better and see better. We agree on that.

But that in no way involves the text itself. And as soon

as you tamper with the text, you change the background and you change the form, for only the technical things have changed.

For me, a Marivaux play must be put on in its 18th century context, and it is at that point that one can understand the characters. When Marivaux first began writing, he felt he owed much to Italian comedy. Later, however, he found his own style. When we speak of Marivaux in an uncomplimentary way, this is, by using the word "marivaudage" which has come to mean talking in an affected and unnatural manner, I think we do him a grave injustice. Marivaux's language is representative of a certain 18th century society—drawing room language. His plays cannot be considered a study of man, but are rather a study of a certain milieu and period. This situation, then, in which he placed his characters may escape today's masses. His extremely pertinent analysis of the human heart, however, does appeal and is understood today.

To distort plays politically just to find new audiences, as we have seen for that matter in France, in the case of Molière's GEORGE DANDIN, and in a rather bizarre way, L'ECOLE DES FEMMES, I find ridiculous, unpleasant, and a betrayal.

Q. As you rehearsed THE FALSE CONFESSIONS, you spoke a great deal about the theme being money and how money affected the life of the characters.

Manuel: There are two things in Marivaux—three things; namely love, goodness and money. It happened that Marivaux lived at a time, 18th century, when people were beginning, little by little, to speak of nothing but money. It is reflected in the plays that appeared during Marivaux's time. Romantic love did not re-appear until the Romantic Theatre of the 19th century: exaggeration, feelings that are a bit ridiculous for our time, loving for the sake of loving without thinking of anything else.

With Marivaux, in addition to money, there is also tenderness and goodness. From his LE JEU DE L'AMOUR ET DU HASARD I would like to appropriate his phrase, "It is necessary to be a little too good to be good enough." I believe an author who could write that phrase is a great author of tenderness, and affection. Marivaux proves it.

One must not fall into affectation in plays of Marivaux. One must remember that the feelings of his characters, even though they are tender, are strong. His people are not talking solely for the pleasure of talking; they speak because they are in love, and there are problems. Strange as it may seem, this is introspective theatre; actors and director have to go deep into these characters, and that is why in the 19th century Marivaux was not acted in France—audiences did not like the plays. Only as late as 1925 did theatres in France begin to play Marivaux.

Now to answer your second question, what are the elements of style: to know and to clarify the thought as well as the style is three-fold. First, *grammatical* punctuation; period, comma, parenthesis, etc., in which one places a different stress, different breathing, different timing. Second, *poetic* punctuation; the laws of verse and prose. Third, that which seems to me most important, the "punctuation" of *expression*; where one places, where one wishes, in tune with the functions of breathing, the sense one wishes to give to a word or a phrase.

Q. Do you feel there is a tangible national theatre style?

Manuel: There are different styles. When one has traveled much one finds, for example, that it is normal for Shakespeare to be staged a certain way in England; with less respect but perhaps more inventiveness in America; perhaps in France with less fantasy, more rigor at times, with as much talent, but less genius.

I have had an opportunity to see Molière interpreted in the United States, in England, and, of course, in France. I found all the styles were extremely interesting when they were sincere, and no attempt was made to put on the plays of Molière to be different, for the sake of difference. As Pirandello said, "To each his truth." We French actors have a truth which we defend. Each of us has. There is certainly a national style without a doubt.

Q. Can a classical play give one the feeling of a period?

Manuel: Yes, and it is exciting; the aroma of history. It is exciting to rediscover a style, to rediscover a language which is not one's own.

The goal of actors, or directors, is *not* to descend to the level of the audience, regardless of how high or low it is. Not to make things easy. It is necessary to raise the audience, to make it believe it is living in the 17th, or 18th, or 19th century.

Q. How important to a production of a classic is authenticity of dress?

Manuel: I think it is extremely important. I find it ridiculous and foolish, for example, to see THE MISANTHROPE performed in modern dress.

Q. May one characterize difference of style between Molière, Racine, Corneille, Marivaux?

Manuel: I will give you my opinion, which doesn't mean it is the truth, as other authorities may disagree. For me, it is a question of stage behavior, articulation, and respect for the text. It is possible to adore a woman and respect her, but I do not think that one can love a woman and rape her! And I believe *not* to respect a text is to rape it. Having a great feeling, a passion for a particular text, does not justify rape. And, in the differences of style, the theatre needs Americans for modern plays; the English for Elizabethan Theatre; but I believe that the theatre has to get from the French respect for the text and, if you permit me, something that perhaps does not exist in America, which is a defect I feel; that is, one must listen to oneself and discipline oneself to speak a classical text. Actors must raise themselves up to the characters. I believe that if an actor wants to perform Racine properly, it is a question of strictness. For us French actors, the unbroken tradition exists—we have it by word of mouth from actor to actor. Actors left to themselves, no longer play tragedy; Racine becomes drama, or worse, melodrama. That is, one retains only the situations, only the lurid actions, not the style, the style of the language as well as of the character, with all that this entails as to behavior.

In plays of Molière, it is the same thing. His characters are no longer heroes, but are good bourgeois or aristocrats in fancy dress. But it is unthinkable that a character of Molière, Racine, Marivaux, would scratch himself or pick his nose. (I exaggerate a bit to make the point.) With adaptation one retains only the structure. For Molière's THE IMAGINARY INVALID, THE MISAN-THROPE, Marivaux's THE FALSE CONFESSIONS, etc., one has to perform it as written, to respect perhaps even more the form than the substance. I feel that it is important because it gives one the method to perform the French classical repertory.

As I said earlier, French tradition is transmitted by word of mouth. Did you know that with eight people we French actors go all the way back to Molière. It's not such a long time. Here whole generations have succeeded one another. I'm not talking about little traditions, little bits, gags, routines that we keep; it is the grand tradition, respect for a style, knowing how to say the verse, knowing how to articulate, knowing how to respect a character.

In working on a role with a student, it is easy to explain to him the differences between Molière and Feydeau. It becomes much more difficult to explain, particularly to non-French actors, that one does not play realism that is cosmopolitan as one plays THE IMAGINARY INVALID of Molière; one does not play Corneille the way one plays Racine; one does not play Labiche as one plays Feydeau; and one does not play Marivaux as one plays De Musset. One has to feel the difference in style, and one can only do that from working on the play, working on the text in evaluating the character. Sometimes there are identical situations, identical characters, but it is not the same thing. One must *feel* these different styles.

(My 'maitre' was André Brunot. He carried the science of diction to a level of perfection. His articulation was a miracle, and his science of the art of speaking verse was as carefully thought out as instinctive. He had a musicality and a rhythm that were extraordinary, taking the trouble to make an audience listen and to make it comprehend. He said to me, "You understand, my friend, if authors give themselves the trouble to write in verse, it is natural—one might say indispensable—that we actors do not betray them, that we speak the text in verse.")

Q. When you speak of classical repertory, what do you mean?

Manuel: A play which, with the passing of years, has been able to conserve its youth, importance and humanity. Such a play can be called classical and will become part of our "classical repertoire." It lasts because it has style; without style there is nothing.

Q. What relevance do Racine, Molière, Marivaux and Beaumarchais have for our contemporary society?

Manuel: Great playwrights, whether they are French or American,

171

have a profound knowledge of man, a sincerity and simplicity which touches us, which strikes a certain chord within us. That is why we actors derive immense joy in serving as interpreters of these men of genius.

Q. How do you train actors to perform the classical repertory?

Manuel: In France, both master and actor have a mission, a love, for classical works. Before analyzing introspectively the roles we are to create, we must know our trade.

In France, we work logically, from the ground up. First of all, one must learn to make oneself heard and understood in the most diverse places. To make oneself heard and understood is not as easy as one may think. Therefore, I use *vis-a-vis* my pupils a formula which might appear paradoxical and perhaps a bit revolutionary. I tell them: imagine you are playing to the *deaf*, to *foreigners* and to *imbeciles*. In other words, let your voice be loud enough, let the timber and tone be rich enough for the deaf to hear. A person who has taken the trouble to come to the theatre whether he sits in the last row of the balcony or in the orchestra, must be able to hear and understand. When I act, I always think of my father who was a little hard of hearing and I imagine that he is somewhere in the audience and my job is to win and hold his attention. Frequently, I force my voice for this reason. You may say that by so doing I hinder the sincerity of the character I am portraying. It would be too easy to say that one captures a character's sincerity by being sincere. This is not so, of course. That is why the introspective approach appears to be a bit dangerous. I also said that actors must imagine they are playing to *foreigners*. Foreigners must be able to recognize words they know, ones they learned in their grammar books and dictionaries. Actors, therefore, must speak correctly, must articulate well; diction must be

172

crystal clear. Now, for the *imbeciles*. One must never take for granted that the author's thoughts are sufficiently clear and well expressed for all in the theatre to understand. It is not the actor's thoughts which are being transmitted, but another man's thoughts. That is why the actor must go to the trouble of explaining these thoughts to make them comprehensible. It is not easy to transmit another man's thoughts with words which are not your own. It sounds easy; it sounds as though I were speaking in platitudes. Why is it difficult? The actor usually feels that he will be more convincing if he appears more human and more sincere. The actor's sincerity, however, cannot and *must not* exist. It is the "character's" sincerity which is of import. Classical roles written for actors are solid and strong. They have perhaps taken on a little patina with changing times. The human heart, however, never changes, though the manner of expressing sentiments and feeling does differ. This is why classical roles are so difficult to act. Words whose meanings have changed during the course of three hundred years, words one no longer uses in the course of conversation must be made to sound new and alive. It is at this moment that the actor must endow his character with sincerity, its own sincerity well articulated, well spoken, well expressed. That is why the classical theatre is a true school for actors. Granted, it is a difficult one but there he will receive rigorous training. The actor is the author's interpreter. What is an interpreter? He is a translator. The actor then translates into a living language something which was dead; printed letters on a white page. The actor infuses life into his character, but not his life, the character's own life. No one in interested in what the actor thinks. What is important is what the character thinks, the way he acts and re-acts in given situations.

Q. What are your techniques for directing classical productions?

Manuel: After meditating on my *"mise en scéne"* for many hours I write it out. I have a little stage in my apartment and I try to visualize what can and should take place on stage; how the characters will evolve, how best I can help infuse life into them. Once at the theatre my conceptions usually change. When working with living beings one gets new ideas and imagination holds full sway. But 85% of directing is casting. If a play is well cast, the director knows the demands he can make upon his actors and if the director has thought about his staging before hand, the production is well on its way. There is one more step to be taken, however, for classical productions. Both director and cast must read as much as possible concerning the playwright in question, the history of the period, criticisms the play received at the time, the costumes, always bearing in mind that modern audiences will now watch the finished piece. As a result of this minute and detailed work, the author's perhaps veiled thoughts and archaic language will be brought out and made to look new.

COMEDY OF MANNERS
(Robert Manuel)

FILM

"Aspects of 18th Century Comedy" (includes scenes from Marivaux's "False Confessions"): obtainable, for rental or purchase, through the Institute for Advanced Studies in the Theatre Arts (IASTA), P.O. Box 1106, Radio City Station, New York, NY 10101 or Gil Forman, 310 W. 56th St., #1B, New York, NY 10010.

SELECTED BIBLIOGRAPHY

Bentley, Eric. *The Classic Theatre:* French Plays (includes English translation of "False Confessions"). New York: Doubleday Anchor, 1959.

Gazagne, Paul. *Marivaux par lui-même. Paris: Écrivains de Toujours, Aux Éditions du Seuil (N.D.)*

MATERIALS AND BACKGROUND

Schneider, Pierre and the Editors of Time-Life Books. *The World of Watteau 1684-1721. New York: Time Inc., 1967.*

Manuel, Robert. *Qu'Allais-Je Faire Dans Cette Galère?* Paris: Éditions Émile-Paul, 1975.

Southern, Richard. *Changeable Scenery.* London: Faber and Faber Limited (N.D.)

MUSIC

Jean-Phillipe Rameau. Operatic Excerpts. Decca DL 9683.

Rameau. Les Indes Galantes. Malgoire, Grande Écurie et Chambre du Roy (F) 3-Col. M3-32973.

GREEK TRAGEDY ELEKTRA

"chorus as theatre"

In the 1930s my colleagues and I began fashioning ancient tragedy in its true, architectural, musical form. Greek tragedy has all the characteristics of a musical composition; in it form and substance are indissolubly tied together in a harmonious unity.

Beginning with the realization of our set plan, our attitude was to preserve whatever had been saved of tradition that would prove of advantage to us. We directed our efforts towards a presentation that would communicate to the modern spectator the tragic emotion and the sacred sense of reverence which struck with such awe the audiences of that time.

From ancient times to the era of Byzantium and on to the present, there is an uninterrupted continuity from which we can extract an abundance of elements to put to fertile use. These enable us to express both the human element, as manifested in the tragedy, and religious element, the sacerdotal, and liturgical.

The mystery of the Holy Eucharist offers a wealth of ideas with which we can emphasize the ceremonial character of Greek tragedy. By studying the evolution of the Holy Eucharist, we discover a great number of substantial analogies and remnants of Greek religion. We think we have been able to take from Christian religion what we judge can serve our theatrical purpose, transmitting it to fit the tragedy we propose to interpret.

Our monophonal Greek folksongs and Greek dances afford plenty of material to enrich our productions. However, we do not use them the way they are today. We trans-substantiate them in order to conform with the spirit of the tragedy. But our inspiration is derived from pure Hellenic sources.

DIMITRIOS RONDIRIS

Born in Piraeus, Dimitrios Rondiris studied law and classics at the University of Athens. Before reaching the age of 20, however, he began, as an actor, his illustrious career in the theatre. He studied drama production under Max Reinhardt, both at his seminar in Vienna and at the Deutsches Theatre in Berlin. In 1934, Mr. Rondiris was appointed Artistic Director of the National Greek Theatre, where he directed about 100 plays from the international repertory. In 1936, he was commissioned by the National Theatre to organize the first Festival of Greek Tragedy, which he inaugurated with Sophocles' "Elektra." In 1954, as General Director of the National Theatre, he inaugurated the Drama Festival at the great, ancient theatre of Epidauros with Euripides' "Hippolytus." He was the Founder and Artistic Director of the Greek Tragedy Theatre (PIRAIKON THEATRON) in Athens. Under his direction they performed not only at the ancient theatres throughout Greece, but enjoyed great sucess touring the European continent and the United States. In 1961, Mr. Rondiris directed Sophocles' "Elektra" for IASTA, and it was revived in 1965 for IASTA's International Classic Theatre Festival in Denver. This interview was conducted in New York, 1961, and in Athens, Greece, 1965.

INTERVIEW WITH DIMITRIS RONDIRIS

Q. How do you define the style for Greek tragedy such as Elektra?

Rondiris: All those who have felt it their sacred and imperative duty to present on the stage the works of the great Greek dramatists have first of all concerned themselves with the problem of the lyric element contained in the chorus. In addition, the tragic style must acknowledge the stature of the characters in the play and the ceremonial nature of the occasion.

Tragedy demands actors of great emotional capacity, actors of great imagination, breadth of vision, and a timeless feeling for life and man's destiny. There is no place for literal-minded people in the playing of the classics.

Q. In your opinion, what is the function of the chorus?

Rondiris: From the beginning of drama the chorus both sang and danced. Their principal characteristic was freedom. The metric composition changed from one stanza to another, but always it was agile, and fluid. The lyric meters in the

179

poetry of Aeschylus constitute a real musical composition with an infinite variety of rhythm.

With the advent of the great tragic poets, Aeschylus, Sophocles, and Euripides, tragedy took on its more perfect form. The lyric element subsided before the dramatic element of the dialogue. At the same time, the part of the chorus was allowed to keep its own place as an artistic contributory factor.

The interpretation of the role played by the chorus requires a long search for a proper resolution. First of all, we familiarize ourselves with the texts as studiously as possible before venturing into thinking out the production in terms of staging. This is an ancient story, poetic in form, born out of religious worship. We try to cater to the need for preserving the ceremonial, ritualistic character of the drama by giving expression to the religious and profoundly human spirit of the tragedy.

The supreme function of the chorus is that of isolating the tragedy making it a thing apart, separating it from everyday reality. The chorus is the poetic concept of the greatest value which had to be rediscovered.

Q.   How do you stage the chorus?

Rondiris: Chorus actors are to incline the head and body offstage, from one side to the other on an eight-beat count, the whole trunk and the head swinging far back; their faces must show all the varied transitions of feeling, sorrow, indignation, joy, reverence, and compassion.

Avoid the sentimental in feelings, the too self-pitying, the too much on the verge of tears. Sorrow is deeper, stronger; their passion is fiercer, wilder. (This direction applies to Elektra as well as to the chorus.)

Know the lines very early in rehearsal. Nothing can be accomplished until the lines are out of the way.

The different verses of the chorus, by their meaning, tell

the actor how they must be read; with what underlying emotion, with what stress and what inflections they must be delivered. The intention of the line gives it its tone, its pitch, its volume, its tempo. In early rehearsals I refer to the relative value of adjectives and nouns. If a noun has not been mentioned before and only the adjective is stressed, the implication is immediately of a comparison between one thing and another. If the adjective is important, then *both* it and the noun are stressed. Failure to do this, with only the adjective stress, could result in several very false readings in the play.

All movements must be clear and definite, not halfway this or that. Interplay of tension and relaxation must always be there.

The choral odes are not a chant. The chorus loves Elektra, but they must keep the rhythm of the beats; I give the chorus actions of consoling and suffering. Distinguish between a period and a comma, and carry the rhythm over a comma. I beat out with my right hand each period, where the downbeat comes. You have no time to do what you want. The rhythm is inexorable. I want passion from the chorus; I want them to see that rhythm is a natural part of everyday speech; I want certain vowels extended, as in words like root and branch; e.g. in one of the expressions of woe; three beats on each vowel. If I had more time, I would write the whole script out in musical notation. At moments I call for "stringendo," a gradual increase of volume, rate and intensity, a term borrowed from music.

The ritual idea of the play constantly recurs; the raised hands, the crossing of arms of the chorus. The turning of the body of each member of the chorus towards Elektra, or Chrysothemis, could be call heliotropic. Any abrupt movement to be synchronized among chorus actors must be felt in each one by counting time, because chorus members cannot see each other; e.g. on Clytemnestra's

181

exit. The chorus must not reveal that they are getting ready, muscularly, to raise; there must be no anticipation of a cue to rise that is visible to the audience. Downbeats must be very firm.

To generalize, there are few silences in the staging of ELEKTRA, few pauses for effect; there are continuous symphonic sounds. I use musical terms, such as crescendo, diminuendo for both the principals and chorus. I require a particular articulation of the words, as a singer approaches words, extending vowels and speaking through them and separating vowel sounds by a crisp enunciation of consonants. In this way, each word is to receive its full value as a sound and not merely its value in the total meaning of a phrase or sentence. This requires tremendous breath control—far more than is generally demanded. It is a matter of technique, not of emotion. Classical plays necessitate a speaking of very long phrases which in turn requires a mastery of vocal technique. The chorus requires lyric speaking for Greek drama started from the dance and the worship of Dionysus. We still do not know at all accurately *how* the chorus was handled; we have only a few indications. But we do know that they had a spirit of reverence and that their relationship to the gods, to the supernatural, even as in the old mystery plays, was very strong. In trying to get a real feeling of worship and reverence into many of the verses of the chorus I say, "We have discovered many things in the world today, but we still do not know *who* or *what* is up there, where they looked for the gods."

Rhythm and one voice-in-unison, along with incidental accompaniment of instrumental music, are used to underline the rhythm. Changes in rhythm do not occur for their own sake or for variety. They are governed by the shifts in feelings and dispositions of the characters.

This changing of rhythms is continuous, following as it

182

does the changing of placement of the chorus. It is in this manner that the poetic word is made to elide into melodious expression, to take the form of song. The same happens with the choric movements which do not employ the feet alone as a means of locomotion through leaps and bounds but by thrusts and schematic motions and gestures. The movements are meant to give vent to human emotions and psychic moods, with the use of the whole body. The movements become passionate and agonized, tense and swift, slow and majestic, following the words as they are recited rhythmically.

This rhythmical recitation reaches out to the confines separating speech from song—to wind up as song. In those moments, the movements of the chorus are akin to dancing. The word "dancing" should not be taken with its modern meaning, but should suggest a way of movement full of dignity and poise, befitting ancient tragedy.

It is this kind of dancing we still can observe today in Greece: real, unmitigated folk dancing, austere in movement, and resplendent in form.

Dance movement must not come about in an arbitrary way, but break forth due to an irresistible pressure exerted by the intensity of the poetic speech. This is not only relevant to the chous, but also must include the principal actors as the protagonists of the drama. There are certain moments when the heroes of the drama air their feelings in a rhythmical speech which evolves into song.

There are also moments when a principal character laments with the chorus and also a moment when the chorus expresses its own feelings and does not make comment either on events or on the feelings of others.

We of the National Theater have worked unrelentingly to provide a solution to the proper style for Greek tragedy. Whosoever has followed the course of our work will be in a position to judge the extent of progress that has

J.D.M.

been made from the first modern performance of ancient tragedy in 1936 up to the present. We hope the lyric element, the chorus, that was once considered to have interrupted the action, has acquired through our efforts its true artistic value and become an element of genuine artistic emotion.

Q.   As a director what is your approach to the actor and the art of acting?

Rondiris: Classical acting is not declamation which is sound without meaning. In the Greek classics the manner of expression is larger because the emotions are larger.

At the National Theatre school we begin with the breath. When we are masters of the breath, we go to the voice. In other words, from speech exercises we move to particular roles. Actors must learn to capture reality and then express that reality with the technical skills of which they are masters. The great poets are not difficult if the actor is master of his skills; they are not so difficult to understand for they are simple.

The actor acts out of a deep fountain of emotion and energy, a concentrated state of being. No one who is not an actor knows the amount of energy that must be used.

The actor cannot give forth this emotion and play the scenes fully all at once. It is impossible. He must work gradually. The actor gives most attention to the voice with breathing exercises every day before rehearsal; then there is less tension and straining. To perform, the actor needs to have absolute freedom and complete discipline. That's all!

The actor must study and read the poet he has to interpret and understand his work very well; and then he must feel it. If he has mastery of his voice and is the master of his acting skills, then he can express it.

I stress punctuation: if you speak with the

punctuation,50% of the work is done. The actor's obligation is to the rhythm of the script, the form. I give the
rhythm, which is painful to the actor's ego, and in doing
so, free the actor. I am convinced I found the rhythm for
the Greek classics among the Greek peasants who had
passed down music and dance steps for generations.

I say to actors, "Don't stretch. Don't try to force what
isn't there. The worst kind of trying is the moment when
you should just *do* it. Be real; find yourselves within the
form. I don't care how big it is—at first. Don't cry or
whine."

The actor must not declaim. There must be serenity in
the center of the tempest. He must be in a constant state
of inner excitement; he must feel the emotions burning inside him, but he must make the verses both intelligible and
beautiful to the listener.

He must know the why and the how of what he says;
observing the need for secondary stresses, the accent on
the main word which each phrase contains; analyzing the
relative stresses of adjectives and nouns.

Actors have to work with the director without explana-
tions, just as a conductor of music works with a group of
musicians who know how to play their instruments. We
discuss the play and the characters first in order that there
may be no discussion during rehearsals.

And once more, the speech, the diction, must be clear;
the audience must understand every syllable! The actor
must be capable of projection in even the largest or most
difficult space. If he has a well-placed and trained voice,
projection is something he comes to feel in order to communicate with the audience.

Actors must strive always to have the largeness of the
feelings in rehearsal or they will never be able to achieve it
in performance. They must try at all times for concentration, inner tension and a sustaining of the emotion

underneath the scene. When the actor is given a direction, he must retain the feeling, stay in the scene.

The most important point of a line is very often at the end, and it needs force and accent to bring out the meaning. Too often the ends of lines may simply die away. For classic plays, far more breath is demanded.

Never mistake the manner for the feeling. Attention must be paid to the form, but the basic thing, the feeling must be there, of course.

I help the actor get a flow of the whole speech by going much faster than the tempo really should be. When the actor has to phrase and keep the speech moving the meaning immediately becomes clearer.

A lethargy in picking up cues will let the whole play fall to the ground; the chain of energy, the dynamic entity must never be broken, for it is like an electric current that passes between actors and audience. Each actor must sustain energy at all times, whether speaking or not.

In the recognition scene: Elektra realizes it is Orestes before her. The suspense in the recognition scene should be overpowering, and it is dependent on the way the two actors play together emotionally and technically. Elektra and Orestes must give the audience the feeling that there is more to come and that the audience cannot wait to hear it. One actor simply hands the scene to the other one to carry on. This technique is again founded on the way people do speak in such a scene in life. It is the selectivity of the lines that makes it art. There is a tempo and a rhythm to this scene which the actor must sense and express, a give and take, a flow between the two that is never allowed to stop or fall.

Orestes has to build his speech in semi-tones, as had Elektra. The narration must be kept distinct at all times from the comments made by the old man, difference is shown by a change in the pitch of the voice. The quality of being royal, the dignity, bearing the inner essence of being a princess or a king, can be very difficult for contemporary actors. To get angry or indignant is not to rage like fishwives. Elektra is a flame, full of pain. She never surrenders. She must have majesty and greatness.

In working to a climax within a long speech, after the actor has built the speech up to a certain point, he then takes it down, but never as far down as the place he had started from, and in the end, the whole speech builds slowly up to its highest point.

A good part of projection is not volume at all, but the desire in the mind to convey thoughts and feelings to the audience. This is an intangible and must be felt by the actor.

To keep the listening body alive and ready for its next speech or action, to have what is said grow out of the whole being, it is necessary to keep the whole play alive. The actor's body must not be apathetic and then, when he speaks, suddenly come to life. Orestes has a long silent time of listening while Elektra speaks to the urn: he cannot simply stand there, limply waiting. Out of all he is feeling while she speaks, which must be shown in the body, grows the tremendous sign required before the actor speaks.

The reason the actor must stand at least an arm's length away from another actor is in order that he may gesture and move freely; also, for appearance's sake. On a bare stage, like the Greek stage, the actor needs space around him for focus and in order to act freely.

Q. Do you use a choreographer?

Rondiris: Yes. The choreographer for the Greek plays not only has specialized dance training, but he must be highly musical. He must understand acting and all that the director is trying to do. He must be able to conduct rehearsals with the chorus so as to interpret the text in the same way as the director, and be part of the unity of the play.

Q. As a teacher of actors as well as a director, how do you work in the early stages?

Rondiris: The first day I give the blocking, the placement of the principals in the scenes. I am right there on the stage with them, sometimes with a hand on a shoulder moving them about and giving them each position. While the actors are getting the blocking, I ask them merely to read the lines quietly, but always in rhythm, of course, not trying to act. After they have mastered their lines, however, the actor must try to put increased meaning and feeling into the scene to try to give the feeling I ask for. Then, if it is wrong, it is my fault, not the actor's.

I repeat often that the weight must be on one foot or the other, so the actor is able to move in any direction at any time (as with a dancer). The actor must learn to take small steps in Attic drama, so that he will always be in control.

At first rehearsals actors read. The chorus sits for the first readings, then stands and delivers the verses with a swaying movement, then finally walks with the words while I, as director, beat time with my hands. The chorus walks in rhythm individually, but in unison with all the others as well. The chorus must be heard and understood; the diction must be clear. In life you may eat (swallow) your words; in the theatre we must hear every syllable. The one may be natural, but the other artistic.

Lines must be read in phrases, not in single words punched out individually; each word within a phrase and each phrase within a sentence (line), as it is said, must convey a meaning in relation to the whole context. The meaning gives the form and the form helps the meaning. They are one and cannot be separated.

In rehearsal I may have one actor read all the chorus

lines while the others mime only the action. Then I check each for correct positions while the actors concentrate on movement alone. Again, I stress: do not stretch delivery out for the effect's sake. Do not declaim; mean it, mean it always.

Crescendos must be created gradually, growing out of what has gone before. I demonstrate how to make a gradual rise by going up in semi-tones, taking one line on an even pitch, then going on to the next line a half tone higher, and with more volume. Do this first on the sound, MMMMMMM; then, on the lines; finally start filling the line with the right feeling.

After much technical work, I demand to have from the actor the soul of lamentation; don't think; feel, act, do it!

When I call for immense emotion from someone; e.g. Elektra, she may say, "But Mr. Rondiris, I have never felt any such emotion." I reply, "You are an artist, aren't you? The artist must have intuition; he must have imagination; he must have perception. What do you mean, you have never felt this emotion?" It is not sufficient for an actor to draw everything from his own experience, to work things out logically, to explain things in words.

Q. What is the next step in rehearsals? Are there strongly distinguished stages in rehearsal, or is this "movement" a gradual and continuous one?

Rondiris: As rehearsals progress, I urge the actor to participate more, to enter in more. Give an emotion in a small way and then in a large way; e.g. use the emotion of happiness and show it in an everyday situation, then in extreme, as both Elektra and Chrysothemis have to do in the play. Unbounded, ecstatic joy comes from a deep well of inexhaustible feeling which the actor carries within himself all the time.

The trained actor must be able to halt his feelings; not

stop them, but the feeling must remain there, ready to be taken up again. The actor has to be able to stop, listen to the director, and then go on. Later on in rehearsals, I will be saying, "louder, softer, slower, faster, etc.," while the actor is in the midst of an emotional scene, and he must be able to hear and follow the direction but not lose the emotion.

Full of the rhythm of the play and of the speeches, I beat the time for the actors almost constantly as I rehearse. In later rehearsals, drums beat the time in certain parts of the play, especially for certain movements and actions of the chorus; this continual beating of time, striking the table, counting and giving vocal attacks where the thought changes, makes the actor feel the dynamics of the play's structure as if a piece of music. The inner tension cannot be relaxed. There must be enough breath to finish lines fully.

In the scene between Elektra and Clytemnestra, there is anticipation; in this scene, the timing of the two women in seeing each other is very important, emotionally and dramatically. The actor knows what is going to happen; as the character in the play, she does not, and her feelings and reactions come as the situations are occurring. This is the challenge, the paradox.

Q. How are relationships dramatized?

Rondiris: Aegisthos is a swaggering man. I bring him on in the play first with his back to the audience, walking from the audience's right, through the orchestra toward the palace door. The chorus is to mime the impact of the blow when Clytemnestra is struck down. All actions must be strong and sharply differentiated in transitions.

The Pedagogus, in the opening scene, must not be too naturalistic (I demand a high-keyed excitability from the start). The actor must keep ever in his soul some images

191

of magnificence. He must never let the ball drop, vocally. When Elektra hugs the urn with Orestes' ashes to her breast, I really want her to cry. The groans of Elektra, at the announcement of Orestes' death are to be the animal groans of an utterly unAnglo-Saxon nature. I want lost, distracted states of emotion. Upon Orestes' appearance, Elektra cannot, in her desperation, believe anyone comes to her with sympathy. There is a difference between intensity and shouting. At the climax of the recognition scene, I want an inhuman explosion. I want hardness, bitterness, aggressiveness for Elektra; Elektra must not let a crying tone come into the voice: I prefer a breathy tone as an expression of passion. I press for an extension of vowels also in the part of Chrysothemis.

As rehearsals progress I stress other aspects of the voice than voice-color; I pay more attention to changes from forte to piano, to metre more than to timbre and color. Actors must not be frightened, but listen for the accents—and start. Listen but don't count. Close to performance it is too late for that. Act! Act! I am the director but I should sing, dance, tease, cajole, and inspire. It is almost as if I am conducting an orchestra, for I set the drummer's tempo with rhythmic waving of hands and arms; I guide the sonorities, pacings and pitches of the choral speeches and songs. As needed, I charge right into the chorus itself to demonstrate a gesture, the kneeling or a dance-like fluctuation of the spine.

I recall that I had Elektra hold her right hand to her breast for long periods, gesturing only with the left hand.

The first song for the chorus comes after the first exit of Chrysothemis. During Clytemnestra's scene, one section of the chorus stands with the weight on one leg, the other leg bent at the knee. For the entrance of Aegisthus the chorus splits into four groups: two upstage at either end of the steps and two downstage on either side. Have a flexible waist. Remember, the mind is master of the body. Have your body at your disposal, but you must also feel. I cannot tell actors to move their arms two inches or a quarter of an inch. They must feel it! For certain scenes the voices of the chorus in unison swell and recede, rise and fall, rush and subside, as they journey toward a monumental climax, find resolution in a whispered sign or culminate in a chant.

I recall a chorus member missed a rehearsal and another chorus member felt as if her leg was missing. That's what I mean about the chorus being one body. The death of Orestes is followed by a scream from Elektra, with no pause. Is it the fault of the audiences or the actors to want to wait an instant? Actors analyze too much; they have to feel immediately.

As the principal characters begin to work without texts and begin to try to enter into the plot situations and the emotions of their parts more fully, important technical work has to begin: keeping open positions to the audience for important speeches; not dropping ends of lines; making the dramatic points; standing away from each other; building climaxes; effecting pitch transitions to show change of thought or feeling, being aware of the dynamics of each scene—its dramatic build which must start in intention in the early part of the scene.

After a run-through, I analyze the technical matters. The drums and the choral music I prefer for ELEKTRA is minor and beautifully sad. As the chorus learns the music and practices with me, supplemented by coaching by a musical conductor, I work with the chorus on attack, phrasing, diction, legato speaking; use a glottal stroke for attack on a line; think "H." After a few days, the change in the choral speaking is remarkable; with mastery of a glottal attack for each line, phrasing and diction improve greatly.

In a scene of anger an actor must give a dynamic lift to the end of his line in order for the other actor to be able to play back to him and make the proper build in the scene. Otherwise, there is no scene, no climax.

Q. Does each play have its own proper style?

Rondiris: Aeschylus, Sophocles, Euripides—to say nothing of Aristophanes—each has a distinct style.

Q. How important to a production of a classic is authenticity of dress?

Rondiris: Sometimes the Greek classics seemed not to have been understood. If they are, all the director and actors have to do is to play them for what they are intended to be expressed. This style is given us by the play itself, and is not superimposed. Bringing the play "up-to-date," changing period, language, conception of character, all this shows a great lack in the directors who do it.

Q. How important is a knowledge of the physical form of the theatre for which the play was written?

Rondiris: Fortunately in Greece, we have many true Greek theatres extant. On our tour we sometimes have to adapt to the proscenium stage.

Q. Do you feel there is a tangible National Theatre style?

Rondiris: Yes, there is a national style. Ancient tragedy was born out of the dithyramb in Greece and today we continue that tradition with a Greek National theatre for the classics.

GREEK TRAGEDY

FILM

"Aspects of the Classic Greek Theatre" (includes scenes from Sophocles "Elektra"): obtainable, for rental and purchase, through the Institute for Advanced Studies in the Theatre Arts (IASTA), P.O. Box 1106, Radio City Station, New York, NY 10101 or Gil Forman, 310 W. 56th St., #1B, New York, NY 10019.

SELECTED BIBLIOGRAPHY

Aristotle. *Poetics, Aristotle — On Style, Demetrius.* New York: E.P. Dutton & Co., Inc., 1943.

Hamilton, Edith. *The Greek Way.* New York: Time Inc., 1963.

Jones, W. H. S. *Pausanias: Description of Greece, Vol. I - X.* Cambridge: Harvard U. Press, 1959.

Storr, F. *Sophocles: Ajax, Elektra, Trachiniae, Philoctetes.* Cambridge: Harvard U. Press, 1951.

Wilson, Edmund. *The Wound and the Bow.* New York: Oxford U. Press, 1965.

MATERIALS AND BACKGROUND

Bieber, Magarete. *The History of the Greek and Roman Theatre.* Princeton: Princeton U. Press, 1961.

Greek Heritage, Volume 1, Number 2 & 3 and Volume 2, Number 6. Chicago: The Athenian Corporation (N.D.)

Green, Peter and the Editors of the Newsweek Book Division. *The Parthenon.* New York: Newsweek, 1973.

A Short Guide to the Sculptures of the Parthenon in the British Museum. London: The Trustees of the British Museum, 1950.

Everyday Life in Ancient Times. Washington, D.C.: National Geographic Society, 1961.

Thompson, Homer A. *The Athenian Agora.* Greece: Aspioti-Elka Ltd., 1962.

MUSIC

Byzantine Chant   Mt. Athos Choir, Abbot Alexos   Easter on Mt. Athos
DG ARC-2533413.

Tilburg Byzantine Choir, Van Dongen   Liturgy of St. John Chrysostom
Phi. 6830194.

INDIA: SANSKRIT

"theatre as a temple"

In India, dancing is religion. Since it is considered the most satisfying and pleasing sacrifice to the gods, every place we dance becomes a temple. In order to sanctify the ground around us, we first say a prayer to mother earth, "Please mother earth, forgive us for treading so harshly upon you." Then we do a small puga or dance of worship. We throw flowers and sprinkle water on the ground and then the stage becomes the temple. We try to make every performance sacred.

Many people think that dancing and acting, in India, consist mainly of hand movements or mudras. This is perhaps because we do use our hands a great deal. But if one watches very closely, one will see that the performer's hands move almost with the eyes and with the entire face. In India, we say, where the hands go let the eyes go. And where the eyes go let the mind go. And where the mind goes let the heart go. Only then can the spectator enjoy the flavor or mood of the performance.

In all Indian culture, philosophy and art are bound close together. For instance, long ago a sage wrote a book about Indian dancing and drama which we still use today. There is a lovely passage in it that says: "To the artist, show the world the true reality of life and from it, those who need ugliness, will pick out ugliness. Those who want beauty will pick out beauty. Those who want lust will enjoy it for it is entertainment. But somewhere inside of them something, if it's a beautiful piece of art, something is going to speak. And this is the message of the artist." Give the reality but in such a way that the truth shines forth.

MRINALINI SARABHAI

In the world of dance-drama, MRINALINI SARABHAI holds a universally recognized position today. She began her training at an early age under Sri Muthukumaran Pillai of Mayavaram. Such illustrious teachers as Sri Ellappa, Sri Chokkalingam Pillai, and the great Meenakshi Sundaram Pillai gave her training in the purest and most cherished forms of Bharata Natyam. She has trained in other countries including Java and the United States where she studied acting and stage technique at the American Academy of Dramatic Arts. She has also studied Kathakali with Sri Kunju Kurup and later, at Santinketan, she played leading roles in many of Rabindranath Tagore's dance-dramas. She then joined Ram Gopal as his partner and danced with him in Bangalore, Calcutta and Madras. But her emphasis on purity of tradition and classical technique soon made her launch out on her own.

Thus equipped, Mrinalini Sarabhai founded Darpana, an academy of dance, drama and music in Ahmedabad in 1948. Since then, her career as dancer and choreographer has come dramatically to life, especially in the field of dance drama.

She has taken her troupe to Europe, South America, Mexico, Egypt, Lebanon, South East Asia, Japan, and America. Dance-dramas and plays have been produced and directed by Mrinalini Sarabhai. She is the first Asian to receive the medal and diploma of the French Archives Internationales de la Dance, a rare honor, and was recently awarded the title, "Natya Kala Sikhamani" in Madras in recognition of her artistic eminence and her dedication to the art of Bharata Natyam.

The IASTA production of *Vasavadatta,* after being presented in the Coolidge Auditorium of the Library of Congress, in Washington, D.C., had its American premiere in New York on November 23, 1963.

The interview was conducted at IASTA in 1975.

Q. Madame Sarabhai, would you tell us something about the author of THE VISION OF VASAVADATTA?

Sarabhai: Very little is known of Bhasa, whose work as a playwright and poet dates back some 2,000 years. It is evident, however, that he enjoyed a great reputation as a dramatist for he is frequently referred to by other writers.

THE VISION OF VASAVADATTA, a prime example of Bhasa's historical plays, revolves around Udayana, Pradyota and Darsaka, whose dates have been accepted as the 6th Century B.C. It is especially interesting to note that writing in the 4th or 5th Century B.C. (there is still much controversy about the exact date), Bhasa deals with King Udayana, hero of a thousand legends, and his beloved Queen Vasavadatta, in human and psychological terms. Bhasa reveals in this play his understanding of human emotion and his command of language both in poetry and prose which led Jayadeva (1200 A.D.) to say of him that he was the "laughter of poetry."

Bhasa was the master of all the nine *rasas* or sentiments of Indian drama, and in THE VISION OF VASAVADAT-TA he employs a number of these: the marriage for love and the marriage for necessity are represented by the King's marriages to Vasavadatta and Padmavati respectively; the sentiment of humor is fully exploited in Vasantaka's character; the sentiment of pathos is embodied in Vasavadatta, alone in her grief, and the heroic sentiment in the character of Udayana, who, throughout the play, exhibits strength in his struggle between reality and illusion. Bhasa excels in a simplicity of style, a sharpness of characterization and in a deep love of nature. He is a dramatist of full-blooded action and his plays are filled with dramatic irony. THE VISION OF VASAVADATTA the most poetic of his plays, represents him at his creative best.

Q. How does one choose the correct style for a production, THE VISION OF VASAVADATTA?

Mrinalini: It's rather simple to choose the style for VASAVADATTA, because we know the period and we know the kind of life the people lived in India at that time. The style, of course, would be the style we read about in ancient Hindu literature; it would be a period piece, and for that we would rely on the ancient Sanskrit theatre which had definite rules as to staging, speech, and movement. This is the oldest theatrical form that we know of. The Sanskrit theatre is based on certain texts including THE LAWS AND PRACTICE OF SANSKRIT DRAMA, by Srendra Nath Shastri. The finest book, Bharata Muni's NATYA SHASTRA, a complete treatise on dance, music, and drama (*natya*) was written about the second century A.D. and is used by dancers and actors today.

The guru (teacher), Bharata, has left behind him a complete treatise on the culture of a world gone by. So we have quite a lot to go on when we stage THE VISION OF VASAVADATTA.

It was my conviction that it might be possible to reconstruct the style of performing of the Sanskrit plays out of traditions and techniques of the classic dance forms of India. In my homeland in West India, Kerala, I found in one of the remote temples a fragment of this particular play, THE VISION OF VASAVADATTA, being performed still by the priests of the temple, as part of a ritual. A Sanskrit classic thus may be said to be rooted in what is the best approximation of the acting style a millennia ago. I utilized my knowledge of the style (e.g. the mudras) of the traditional classical dance forms of India and the patterns and the staging of the fragments of THE VISION OF VASAVADATTA as I observed it in the temple as performed by the Hindu priests.

Music was used extensively as background for and to underscore the performing of the play.

Q. Although Sanskrit theatre, as it was known a thousand years ago, has largely died out in India might it be said that you have rediscovered the style?

Mrinalini: Well, one can still find traces of it in South India where they still do this kind of drama in the temples. In India, dancing is supremely devotional, and the art cannot be separated from its religious source.

We can trace dancing back through the ages through the sculptures on temple walls, through learned gurus, and through ancient manuscripts. Scholars have found that the dance movements mentioned by Bharata are all depicted at the Chidambaram Temple of Siva. There are one hundred and eight in his treatise. Above each movement depicted verses from Bharata NATYA SHASTRA are inscribed. The temple itself was built over a period of 1300 years, from the sixth to the nineteenth century. Here in this temple, according to tradition, Siva danced his cosmic dance which has been immortalized by sculptors and which has become the symbol of the dance today.

A striking difference between the Chidambaram and the Siva temple of Tanjore is that many of the figures in Chidambaram are of the feminine form as opposed to the sculptures of the male in the eighty-one postures beautifully depicted in the tower of the Tanjore Temple. Both adhere exactly to the principles laid down in the NATYA SHASTRA.

The art form is still, I think, completely the style of the Sanskrit theatre. It has deteriorated a bit in the style of dress, and it has become very popular. But yet the form is very clear. It was definitely a kind of total theatre where the actors danced and sang and spoke, and they were gifted in being able to do all these things together. I think the difficulty today is to find actors who sing very well, who dance very well, who speak well, and who move well.

Q.   Do you feel there is a tangible national theatre style?

Mrinalini: I think there's a natural "experience—style"—if there's a word like that—where the kind of feeling for things is symbolic and religious and has a background of the same theatre.

In the folk theatre of India you find much more of a national style. Not in any other form of theatre, and certainly not in the dance. When you see Indian folk theatre, you really can say that there is a definite style; the type of dialogue, the movement of the actors and the rather broad humor. All these are characteristic and similar in folk theatre all over India.

Q. Does each play, even a Sanskrit play, have its own correct style?

Mrinalini: We perform a Sanskrit play as you would an ancient Greek play, which definitely had a style one can follow. As for modern plays, American or German or English, we Indianize them all in the sense that we try to make them as Indian as possible so that our audiences can understand them.

Q. As a director, how do you clarify for an audience the historical and social pressures which dictate behavior and relationships?

Mrinalini: Actually, what I do as a director is to take each play as a separate experience. I don't try to think of it as historical. I tell my actors for a VISION OF VASAVADATTA that the problem is really one of love. Suddenly, I find the play becomes very clear to them. There were certain concepts the American actors couldn't understand; why a man had two wives and how he could be married twice. I said, "It's the same in your country, except that you may divorce and remarry." In ancient India they believed that was unfair to the first wife; that she also should be as important as the second wife.

Economic social divisions still exist today. We don't often write of kings and courtiers, but of the rich and the poor. These are universal problems, and I think when the director talks of people as human beings, the director tries to make actors and actresses feel that each of the play's characters is an individual human being who would react the same way as anybody else today. Even in VASAVADATTA, the king had to marry again to protect his kingdom. He hated to do it, for he hated to make his second wife feel that she was not loved. Now, this is a very human situation so I would always try to get at its-humanity and at the universality of the problem rather

203

than take it as an isolated period play.

Q. As a director, what do you see as the elements of style?

Mrinalini: That really is a difficult question. I wonder if style has any elements? Style, to me, is divided into two aspects: one, the style that one has studied and learned as being a part of the past, and then there is the style that is one's very own. My individual style I would call the present or the contemporary. The style of the past, of course, we have talked about as a certain stylization of movement, dress, etc.

For any modern play, I think that the director may concern himself with a very, very individual style. The actors or actresses one works with have a style of their own; their thinking is their own. This is where I think it is very important that the director understand the actors as human beings, for very often, directors try to superimpose their own personalities on the performers. Directors have to express their ideas, but they also must let their actors and actresses speak out and give expression to what they feel. I really try to share experiences with the actors in creating the world of the play; we are all in it together. Creating a play isn't any different from the world around us, how we have to act in real life. We build on that to make the play. But the inner life of the play must be a shared life.

Q. Is a knowledge of the manners of the period important?

Mrinalini: What you really have to get across is the feeling of the period you are portraying. You may use any mannerisms or styles, if you can get across the experience and the mood. For instance, I tell people that wherever I dance, whether it be a lecture hall in Brooklyn or a theatre in New York or Paris, there the audience must feel that it is a temple in India. We dancers must be able to transmit that feel of India, not Indianess, not by means of costumes but by the feelings evoked when the spectators see the dance.

Some, when they see the dance, are completely surprised by a kind of sacred feeling—I talk of sacred at its deepest level. They have reacted to it with something within themselves.

Now this, I think, is more important than if I had surrounded myself, let us say, with temple scenery, or a shrine and a lamp and all that. Usually we don't have any scenery; it's just a bare stage. Even in acting a play I think this is more important. Of course, if you can bring in something of the visual style, that's important, but certainly it's not *the* most important thing.

Q. How important is authenticity of dress?

Mrinalini: I would like it to be as authentic as possible. certainly. But sometimes certain dresses might not have a theatrical beauty about them. So there I think you can cheat a little and use materials that are modern or especially beautiful but that suggest a kind of style. Many people asked me why I hadn't used elaborate head dresses for VISION OF VASAVADATTA. When I looked up the period through pictures, I found that head dresses were a much later invention and rare. At the time of the play, only two pieces of cloth were used for covering the head, which I used throughout, and one can see the variety we achieved with two pieces of cloth: the men wore two pieces; the women, as well, wore two pieces, and there were many different variations. Now some might argue that in the Buddhist period there were crowns, but I felt that crowns just didn't go with the actors and actresses we had, and our American actors looked much more genuine without them. Their simple and ordinary hair styles made them seem Indian. In fact, many asked me whether the blond girl, who took the part of Vasavadatta, was Indian! This is something I think that shows the play came across. And, this is what was important: the style was there and the

205

basics, ornaments and so on, were there, but it was not an exact imitation; e.g. of paintings.

The costuming of the characters in the play may basically be quite simple: for the men, the wearing of the dhoti. A possible variation for certain of the elderly or priestly men characters can be the long loincloth. The materials of the costumes can be of silk and authentic saris, or they can be of cotton with some kind of border. Each character (both male and female) may wear the red dot on the forehead.

As for jewelry, the female characters may wear bracelets, earrings, anklets, and strands of beads or metal chains woven into the braids if they are long. As for the men, earrings and arm bands may be used. In the case of both male and female characters, amounts of jewelry should be used with economy and taste.

Since to the Indians even today, the stage floor will have been consecrated, both male and female characters perform the play in bare feet. Even when the text is referring to the locale of the scene as exterior (and in life Indians might wear sandals), even so the actors performing on the consecrated stage floor do so in their clean bare feet. The soles of the feet of the young female characters may be lightly rouged.

Q. Is it important to know something about the physical shape of the theatre in which Sanskrit plays were performed?

Mrinalini: We know that these plays were performed mostly in the open air or in the round; that much we do know. However, we have to work with stages which are mostly the proscenium stage of today, and I find we don't much bother about that. Actors can seldom choose their theatre: few actors or directors get theatres built for them.

I think it's better to create—again I come back to

this—that which is inner and not outer. I find that if you work from the inside out, you really can create anything, anywhere, if that is what you really want to do.

However, since the recommended setting for the Sanskrit play is basically a platform, the IASTA production covered the deck of the stage with slabs of closely joined and sealed beaverboard. These then were lacquered black. Then the black surface was highly polished with wax, giving the appearance of a highly gleaming surface. This was also effective for the acting and whatever dancing was involved. Black velours delimited the acting area on stage. It was our special concern to keep the stage lighting off the velours. Although a very simple bare stage works for a Sanskrit classic, for decorative relief we used three rosettes of approximately three feet to six feet in diameter in primary colors, as in folk art, suspended above the acting area of the stage. A keynote to the style of the production was miming of most of the hand properties. Set props were extremely simple: a bench, a bed, a chair. Since India has always been a hot and tropical country, the bed and chairs were very low to the floor. In order to enjoy the cooler air close to the earth and floor, much of the action was sitting on the ground, squatting, crouching, kneeling.

Gesture is very basic to the style for the play. Appropriate mudras were taught which fit the imagery in the speeches. All mudras are not simple, and the mudras were kept at a minimum to avoid an over-fussy and distracting amount of gesticulation on the part of the actors. Economy and selection were keynotes.

Q. How important is it for the director of a Sanskrit play to learn about India, its customs and climate, to invest the production with reality and style?

Mrinalini: I do think it is important and the best way to learn, as did

IASTA, is through an Indian director. I think it's important to learn as much about India as possible, but a theoretical knowledge is just not enough. One has really to feel India. I find that many people have read a lot but know so little; whereas one visit, being just once with an Indian, talking, working with somebody Indian, gives much more. That's why dialogues resulting from bringing in directors from other countries to stage classics are so important and valuable.

SANSKRIT

FILM

"Sanskrit Drama" (includes scenes from Bhasa's *Vision of Vasavadatta*): obtainable, for rental and purchase, through the Institute for Advanced Studies in the Theatre Arts (IASTA), P.O. Box 1106, Radio City Station, New York, NY 10101 or Gil Forman, 310 W. 56th St., #1B, New York, NY 10019.

SELECTED BIBLIOGRAPHY

Baumer, Rachel Van M. and Brandon, James R. *Sanskrit Drama in Performance*. Honolulu: The University Press of Hawaii, 1981.

Brandon, James R. *Traditional Asian Plays*. New York: Hill and Wang, 1972.

Lal, P. *Great Sanskrit Plays*. Norfolk, Conn.: New Directions, 1964.

Mitchell, J. D. "The Sanskrit Drama Shakuntala: A Psychologic Sounding Board for Hindu Culture." *The American Imago*. Massachusettes: Winter, 1959.

Mitchell, J. D. "The Theater of India and Southeast Asia." *Asia and the Humanities*. Bloomington, Ind: Indiana U., 1962.

Mitchell, J. D. "The Theatre in India." *Catholic Theatre*. Davenport, Iowa: 1957.

Shastri, S. N. *The Laws and Practice of Sanskrit Drama*. India: Chowkhamba Publication, 1961.

MATERIALS AND BACKGROUND

Coomaraswamy, Ananda. *The Dance of Siva*. New York: The Sunwise Turn, Inc., 1924.

Coomaraswamy, Ananda and Gopalakrishnayya, Duggirala. *The Mirror of Gesture*. New York: E. Weyhe, 1936.

Irwin, Vera Rushforth. *Four Classical Asian Plays*. Baltimore: Penguin Books, 1972.

MUSIC

India Today   Mrinalini Sarabhai   Intersonar   SPL 750.

THE MEDIEVAL:
MARY OF NIJMEGHEN

"religion as theatre"

J.D.M.

Unlike the Greek tragedies, for which there have been no authentic celebrants for 1500 years, religious plays of the West, e.g. EVERYMAN, the York cycle, MURDER IN THE CATHEDRAL, like the Noh theatre of Japan, are part of a living and continuing faith, using symbols and iconography still actively embedded in the audience's mind.

To discover whether these medieval plays are so naive and lacking in craftsmanship as to be unable to capture the attention of a modern audience, IASTA turned to a Dutch master of the medieval style. Mr. de Meester's production of MARY OF NIJMEGHEN proved that finding the intrinsic style of a text determines the audience's response.

JOHAN de MEESTER, IASTA'S distinguished visiting director from Holland, has been actively involved in the theatre for 50 years. He began his career as an actor, turned to directing at an early stage, and in 1924 became the artistic director of the Flemish Popular Theatre in Brussels. Upon his return to Holland in 1929, he directed plays, operas and musicals until 1937, when he became the co-director of the company *Residentie Toneel* in the Hague. After ten years with this group, Mr. de Meester became the co-director of the Nederlandse Comedie of Amsterdam. He remained with this company until 1962, when he left to direct plays for other companies, as well as for television and opera.

In his long and impressive career, Mr. de Meester has directed, in addition to Dutch plays, many foreign plays such as "Measure for Measure." "Death of a Salesman," and "The Tales of Hoffman." For the past 15 years, he has been the director of the famous Dutch "Everyman," which is performed annually at the festival in Delft.

Mr. de Meester's IASTA production of "Mary of Nijmeghen" at the IASTA Theatre, New York, May 2, 1965, marked his first visit to the United States. He had previously directed productions of "Mary of Nijmeghen" in The Hague and in Brussels.

The interview was conducted in Amsterdam, Holland, 1972.

INTERVIEW WITH JOHAN de MEESTER

Q. How do you choose and define the style for a production?

de Meester: What an elusive word! The director, the actors and everybody in the production has to find his style in the play itself. You have, I think, to look to the text that comes directly from the author, as an individual and as a poet. Then you have to consider the time that he lived. Not only is a text born out of the conflict that the author had with the world around him, but what comes only from him, the author. You find the style of a play best by thinking of both things at the same time: taking the inner and the external conflict, fundamental enemies. What comes out of the conflict is a way to come to the style. Having said that, I must admit that in MARY OF NIJMEGHEN there is no antagonism between author and his social milieu; the period is Gothic with the one philosophy of Catholicism. Maybe one may find the style in the fact that Mary is the fundamental character. She and her uncle believed in the *only* truth of the Middle Ages: the one God, the one religion; Catholicism. That was truth for everybody.

Drama arises out of the girl's going out from that quiet village to meet the world of evil influences. The style is a conflict between the quiet, private world of Catholicism and the outer wild world.

Q. Can a Medieval play recreate for an audience a feeling of another time, another way of living and thinking and feeling?

de Meester It is important from time to time, to perform primitive plays like MARY OF NIJMEGHEN. In their simplicity, these plays sometimes tell us more about the fundamental and essential value of drama than later plays by more sophisticated writers. The unknown author of MARY OF NIJMEGHEN was not a highly trained poet as were many of the later Renaissance playwrights. He was probably a member of one of the many rhetoric clubs that existed throughout the Netherlands in the 15th and 16th centuries. These clubs made it possible for craftsmen, merchants and members of the intelligentsia to collaborate in their spare time in the writing and producing of masques and plays.

The playwright of MARY OF NIJMEGHEN knew little about the refined and complicated techniques of renaissance poetry, but this was more than balanced by two different and essential qualities: an instinctive and unspoiled sense of drama, and a deeply religious view of life which he communicated in his drama. He tells us a simple story about a young girl who is seduced by the devil into a life of sin and shame. But even in her deepest disgrace, Mary never gives up her love and veneration for the Virgin Mary, and in the end her soul is miraculously saved from damnation. For this simple story our unknown author has found, with unerring instinct, an equally simple but remarkably strong dramatic form. His dialogue is alive and comes straight to the point and his characters, like a woodcut, are drawn in few, but bold strokes.

The figure of Mary is, even for a modern audience, interesting and moving. She is not primarily interested in money and luxury. The devil succeeds in seducing her only by promising to teach her the "Seven Liberal Arts" and to turn her, in a few weeks time, into an accomplished scientist and poetess. Mary is a highly original forerunner of all the modern women who throw away quiet happiness for the sake of a glamorous career. Just as Mary may be regarded as an early female Faust, so one-eyed Moenen is an amusing precursor of many devils of later times, including his famous great-grandson Mephistopheles.

Q.   Would you characterize some specific elements of style for the Medieval play?

de Meester: We must remember that in the Middle Ages time was a 'slow moving' time. In MARY OF NIJMEGHEN the narrator has a special feeling for each character, as would the playwright. The narrator should suggest a quality found in an old Flemish painting. He talks as if he were talking to children. He must not be stagey. He believes in what he is telling his spectators.

The devil is an underdog, and he fears defeat. In earlier Medieval plays, he was always a clown. Here, he is a bit more modernized, but he is still almost a clown. However, the devil (Moenen) must not be made too modern. He is always a little sad and easily hurt. For instance, the fact that he is allowed to masquerade as a man but has only one *eye* is painful for him to mention. The meanness of Moenen is in the *small* movements. When Moenen asks Mary to give up her name before she can travel with him, he has an uneasy feeling. Then, when he says, "There was once a Mary who did great harm to me and my friends." Moenen's voice should get deeper, as if from some voice from below. Later, it's not easy for Moenen to come back from hell—to talk to Mary again.

Mascaron is a different kind of devil. A devil is just not a devil. Unlike Moenen, Mascaron is angry and means his demands to be taken absolutely, tragically and seriously.

There is no psychology to the character of the aunt. She is just a picture of political madness. She enters as a tired being filled with air, and the attendant has forgotten to turn off the switch. The actress must bring to the part of the aunt a proper amount of fury and a kind of fury and a kind of comic quality at the same time. The aunt thinks, "I'm such a tragic personality." The aunt likes to be overly dramatic; she enjoys this; she is moved only by fury, fury, blind fury. The actress doesn't have to do anything. That is, once she feels it, it will be there.

Emma's (Mary, after her name was changed by the devil, Moenen) song of praise to the seven liberal arts seems unnecessary to the play, perhaps as similar instances of exaltation in plays such as EVERYMAN seems at first, but it does have a purpose. It shows that Emma (Mary) had followed Moenen for noble reason; e.g. her love of learning an art.

Jesus (in the play within the play) is turned almost into a Jewish God, or the God of Wrath that we find in much of the Old Testament. God must speak slowly and simply. When his anger rises, he still keeps the tone low. He regrets that he must bring punishment on mankind.

On the narrator's final line in the play, "Accept this thankfully and without complaint," the narrator should be talking directly to the audience in a real appeal. It is as if he were saying, "Don't say that our stage is too small or ask for your money back."

Q. Do you think it is possible to make of MARY OF NIJMEGHEN a modern play?

de Meester: Certainly, one time we tried to make a musical out of it. I'm sad to say it not only didn't succeed, but it ended as a catastrophe.

Q Is there a national theatre?

de Meester: Holland is the last country in the world to have a national theatre style! We have very few dramatic authors. Heijerman is probably our last and maybe our only theatrical author.

Q. What ought an American stage director know about the Dutch characters in Heijerman's THE GOOD HOPE?

de Meester: Heijerman's play is highly realistic, and the best part of his writing is his realism. The style for Heijerman is "photographed life" as it is in Holland, staged as realistically as possible.

Q. I'm thinking of my first impressions of Holland, the high varnish on the steps, the steepness of the stairs of the Dutch houses; everywhere flowers and flower boxes. Such detail enters into style, doesn't it.

de Meester: Yes, such things tell you that the Dutch live *in* their homes and *in* their gardens. They give much time and also much money to them. I don't think there's any people that are more homey. Our preoccupation with our own little homes and our own little gardens in part of the national style—definitely.

The houses are very narrow, that's why we have those steep stairs. All these details reflect the narrow character of the country, its cities. The Dutch way of life is in Heijerman's plays. In Amsterdam, a Dutch friend was phobic about foreigners. She couldn't stand the idea of a foreigner being under her roof.

Q. Are the Dutch, traditionally, 'closed in.' insular?

de Meester: Yes. There are still a few of the villages where, if an inhabitant does something of which the village doesn't approve, i.e. adultery, he is stoned by the villagers. Or, they are bound to a horse and carriage and dragged through the village; all the villagers jeering them and shouting at them. Very severe and very Protestant, of course, and very old-fashioned. Two world wars have not changed them.

Q. How does the director clarify for an audience the historical, social pressures which dictate behavior in relationships?

de Meester: Oh, that's a wonderful question, I think. Sometimes it's relatively easy. I directed TROILUS AND CRESSIDA by Shakespeare for the Holland festival. It was easy at the time to make clear to a public, still quite near to World War II, an empty war play by Shakespeare. Shakespeare shows so clearly in that play that war is horrible, and one of the ways a director shows how horrible war is, is to make cruel fun of war, making caricatures of Greek heroes.

Q. In MARY OF NIJMEGHEN is it important for the director to communicate to his actors the relationships that existed between the religious and the lay characters of the play?

de Meester: Certainly! But in Holland I had no difficulty directing actors as priests or how to behave in front of a priest.

Q. If a director wants to give his audience an experience he has to come to terms with the play, right?

de Meester: Yes, you have to come to terms with the audience and with the play. You asked me how do you find the style of a play. The answer is to find the one basic idea of the author. Each author, Shakespeare, for instance, has one basic idea, and I think that is the way to find the style of the play. You ask yourself, what did the fellow mean? Why did he write RICHARD II? One answer to RICHARD II is certainly to reveal the divine right of kings. From there on with the play, taking other things into consideration, one finds the style of a play.

Q. In Delft, for your production of EVERYMAN, how important was an awareness of the physical shape of the theatre, or acting space, for which the play was written?

de Meester: The play is very simple. We performed it in that old building in Delft called the Court of the Prince, the Prince of Orange. (He was killed there.) The very simple architecture was effective, an ideal scene for that play. And I'm sure EVERYMAN was a success, only there, because of that building. Taking the play from the Court of Prince of Orange to a beautiful church overwhelmed it. It was not a success anymore.

For the first year of the Holland festival we did Euripides' IPHIGENIA. We did it with a modern painter as designer, and modern music—but we did it on Greek principles; e.g. in an arena, audience three-quarters round, and an indication of a palace as background. All the players wore masks; chorus was of many voices singing to a small orchestra. The music was the base for the movement of the chorus. Fifteen dancers led the movements of the chorus. That year we carried out as much as possible, an acting style grounded in the tradition of the Attic theatre.

For the next Holland festival we did the same Greek play, the same translation, same actors, but on a conventional proscenium stage, without masks, without music. True, some of our actors preferred the modern or realistic way, because they, as actors, could show details of feeling since their faces wore no masks. For me the production had lost all style and greatness. It had become an individualistic play with some dramatic moments, more or less sentimental. It had been a very strong thing with the cleanness and hardness of Greek drama, resulting from our choice of style and through using the orchestra circle. Greek plays should always, as much as possible, take the shape of the Attic theatre. The Greek physical theatre is the spirit of the play.

Q. For the actor, the mask is an interesting challenge?

de Meester: He must express more with body and acting voice; expressing solely with the face results in expression of small sentiments: small and, yes, human, but individual feelings. Greek playwrights didn't write for the small feelings of the modern individual; they wrote for the great strong line of religious drama.

Q. The simplicity of your IASTA production of MARY OF NIJMEGHEN was true to its original staging in medieval times, wasn't it?

de Meester: The play is so simple, that as soon as one stages it in a big way, the play is lost. It is a small intimate play. The most remarkable quality of the play is that it is truly a miracle play; it turns the supernatural mystery of Mary's conversion into dramatic reality and offers a challenge to players of all countries to make their audiences believe in the unbelievable.

MEDIEVAL

SELECTED BIBLIOGRAPHY

Purvis, J. S. *The York Cycle of Mystery Plays.* London: S.P.C.K., 1962.

Purvis, J. S. *The Flood.* London: York Festival Society Limited, 1966.

Southern, Richard. *The Seven Ages of the Theatre.* New York: Hill and Wang, 1961.

MATERIALS AND BACKGROUND

Stage Design Throughout the World Since 1935. New York: Theatre Arts Books, 1956.

Editors of Time-Life Books. *Seven Centuries of Art.* New York: Time Inc., 1970.

Foote, Timothy and the Editors of Time-Life Books. *The World of Bruegel C. 1525-1569.*

Russell, Francis and the Editors of Time-Life Books. *The World of Durer 1471-1528.*

Zarnecki, George. *Art of the Medieval World.* New York: Abrams, 1976.

MUSIC

Instruments of the Middle Ages and Renaissance   Musica Reservata of London 2-Van. 71219/20.

Medieval Instrumental Music   Rogg CMS/Oryx 1509.

NOH

"theatre as skill and concentration"

L.T.M.

The Noh play seeks to inspire wisdom and deals with the paradox, life and death. Like Western classical drama with its noble simplicity and quiet grandeur, Noh tends to be moralistic, intellectual, and abstract, with less emphasis upon the passionate and sensual feelings. This does not mean that there is no depth of feeling in the Noh or classical form; it is only of a different quality.

Noh represents the opposite pole of the younger Kabuki; it tends to encourage greater contemplation, turning inward. When a person comes out of the Noh playhouse, he is supposed to come out wiser.

The background, or set for a Noh play never differs, always being the back stage wall with its picture of an ancient pine tree, regardless of whether the scene of the play is laid on the sea, in a palace or on a moonlit beach. A low door called in Japanese the "hurry up door" provides entrances and exits for the Noh chorus and minor characters.

The bridge to the left of the Noh stage is called "hashigakari." It is 18-45 feet in length. Along the audience side of this passageway, (hashigakari) pine trees are planted, the one nearest the stage being the tallest in height, each of the others being proportionately smaller. When the hashigakari is used as an extension of the stage area, these three pines are to create the illusion of perspective.

Noh costumes are highly-formalized, rich of fabric, and severely simple in line. The patterns on the garments are of a symbolic nature and show large bold designs of extravagant beauty and sensitive delicacy of detail. The white glove-like conventional footgear is known is Japanese as tabi.

The movement in Noh is highly symbolic and stylized. The sliding step seems to have had two origins: one is the characteristic walking of the court ladies. It is a gliding movement of the whole body.

The other sliding step derives from the idea of the motion of a ghost. A ghost, of course, has no feet and so it moves neither up or down. This effect is attained through this unique gliding motion of the feet and a position of the body that doesn't change levels giving an impression of elegance which is characteristic of the Noh. In contrast, there is movement of the whole body in Kabuki and Western dance.

The stamping of the Noh actor's foot is probably connected with primitive stamping of ritual dances at Shinto Shrines. Its purpose was to quiet the spirits of the earth and of the dead.

Due to the stylized form of the garments and the stiffness of the garment material, the natural contours of the human body are almost entirely negated. Within the form molded by the stiff garment, the performer holds his body in a position which is actually unnaturally bent slightly forward from the waist, allowing the garment to form the line, with his body conforming within. This posture also allows him to be always in preparation for the next movement, and is a posture of alert attention and readiness. This quality of hiding the lines of one's own body within formalized lines is most characteristic of the Noh.

The mask serves the similar purpose of hiding the performer's individual features: even the unmasked face never shows any sign of emotion or change of expression.

The style of the Noh is of singular rarity because it is the oldest Japanese theatre, (circa 1336 A.D.) largely unchanged to have come down to us. It is of a special interest to the West because, like the ancient Greek theatre, it has a chorus. Likewise, it combines in a veritable seamless style mime, dance, music, song, and poetic speech.

Although present day performers of Noh skirt talk of religion in their theatre, the disciplines under which the actors train and perform suggest a religious order.

Sadayo Kita is a 16th generation performer and teacher from the Kita Noh Troupe in Tokyo. The Kita School of Noh was founded in the 17th century by Hichidayu Kita, a Samurai of the *Toyotormi* clan, and through the years it has produced celebrated performers and teachers, as well as Noh scholars, such as Kenbosai Kita, an 18th century performer and scholar whose books on Noh are still in use. Roppeita Kita, grandfather of Sadayo Kita, and one of the most venerated Noh artists alive, was still teaching advanced students at the age of 90. Sadayo Kita's father, Minoru, is not only a performer and teacher, but a respected writer, composer and lyricist who has created many new Noh pieces.

Sadayo Kita made his professional debut at the age of four and has been working in the Noh medium for more than 40 years. In 1950 he won a prize at the first Noh Association Contest. Mr. Kita performed at the International Venice Bienniale Theatre Art Festival in 1954, and in 1957, at the

225

Théâtre des Nations in France where he won a prize from the National Academy of France.

Sadayo Kita directed the Noh play IKKAKU SENNIN for the Institute for Advanced Studies in the Theatre Arts at the IASTA Theatre in New York, in 1964. The interview, in Japanese, was held in 1975 at the Nippon Club in New York. Mr. Kita encouraged both Akiyo Tomoeda of the Kita troupe and Miyoko Watanabe of the Nippon Club to join him in response to the questions.

INTERVIEW WITH SADAYO KITA

Q. How do you define the style for a production of the Noh play you directed, THE ONE HORNED HERMIT (IKKAKU SENNIN)?

Kita: Noh plays fall into five categories: plays about gods; about warriors and Samurai; about young and beautiful women; plays usuually dealing with madness; and finally the last category, plays about wizards and monsters. THE ONE HORNED HERMIT (IKKAKU SENNIN) belongs to this last type. IKKAKU SENNIN has comparatively little Yugen,* that indefinable essence or spirit of beauty that the actor can physically experience with his body while performing, or that the audience can experience while watching the performance. THE ONE HORNED HER-MIT does have a great degree of dramatic quality lacking in other types of Noh, but it is not sufficiently distilled to be considered a Noh piece of the highest rank. Therefore, to perform this fairy tale with its elements of entertainment, without making it similar to ordinary drama, demands of actors a tremendous amount of skill and concentration.

Q. Does each play have its own correct style?

---

*The Japanese *kanji* or Chinese characters were adopted by the Japanese more than a thousand years ago; the characters for *Noh* read as Chinese mean "to be able;" *Yugen* read as Chinese means: "subtle, containing a philosophical aura."

Kita: In Noh there *is* a correct style, but depending upon the individual actor, the way of expressing the form *(kata)** differs.

As for myself, I endeavor to preserve the definite style, form *(kata)* as is. I do not know about the performers who will follow (i.e. the next and succeeding generations), but I believe tradition should be passed on, for tradition is a living thing; it is handled by people, and depends upon the feelings of people and their social environment. It does change.

Q. How does an actor help an audience to have an appreciation of the Noh?

Kita: When I know the audience is to be students, my goal as actor is to have the audience understand what I am doing. It is said that Zeami would observe his audience, analyze their social status or class, and then decide upon his performance. Today, I would not attempt to do this. Zeami's times were different. But, for students or children, I would endeavor to select numbers easily understood. I would not change them. I do give special thought to the performance because if the children do not understand, it is futile to perform for them. I give demonstrations in the United States and through film; some Japanese people object. They say it is improper of me to go to America and give demonstrations. But, gradually, even in Japan, it has become necessary to explain and instruct. To show the Noh in its true, full form, first it is better to arouse interest in the Noh. Those who have opposed this have reproached me personally. I do not listen to them.

Q. Is a knowledge of the manners of the period and of the social structure of the period important?

---

*The character read as Chinese means: "style or mode."

Kita: Tradition is above social environment and manners. Tradition still exists today. Were one able to look back and to observe Noh of the Muromachi period (1336-1568), one would see there is still some continuity with the past. If there were no continuity, a tradition could not exist. A past may not exist, but it informs.

Q. How important to a production of a classic is authenticity of dress?

Kita: It is so important that it is best to have the original costume. In Noh, if possible, one wears old costumes because it gives more depth to the performance. The quality of the costume may be good enough, but due to wear and tear, as years go by, one sometimes has to wear costumes made today. It is not like making identical street clothes, same fabric, etc., which is possible today. The patterns on the DOJOJI play's costumes are fixed according to each respective Noh school, but on the other hand, the HAGOROMO play does not have a rigidly fixed pattern. There are certain colors for young and old characters. For the FUNABENKEI play the pattern on costumes differ according to the taste of the actor. The Kita School DOJOJI costume has a pattern which is standard. Interestingly, the Kita Troupe actors who have performed it several times desire a change; some even have worn a costume like that of the Kanze School. However, for a first performance, the actor must wear the standard costume. Even when an actor makes a change, he must know in depth the authentic costume. Of course, it is best to wear the ancient costume. But since it has become a treasured work of art, an actor may not use it often.

By contrast Kabuki does not strive for authentic apparel, that is, style of costumes worn at the historical time of the plot. Kabuki's aim has always been for a theatrical effect of beauty rather than an historical authenticity.

Q. How important is a knowledge of the physical form of the theatre for which the play was written?

Kita: The bridge *(hashigakari)** is a part of the Noh stage even today; a long time ago there were two bridges. But through the ages the Noh troupes refined the stage to its present physical form and decided it was best. The form did not change according to plan or orderly change, but the physical shape of the stage and theatre went through many stages; e.g. there was a period when the *hashigakari* was located at the very center of the stage. Noh actors have decided that the shape of their theatre, as we see it today, is best.

Q. Did Zeami, who wrote the great plays for the Noh Theatre, influence the evolution of the shape of the Noh stage?

Kita: Yes. For the play HAGOROMO, Zeami used the bridge very effectively for the climatic exit but Zeami had not written HAGOROMO with a bridge in mind. Hence, HAGOROMO as a text existed first, and later changes were made to take advantage of the Noh stage. Thus, the manner of performing HAGOROMO changed. We of the Noh Theatre do not know the physical characteristics of Zeami's stage. A definite stage probably had not been established.

There is a big difference between today's Noh and that of Zeami's time. (There is a record of time of performances which has come down to us.) At present, for a day's performance, we perform five plays. In Zeami's day, within the same time, three times this number were presented. HAGOROMO takes about one hour today; in former days it was performed in 12 or 13 minutes, it

---

*Read as Chinese, the characters mean "a hanging bridge."

would seem. Such seems impossible when we think of HAGOROMO today, but that shows the change of taste in different periods.

During the Tokugawa era, the content of the Noh deepened. Perhaps some may object to my saying this, but although the original and early Noh was good, it was the later generations that refined it and perfected it.

Q.   So the pace was faster in Zeami's time?

Kita: Yes, and I think it fit the social environment of Zeami's era.

Q.   Mr. Kita, you have performed on proscenium or Western-type stages where the audience is out front; by contrast, in the Noh Theatre the audience, more or less, surrounds the actor. Do you, as a performer, feel isolated when performing behind a proscenium?

Kita: I was brought up acting on the open Noh stage. Noh should be performed abroad in theatre-in-the-round. For the Noh actor, the longer the bridge, the better it is for the performer. A great number of the Noh play characters are ghosts; a long entrance gives the right feeling.

At the Kita School, there are four ways possible to perform HAGOROMO. Originally the text said the angel rose to heaven and the performance ended on stage in view of the audience. Then, the actor simply made his exit. Exiting on the bridge was a change; a developing sense of dramaturgy made use of the bridge, enabling the angel to dance to heaven and disappear through curtained exit (agemaku)* before the piece ends.

The performance symbolically ends in mist and the actor goes around and around and glides backwards into the curtained exit. This shows that the angel is happy to

---

*Read as Chinese, it is very descriptive: "to flash the curtain."

return to heaven. As I performed it, the actor makes an exit facing the curtained exit.

Q. Was there some attribute of your grandfather Roppeita's acting of Noh that was especially outstanding?

Kita: He continued the samurai life and strictness of the Kita School. There were plays that only he could do. He was very good at performing what had already been choreographed. But my grandfather would also do research and create new numbers.

Q. Is it possible to cite which are the most important skills to be developed?

Kita: All the skills of the Noh actor (movement, voice, etc.) have equal importance. Perhaps one might say that song is a bit more important, because if the actor doesn't sing well, he lacks form.

Q. In a rapidly changing Japan, do your students want to change the Noh, to introduce innovations?

Kita: Our students haven't gone that far yet. We must preserve the art of our Noh school, so students are not preoccupied with change. Often students and members of my troupe will observe performers of other schools, and find other interpretations excellent, and at times even better than their own. All, however, feel it is most important to preserve the tradition of one's own school rather than to make changes.

NOH THEATRE

FILM

"Aspects of the Noh Theatre:" obtainable, for rental and purchase, through the Institute for Advanced Studies in the Theatre Arts (IASTA), P.O. Box 1106, Radio City Station, New York, NY 10101 or Gil Forman, 310 W. 56th St., #1B, New York, NY 10019.

SELECTED BIBLIOGRAPHY

Brandon, James R. *Traditional Asian Plays.* New York: Hill & Wang, 1972.

Haar, F. *Japanese Theatre in Highlight.* Rutland, VT: Tuttle, 1959.

Ichikawa, Sanki. *Japanese Noh Drama, Vol. I - III.* Tokyo: Nippon Gakujutsu Shinkokai, 1960.

Keene, Donald. *Noh, the Classical Theatre of Japan.* Palo Alto: Kodansha, 1966.

Keene, Donald. *Twenty Plays of the Noh Theatre.* New York: Columbia U. Press, 1970.

Malm, William P. *Japanese Music.* Rutland, VT: Tuttle, 1959.

MATERIALS AND BACKGROUND

Bayrd, Edwin and the Editors of the Newsweek Book Division. *Kyoto.* New York: Newsweek, 1974.

De Bary, William T. *Japanese Tradition.* New York: Columbia U. Press, 1960.

Ishimoto, Tatsua and Kiyoko. *The Japanese House, Its Interior and Exterior.* New York: Crown Publishers, Inc., 1963.

Kawasaki, Ichiro. *Japan Unmasked.* Palo Alto: Kodansha, 1966.

Morris, Ivan. *World of the Shining Prince.* New York: Knopf, 1964.

Rudolfsky, Bernard. *The Kimono Mind.* New York: Doubleday, 1965.

MUSIC

Danielou, Alain. The Music of Japan. (Phonodisc) Bareureita Musicophon BM 30L, 2012-2017   6 albums.

Japanese Noh Music (Phonodisc) Lyrichord LLST 7137.

Seami, 1363-1443. Hagoromo and Kautau   Caedmion TC 2019.

FRENCH NEO-CLASSIC: PHÈDRE

"the iron corset as theatre"*

*le corselet de fer

"The Royalty of Language," the title of a chapter from a work of Thierry Maulnier devoted to Racine, seems to me to be the key to the true interpretation of PHÈDRE.

It seems impossible to substitute the language of Shakespeare for the language of Racine. To this impossibility the poet, William Packard, addressed himself, and he deserves much credit for retaining the spirit of Racine while preserving the difficult, but absolutely necessary alexandrine rhythm. And is it not this rhythm which pounds in the hearts of heroes?

All of my actors felt it, and all of them tried to arrive at the sublime poetry inherent in it. But by what means? Simply, by means of the "perfect actor" using synthesis of the three actions: verbal, physical and interior. Our goal had to be the true music of Racine's art. It takes great ambition to do a great play, but Racine lives by the nobility of his style, by the inexorable rhythm which is singularly his. The love of the actors was equal to this challenge, and it led them to the discovery of this most French of poets.

It is my hope that our professional colleagues, through this production, may discover the rhythms and passions of the world of Racine where

". . . tout n'est qu'ordre et beauté . . ."

(Baudelaire)

PAUL-ÉMILE DEIBER

Paul-Émile Deiber is today's director for the supreme challenges of the French theatre . . . the 17th-century tragedies of Corneille and Racine. As an actor, his roles in the repertoire of the Comédie-Française range from the classicism of Racine and Corneille, (he has played both Hippolyte and Theseus in "Phèdre"), the romanticism of Victor Hugo and de Musset, the farce of Labiche and Feydeau, to the modern theatre of Montherlant. He is also acclaimed as this generation's Cyrano.

As a director, M. Deiber is equally impressive. He is the producer of all recordings of the classics made by the Comédie-Française. One of his popular productions of Racine's "Bérénice" was staged in the ruins of Carthage in Tunisia. He also has directed for the Paris Opera.

In 1962, M. Deiber was accorded the much coveted honor of preparing the annual Homage à Molière. For this occasion, he wrote "La Troupe du Roy" which dealt with the fortunes of the original Molière company.

In 1966, M. Deiber's IASTA production of PHÈDRE with Beatrice Straight, Mildred Dunnock and Reid Shelton at the Greenwich Mews Theatre in New York set an international record with 100 consecutive performances.

INTERVIEW WITH PAUL-ÈMILE DEIBER

Q. How did you choose and define the style for this production?

Deiber: Racine's style is very precise. The first thing is to find the rhythm of Racine's language, the rhythm of the verses. His language is the rhythm of the heart. Racine himself taught La Champmeslé, the first actress to play Phèdre. In the Tuilleries Gardens Racine taught Champmeslé to deliver the verses as precisely as if she were a singer. If we consider language old-fashioned and ignore it, we will only play the *sentiment au premier degré:* the emotions; I think it is criminal to just play the action—what happens.

Q. Since Racine is the supreme example of neo-classic tragedy, how do you characterize French classicism?

Deiber: What is theatrical reality for one age must not be confused with the reality of an earlier or a later age, or of the contemporary age. Ceremonial, ritualistic, even artificial behavior has existed in different cultures, at different social levels and in different epochs. An attempt to recreate on a stage the characters of the plays of Racine as if they are as casual as middle-class twentieth century man, is doomed to failure. Their reality is of the Court of Louis XIV of seventeenth century France preserved in a particular form, the Alexandrines. The rediscovery of that special world is through the text, and all that the actor and director can evoke from the text of that moment of human history. The etiquette of the seventeenth century Court of Louis XIV is the basis of the "motivation" of the characters of PHÈDRE. For example, at the first meeting between Aricie and Hippolyte she bows. His "madame" is of the etiquette of seventeenth century France. Thereon he expresses sentiments and relates physically to Aricie as a future "bon roi." Hippolyte is a king potentially.

Since Racine is the supreme example of neo-classic tragedy, what may be said to be French Classicism? French Classicism may be characterized as: (1) moving "statues;" (2) demigods; (3) intense feeling but internalized. It is avoidance of loudness, shouting, cries. When the comment is made that such cries add syllables to the twelve syllables of the alexandrine line, one is reminded of the French respect for logic. Neither is it gasping or clutching, for such exceeds the economy and taut restraint of classicism. When there is overt expression of big feelings, it's *drame*, in excess, it is *melodrame*. Victor Hugo's RUY BLAS or Rostand's CYRANO demand a full voice, the open-stop all the way. These are romantic dramas.

The neo-classic tragedy is the antique world as seen through the eyes of seventeenth century man, renaissance man. There is not the big feeling, freely expressed, welling up out of the unconscious as is reflected in the tragedies of the antique Greek world—so remote from modern man.

Q. How have you directed PHÈDRE?

Deiber: For the first two weeks of rehearsal the cast sat in a large circle around the table with their director. The time was devoted fully to reading, and an examination and an analysis of the verse. I devoted six weeks "at the table" with my French actors studying the verse of Racine's BÉRÉNICE. I frequently held up a French text and said, "All is there in the text. Racine has thought of everything.

It is not I that is guiding, but it is Racine."

For the American actor the first challenge is the long speech which sometimes may cover four pages on the actor's text (script). This long speech is referred to by us as a *tirade*.

Rehearsing at the table, the crescendos and the diminuendos of these long speeches were carefully plotted, even dictated by the director. Since I am as much an actor as a director, I do not hesitate to tell each actor where to breathe. Since breathing is of such prime importance in negotiating a speech of unusual length, I shared with the American actors a technique for breathing that as an actor I was instructed in at the Conservatoire in Paris: "The actor must not breathe at the end of a phrase—revealing to the audience his need for breath and support for his voice; but the actor develops the technique of breathing into the phrase that lies ahead."

As the first two weeks of examining the verse and of understanding in depth the text drew to a close, I revealed my musical approach to Racine's PHÈDRE. I suggested as a metaphor the symphony. In the first act Hippolyte introduces the musical preparation, the first theme of the symphony; he confesses his love for Aricie. The next musical theme of the first movement, is PHÈDRE's confession of her love for Hippolyte to Oenone. Thus by analogy the first act is like the first movement of a symphony. "Racine is music."

I devoted the next two weeks to the placing of the actors, creating the *mise-en-scene* with high spirits. This work for the actors is "putting them into the iron corset." Having locked you into it, I demand then that you convince us in the audience that the iron corset does not exist. The challenge now was to mesh the verbal "iron corset" with the "iron corset" of the physical action. All blocking had been carefully worked out in advance and was pre-determined—down to millimeters. I was sternly authoritarian in dictating the movements. I worked very quickly. All is in the text. Racine has created a ballet, and the physical movements and action arise out of the rhythms of the verse—are dictated by the verse.

The first run-through concentrated on coordinating the gesture and movement with the verbal rhythms (mastered at the table). My mandate had been for all the actors to have memorized the text of the play, be free of their scripts, *before* putting them on their feet on stage, and giving the blocking.

Since I knew Americans like to learn their lines *with* the movement and gestures and actions of a play, this was both a challenge and a source of distress to these American actors.

Along the way from the first day, I had sought with the actors the third goal: the attainment of the interior action or rhythm.

Q.   There are three types of rhythm; verbal, physical and interior?

Deiber: Yes, and each scene has a rhythm, too, and each act a rhythm. And for the full play, a rhythm, to coordinate the rhythm of the verse with the physical movement for harmony.

Thus the goal was, for as much as two weeks of two run-throughs a day, to set in motion the rhythms of the play—as dictated by the alexandrines: couplets, caesuras, beats, *enjambment,* and the emotion expressed. Unnerving as it may have been for some of the American actors, I persisted in beating out from time to time the rhythms, the pulsations, indicating as an orchestral conductor the climaxes with my pencil on the director's table.

By the time the week of technical and dress rehearsals had arrived, as a director I assumed my work for the actors had been done.

Q. You have spoken of the perfect actor. How does the perfect actor deliver the verse of Racine?

Deiber: There is strict adherence to the rhythms, the music of the verse. The French alexandrine is made up of twelve syllables: six long beats alternating with six short beats. Rhyming couplets are characteristic of the alexandrines.

In the whole text of Racine's PHÈDRE there are only two or three run-on lines as written by its author, but I encouraged some additional running-on *(enjambment)*. However, I insisted that the actors exercise both restraint and taste in taking this liberty with French classicism.

The caesura (or hemistsch) always comes after six syllables: the actor should explore it and use it; the actor's inner metronome should be aware of it. It can lead the actor, often, to Racine's intention; for interpretation of line, scene, character.

For variety, the "rest" can be made after three syllables, or after nine syllables. As for the rhyming couplet, use it, do not deny it but don't be enslaved by it.

Repeatedly at rehearsals, I would reiterate, "Le corselet de fer" (the iron corset of alexandrines), of couplets and rhythms must be put on by the actor; he must wear it but create the illusion it does not exist—nor trouble, nor restrain him.

My picture of the perfect actor is that the verse rhythms —the music—dictate the rhythms of his and her physical movements. These physical movements need to be meshed, integrated with the verbal utterances. A demigod moves as if his legs were of iron. After a performance the actor (performing in the classics) should be exhausted as a result of the demanding physical exertion.

Concerning PHÈDRE's first entrance, if someone does not know the story of PHÈDRE, and sees her first en-

D.C.

trance on-stage, the person should be able to say, 'Aha, I know what is happening to her; she is dying of love.'

Concerning PHÈDRE's death scene, if the actress goes too fast she won't be believed. It must be a death of complete calm and tranquillity. Racine himself says: ". . . descend more slowly to the dead."

In classical acting the actor's movements and gestures are full, large, controlled, but economical and measured, in rhythm with the verbal rhythms. For example, the fingers of the actors in gestures are not spread, but held together. The actors in PHÈDRE, with some exceptions, never look at the stage floor. No actor moves at the same time as another actor. Therefore, no actor—generally—moves as another speaks. All gestures and movements are weighted and significant.

Gratuitous movement distracts an audience from hearing the verse, savoring the verse, grasping the twistings and turnings (convolutions) of the characters' feelings being explored by the actors.

The requisites of the perfect actor include carriage and posture, leading to physical action in rhythm with the verbal music of the text; this makes of the physical action a bullet. Articulation must be optimum at all times; breathing must be plotted, calculated, exact at all times.

The actor does not move after a phrase or between a phrase: he moves and breathes into the phrase ahead. In a long *tirade* don't rush into the long speech; take plenty of time, make the audience feel that what is coming is of greatest importance. Don't move. Dominate the long speech. Do not be dominated by it.

The voice is always fully supported, never pushed to its limit, always creating the illusion that there is vocal force in reserve, that the resources, physical, vocal, and emotional—in reserve are limitless. In the classic, the characters are gods or demigods. The insecure man, the impotent man or woman shouts and forces to the limits of power. Omnipotence—the heroic of classic tragedy—is created by the illusion of limitless powers.

The actor must avoid the error of striving to express strong feelings through prolongation (hanging on to) the vowels. It disrupts the rhythm. The actor must learn to express the feeling without distortion of the word, and on the word. As a corrective, focus the attention to moving quickly from the vowel to the consonant.

Interior action is in harmony at all times with the music of the text. *It is the text* that is being presented to the public.

Q. Would you specify other characteristics of the style of acting for PHÈDRE?

Deiber: In the spirit of the classicism of the seventeenth century, there is the greatest economy of physical contact between characters. When contact between characters (actors) occurs, it is climatic.

The gaze of the actors is at all times high, but never much above the plane of eye level. The demigod, e.g. Theseus, talks to Neptune largely as an equal, not as a suppliant or as a mortal. In this feeling there is, out of mutual respect, a quality of reverence; e.g. when Theseus goes to invoke the aid of Neptune for the revenge he seeks on his son.

As in the great canvasses of the renaissance painters, strong focus is sought at all times. Being surrounded by space is one major source of heightened focus. The tendency in renaissance and baroque art is movement out, even breaking out of static space, brushing the bonds of a frame. Thus, the thrust of the actors is "out front," playing out and down on the apron; there is a projection of feeling and personality out into the audience.

As an example of this, I designate specifically the placement of the gaze of the actors at the different vertical planes of the auditorium of the theatre. Inter-character relatedness is never at the expense or loss of relatedness to the audience. The thrust is always out front, even at the expense of the characters in the scene not having direct contact; e.g. the "symbolic marriage" of Hippolyte and Aricie in Act V. Here Hippolyte leads on a diagonal from upstage right to down left center and he is followed in measured rhythm and step by Aricie. This is a symbolic marriage but there is never body contact during this rhapsodic and lyrical marriage scene.

The seventeenth century tragedy has a form, a shape. For it to have been meaningful in its own age, it had to have an inner humanistic truth. If it is deserving of our attention today, both its design (form) and inner reality must have validity. The fact that the rediscovery of its extrinsic style may result in conscious, even mannered style, does not mean that it is a hollow or dead tradition.

Q. Is it the tendency of modern actors to act *between* the words and to throw away or ignore the words?

Deiber: To act between the words is a mistake. If you act what Racine has given and are aware of the stress and the rhythm of his language, the verses will do much of the work. You have to follow Racine. He is very strict. His art is as demanding as playing Bach and the actor must be disciplined to find the right way.

Racine's method is simple and concentrated. Inside, the actors have to be very rich, but outside it's not difficult. But to bring everything inside, with an internalization, *minimum of voice, minimum of gesture,* that's the big art!

But not just one person acting; I want the whole ensemble acting. Everybody. Sometimes it is difficult. To have one actor play PHÈDRE, acting and speaking very well in the style, and have another actor near without style is terrible. The actor cannot play alone.

Q. How do you visualize PHÈDRE? The lighting, the sets, the costumes?

Deiber: Let me elucidate my stage-lighting scheme; Act I is early morning, with the stage light predominantly striking across the columns down stage left. Act II is from 11:00 a.m. to 2:00 p.m. Act III covers the same amount of time, or when the sun is at its full height in the heavens. Act IV is late afternoon. Act V is evening with the sun declining in the West, or offstage right. The rising and the setting of the sun take place during the action of the play. It parallels the imagery of the play, to PHÈDRE's last line about the daylight, and it is a visible display of the unity of time which Aristotle describes as the rising and the setting of the sun.

In the decor the use of the vanishing point, the forced perspective, is appropriate to renaissance man's preoccupation with focusing on the nature of feeling, and the analysis and dissection of feelings.

The delight in plumes and ornament of the court of Louis XIV is no longer appropriate for the seventeenth century classics. Therefore, for settings and costumes we turn today to Italian painters of the renaissance. For PHÈDRE a painting depicting Alexander the Great by the Italian painter Veronese provided the silhouette for the PHÈDRE costumes.

The arms and legs of the actors must be covered. Bare limbs—which would be appropriate for a Greek tragedy— connote free and full physical movement; thus such costumes would mislead the neo-classic actor into a violation of the restraints of the three actions, as outlined above. Visually for the spectators and tactilely for the actors, the clothed and covered extremities of the body promote internalizing, holding within the intense feelings.

(It raises a question: might it not be possible to have even the actresses wearing gloves?)

Q. How does one clarify for an audience the social pressures which dictate behavior and relationships?

Deiber: It's very difficult. In France now it's difficult to find the people who have enough theatre culture, enough knowledge of the French language, to perform Racine. Actors have to be very modest to act the plays of Racine.

Q. Can PHÈDRE be compared to a Greek play?

Deiber: I think PHÈDRE is easier. At the beginning of this century the French actors played PHÈDRE at the Comédie-Française with the big cry, big movements. Such performances came after the Romanticists and they wanted something exaggerated.

Q. How important is a knowledge of the physical theatre of the period?

Deiber: In the 17th century, Racine was played in a very small theatre. The Théâtre Hotel de Bourgogne had three hundred seats, very small. The actors could speak very softly. The Comédie-Française, with its twelve hundred seats, is a big theatre. Actors have to project and that is against the style.

Q. How important to a production of a classic is authenticity of dress? What about modern dress?

Deiber: It's completely crazy. You remember that all the tragedies of Racine played in the costumes of the 17th century. It was their interpretation of Greece and Rome, but adapted in the style of the 17th century. I saw, in my youth, tragedies of Racine and Corneille played in the true Roman or Greek costumes. The last performance of PHÈDRE at the Comédie-Française was in the real 17th century costumes, feathers and all, like the original production of 1677. It was not a success. The critics were really against it because it was too stiff. The style of the 17th century is also difficult for the designer.

Q. What advice do you have concerning the style for Corneille?

Deiber: The first successful classic of the 17th century? The verses, of course, are very beautiful. The language is classical. But, to give advice as to how to produce LE CID is very difficult. My way was to bring forward the love story, and I put the actors in the costumes of the original period.

Q. Is it important, as we did with PHÈDRE, to try and get the rhythms of the verse into English?

Deiber: No, that's not so important. The verses are not as musical as the verses of Racine. In some pieces, yes, in POLYEUCTE. The sentiment in Corneille is always between love and duty. Racine, in my opinion, is more pure. They are two different styles.

NEO-CLASSIC

FILM

"Aspects of Neo-Classic Theatre Style" (includes scenes from Racine's "Phèdre"): obtainable, for rental and purchase, through the Institute for Advanced Studies in the Theatre Arts (IASTA), P.O. Box 1106, Radio City Station, New York, NY 10101 or Gil Forman, 310 W. 56th St., #1B, New York, NY 10019.

SELECTED BIBLIOGRAPHY

Barrault, Jean-Louis. *Phèdre de Jean Racine.* Paris: Éditions du Seuil, 1946.

Racine. *Phèdre.* (Translated by William Packard.) New York: Samuel French, Inc., 1966.

MATERIALS AND BACKGROUND

Gaxotte, Pierre. *Versailles que j'aime . . .* Paris: Aux Éditions Sun (N.D.)

Barrault, Jean-Louis. *Reflections on the Theatre.* London: Rockliff, 1949.

MUSIC

Michel de Lalande and Nicolas Bernier. Fastes et Divertissements de Versailles, Vol. 3. Philips LIL 0009.

Concerts Royaux (4) Harnoncourt, Vienna Concertus Musicus (No. 2) François Couperin Van C-10029.

FEYDEAU

"the Swiss-watch as theatre"

D.C.

Feydeau is a mathematician, an astronomer, a chess player and an inventor. In a Feydeau play, the events and action develop with the precision of a well-groomed machine. After the *Quid pro quo,* the imbroglio. Tangles, mixups, utter confusion prevail. For it is impossible to cut a single word, in a Feydeau play. And the astounding part is the certainty, the absolute knowledge that all this is ruled, explained, justified in the most extravagantly uproarious style. Not a single event, not a single sentence of which you cannot say;—But, of course! It couldn't be otherwise. Yes, Georges Feydeau is a very great comic author. The greatest, second only to Molière. The miracle of Feydeau is the rhythm that shakes, pulls, pushes. Feydeau's plays are just as forceful and inexorable as tragedies. They are the image of destiny, fatal destiny itself. In front of Feydeau, one strangles with laughter.

MARCEL ACHARD

PAUL-ÉMILE DEIBER, a member of the Comédie-Française for twenty-two years, is among the leading actors and directors of France. He is today's director for Corneille, Racine, Molière, Labiche, and Feydeau. His directing of American actors in Racine's PHÈDRE in English was his first staging of a play outside of France. As a result of the success of the PHÈDRE, both in New York and London, he joined the roster of stage directors at the Metropolitan Opera in New York. Among the new productions of operas he staged for the Met are: ROMÉO ET JULIETTE, NORMA, WERTHER, and PELLÉAS ET MÉLISANDE. This interveiw took place in New York in 1972.

> **Q.** Paul-Émile Deiber, you have acted in many different styles at the Comédie-Française: Molière, Corneille, Racine, and Feydeau. What is the style for Feydeau? Jacques Charon of the Comédie-Française said that the key to acting Feydeau is *parlez large?*
>
> **Deiber:** *Parlez large?* Literally, it means "speak broadly." You know, it seems as if the actors are talking at the top of their voices. Yes, Charon would have used that phrase to describe the vocal quality. As for the tone used in

Feydeau, it is brilliant.

We French actors speak a little bit over, above, normal speech, when we *parlez large*. Ah, but the major thing is that immediately the audience is laughing, the actor must top that. (Deiber's voice rises in volume to illustrate what he means.) You speak over the laughter, not wait until the audience has finished laughing. You must go ahead. On! On!

Q. Can one play Feydeau . . .

Deiber: Modern? I don't see that as interesting. No, it's not interesting, for Feydeau is too much in his own time; plays set in a hotel, or, to be more specific, a man's bedroom. It's more funny, I think, in his pre-World War I costumes. It's not that I like only the classics; it's just not the same problem. You can find another way, of course; you can try to play Feydeau tragic.

Q. Tragic? Feydeau?

Deiber: All the situations in Feydeau are always tragic situations.

Q. For the characters the situation is tragic, so the actors must never play to the audience for laughs?

Deiber: It's a tragedy for the characters. The actors ignore the laughter and just keep pushing.

Q. That's the best way to get more laughs?

Deiber: Play it very intensely, that's best. There's nothing more tiring than to play Feydeau, it takes so much energy. I, too, have played Feydeau, and after a performance I am completely dead. One has to fight against the laughter: you have to 'fight' with the characters on stage. When I played the General in UN FIL À LA PATTE, (CAT AMONG THE PIGEONS, the title when performed in London in English), the expenditures of energy was terrible. The General is a wild man; he wanted to kill the poor rival; he

251

really loves the girl; he is fighting everybody. For the rival, too, it's a big tragedy.

I remember Jacques Charon saying his English actors in Feydeau's FLEA IN HER EAR didn't know what they were in for; after each performance they were just completely dead. They found they had to rest all day. Even Charon couldn't speak anymore; he was very, very tired while playing CAT AMONG THE PIGEONS each day for a whole week at the New York City Center.

Q. Is Feydeau, as performed by French actors, played fast?

Deiber: Yes, we play Feydeau very fast; it is the movement, the tremendous movement. I think the best result for the audience is to give the audience no opportunity to breathe. There's one comic effect after another; bang, bang, bang, always faster.

Q. Do you sacrifice communication, or do you always have to be understood?

Deiber: The words are not so important in Feydeau, as in Racine; some key words for the scene in Feydeau must be heard and understood. Actually, it's almost impossible to compare the styles of Feydeau and Racine.

Q. In Feydeau, is the articulation crisp?

Deiber: When the French play Feydeau, or any fast-paced play, their diction is always very good. It is a well-known fact that the French people love their language and are fastidious about speaking it well.

Q. You directed IASTA's American actors in GLADIATOR'S THIRTY MILLION by Labiche. What were your problems as director to get out of non-French actors the style for Labiche?

Deiber: I think I have more difficulty to find the real way with Labiche than with Racine. It's curious, but Labiche is so

French. Of course, Racine is French, too. But the French humor of Labiche, you know, is something very different. Charon was very successful directing Feydeau with English actors, but Labiche is something else: he's not Feydeau. Labiche *is* French!

Q. Then, how do you distinguish between the style for Labiche, the style for Feydeau?

Deiber: Comic events in a play of Feydeau are more intense; they pile up faster in Feydeau than in Labiche. Situation is more important in Feydeau, and character more important in Labiche.

Q. Is Labiche more serious a playwright with a message?

Deiber: Perhaps, for Labiche's satire is directed against bourgeois society in France. Feydeau relies completely on crazy confrontations. The second act of LE DINDON (THE TURKEY), in a hotel room, is played at a dizzying pace with entrances and exits throughout. The scene builds fantastically.

Q. Is Feydeau concerned with man's . . .

Deiber: . . . Problems? He rather enjoyed them. Labiche, on the other hand, had his little war with the French middle-class; he wanted to change the bourgeoisie. In Feydeau's one-act play DON'T WALK AROUND NUDE there is a brilliant character of the husband, who is wrapped up in his career in politics, as a deputy in the Parlement. The wife, Clarisse, must be a little woman. In French, we describe her as "piquante." She has temperament, is a little bit, but not quite, crazy; she doesn't think about the gravity of things. She wears a nightgown with a hat, in the afternoon, in her apartment!

Q. In America, she would be called wacky. Are there similar characters in other Feydeau comedies?

Deiber: Yes, yes. The same characters in FEU LA MÈRE DE MADAME, in LE DINDON; the same characters everywhere in Feydeau. The playing has to be brilliant and fast. The cues have to be picked up very fast, with overlapping of lines. Basically, it is so fast it is more tiring than playing a five-act tragedy.

Q. I've seen you play CYRANO DE BERGERAC.

Deiber: It's fast, also, but you can act more slowly in verse.

Q. How did you pace the long and entertaining speech of "the nose" from CYRANO?

Deiber: The playing is brilliant because first, Cyrano is a heroic character, and the lines are in verse. You don't have to search to look for something natural. Cryano is an historical character, in a period costume; the play is not modern.

Q. Does the French actor play Molière faster than Feydeau? Is the speed of delivery in Feydeau an illusion?

Deiber: Sometimes that is true.

Q. I've seen you play Alceste in Molière's THE MIS-ANTHROPE.

Deiber: There's danger in playing too fast in THE MISAN-THROPE. But, if it's too slow, Alceste becomes an old man. He's young; a man of forty-five years. When Molière wrote this play he was forty-four. But I think the character is younger than that, and practical for today. THE MISANTHROPE, Alceste, is for us, boring, you know, if he is *not* played very young. He is like a teacher.

However, Feydeau must be overplayed; everything must be fantastically precise, too. The Comédie-Française for a long time played the whole Feydeau repertoire, always with the same people. We were friends; we learned the words, and we came together . . .

254

Q. An ensemble?

Deiber: Yes, an ensemble. It was a big ensemble by this time. Like chamber music, it was unbelievable: perfection!

The stage directions for Feydeau have to be very precise also. It's *moto perpetuo,* perpetual motion. Feydeau is always as precise as a Swiss watch.

Q. Is it impossible to change or remove the stage directions?

Deiber: Some stage directions of Feydeau's may be cut, of course. When I directed Feydeau's UN FIL À LA PATTE in Vienna (in German), it was an interesting experience. I found that I could not change the directions as Feydeau conceived them. They are locked with the words. Some people I knew (in Paris) decided to depart from Feydeau's stage directions. Feydeau wrote "The door is right; the table is here." If one changed those directions, after two-weeks rehearsal, the cast would be asking, "What are we doing now; we cannot do this." All would become too difficult and one had to go back to the original Feydeau version. His is fantastic organization in stage directions. One cannot successfully do it another way because Feydeau is so exact. With Molière, Racine, changes are easy. But Feydeau's directions are very important.

I remember in his play UN FIL À LA PATTE when a character brings the Figaro newspaper to the house, five characters have to be on stage, each in a precise place, otherwise all goes wrong. Everything is written down by Feydeau, and he is right. He knows stage business perfectly; he was a fantastic organizer. All his stage directions have a reason. Yes, Feydeau is always fascinating.

Q. Simple but ever comic.

Deiber: And dramatic, too. For the actor, it is never a let-up in energy. It's exhausting! His plays should alternate with other plays in repertory. To play Feydeau eight performances in each week is killing for the actors.

FEYDEAU

SELECTED BIBLIOGRAPHY

Anonymous. "Forms of Shock Treatment for a World Out of Plumb". *Times Literary Supplement*. New York: June 18, 1971.

Bentley, Eric. *Let's Get a Divorce! and Other Plays*. New York: Hill and Wang, 1958.

Lorcey, Jacques. *Georges Feydeau*. Paris: La Table Ronde, 1972.

Pronko, Leonard C. *Georges Feydeau*. New York: Frederick Ungar Publishing Co., 1975.

Shapiro, Norman R. "Suffering and Punishment in the Theatre of Georges Feydeau". *The Tulane Drama Review*, Vol. 5, No. 1., September, 1960.

Shapiro, Norman R. "Introduction". *Four Farces by Georges Feydeau*. Chicago: U. of Chicago Press, 1970.

Shenkan, Arlette. *Georges Feydeau*. Paris: Seghers, 1972.

MATERIALS AND BACKGROUND

Schneider, Pierre and the Editors of Time-Life Books. *The World of Manet 1832-1883*. New York: Time Inc., 1968.

Impressionism: A Centenary Exhibition. New York: The Metropolitan Museum of Art, 1974.

Antoine, André. *Memories of the Théâtre-Libre*. (Translated by Marvin A. Carlson.) Coral Gables, Fla.: U. of Miami Press, 1964.

Wiley, William L. *Formal French*. Cambridge: Harvard U. Press, 1967.

GERMAN ROMANTICISM: Schiller

"storm and stress"*

*Sturm und Drang

In Germany, Austria and Switzerland the plays of Goethe and Schiller are known, performed and admired; but with the exception of Friedrich Schiller's MARY STUART, the plays of these famous authors are admired but rarely, if ever, performed on the English speaking stage.

Neither are these "storm and stress" dramas of romantic theatre found on American college reading lists; nor are they studied in depth in courses of dramatic literature. It is conceivable that were it not for the two fat roles for great actresses, Schiller's MARY STUART would have been neglected.

Are Goethe's FAUST and Schiller's THE ROBBERS, to name but two classical plays rarely absent from the repertories of the German language theatres, beyond the stage facilities of theatres outside Germany? In size, these plays are no longer than the plays of Shakespeare. Moreover, the emergence in the United States and England of the thrust stage, which has fostered numerous productions of almost all of Shakespeare's plays, now makes accessible these sprawling 18th century theatre pieces. We know that German audiences sit enthralled before productions of these plays and seem not to be put off by a first act that lasts for two hours. The highly charged style which these stormy plays demand may seem too great a challenge to us causing them to be left on our library shelves rather than to be performed on our stages.

IASTA determined to meet this challenge by engaging for an American production of Schiller's LOVE AND INTRIGUE, a master of German stage design and direction, Willi Schmidt.

After being graduated from the University of Berlin, where he studied philosophy and the history of arts, Willi Schmidt served as assistant to Rochus Gliese, a famous German stage designer.

Professor Schmidt has been a stage director at the Schiller and Schlosspark Theaters in Berlin; the Schauspielhaus in Hamburg; the Schauspielhaus in Düsseldorf; the Schauspielhaus in Wuppertal; and the Burgtheater in Vienna. He was a Professor of Stage Design at the *Hochschule für bildende Kunste*. Schmidt has directed plays from all the principal literary periods, including works by Sophocles, Shakespeare, Molière, Goethe, Claudel, Giraudoux, Anouilh, Shaw and Pirandello. In many instances, he designed the sets of the productions also.

IASTA chose to inaugurate its program with a play by Friedrich Schiller to commemorate the 200th anniversary of the birth of this great German romantic poet and playwright. This play, the basis for Verdi's opera, LUISE MILLER, was written by Schiller at the age of 25, and reflects some of his personal experiences as a youth in the dukedom of Württemberg.

LOVE AND INTRIGUE was presented early in 1960 at IASTA's theatre in New York. The interview was current with the rehearsals and continued through correspondence over the years.

INTERVIEW WITH WILLI SCHMIDT

LOVE AND INTRIGUE is a play that stands midway between prose and verse. Here is the young Schiller writing poetic passages that could not be contained in a prose paragraph, needing the strength of verse to keep his revolutionary ardor from flying off the page. Mixed with the daring poetic outpourings of the young revolutionary are his more down-to-earth pictures of a rising German bourgeoise. There is an interesting dichotomy between the play's poetic flights (LOVE) and the earthbound, tense prose (INTRIGUE). It is almost as if Schiller were equating love with poetry and intrigue with prose. The play was written at the time of the American Revolution. This play was one of the first in Germany to have a commoner; one of the first in Germany to represent the bourgeoise in a positive light.

> **Q.** How do you choose and define the style for a production? As director? As designer?

> **Schmidt:** The style is present in the work itself. Schiller can be played in many different ways, but the true style emerges always if the actors allow it.
>
> Since my childhood, I have seen Schiller performed. Naturally, the 'style' is present in my bones. But the deeper, truer essence is to be found by anybody, American or German. That can be found by a thorough study of the text, a kind of osmosis, or by the actor and the director absorbing the hidden meaning by a constant re-reading of the external form. If the poet is great, he will begin to take hold of your soul, and gradually you'll

become him. He will live again through you, and work his wonders through you. This is not a metaphysical approach; it is merely an organic way of getting at his truth. The director listens for the author's melody and rhythm . . . the breath and spirit of the work.

A dramatic genius like Schiller knows very well what he has written, and all we have to do is to get inside of his spirit. That means to think his thoughts and feel his feelings. The attempt to be more clever than he, and to approach the play from the outside instead of the inside, can only lead to bad results. A playwright of his caliber writes all the motivations that an actor needs to interpret his part. The playwright has seen and conceived his play as a totality.

Q. As a director what do you see as the challenge of Schiller's style?

Schmidt: Schiller is a challenge in sustaining characterizations and movement, without the deep motivation of more complex characters. Schiller's language is difficult. To act Schiller requires the ability to distinguish between varying levels of intensity.

I have directed in Germany and in Austria. A guest director finds an ensemble so the task of auditioning actors for the play is eliminated.

For best results of any production, the director needs an ensemble—a permanent acting company. An ensemble is not just a group of actors which accidentally come together, but it is an ensemble in which each new member knows the others through experience, has worked together for a period before and has worked with the same director. It is a group where the spirit of give and take is permanent.

The important and the great times of the theatre have always been when such a permanent acting company—

the ensemble as I have called it—had an author in its midst. I use many hours to audition actors to find out if the actor is suitable for the part. "Why do you make it so difficult for yourself," I am asked.

No director in the whole world, even a genius, is able to judge within a few minutes, the qualities of actors, and it is against my feeling of respect for the ego of the actor to judge him in so short a time. I try to be thorough and I rehearse for an hour or even longer with each actor.

Q. Do you feel there is a tangible national theatre style?

Schmidt: A national style? Yes, and each major playwright has a style.

Q. How do you direct Schiller?

Schmidt: I am afraid I may disappoint you very much in saying that I have not developed any method of how to direct a play. I am even inclined to say that it is dangerous for a director to have one simple method for directing Aeschylus, Shakespeare, Chekhov, O'Neill, or Thorton Wilder. A director must be as free as possible and ready to be inspired by the author. I try to become inspired by the spirit of the play, to become the right hand of my author. If he is a poet, I need sensibility, imagination and fantasy to bring to life the written lines of the author. Drama on the printed page is dead and lifeless and demands urgently to live on the stage. The director begins with reading over and over again the work which he intends to direct. He makes an intensive and thorough study of the work—almost a word by word reading. Reading the play in this specific sense, the director anticipates the production. The dramatic accents appear in his mind and the characters of the persons acting are in his imagination before his first rehearsal. He connects the characters of the play with the individuality of the actors he has chosen for the parts. He hears with interest the consonants and the dissonants of their voices and he anticipates the movements and the gestures of his actors in his mind.

The sequence and the visual side appear. It is therefore not an impartial reading that the director does, but from the very first moment, the reading demands a transposition into the dramatic. It is rare, indeed, that a play can be played without cuts, but cutting is a difficult responsibility.

I expect the actor to come as free as possible to the first rehearsal, not to be preoccupied, but to be open, to work with the material which the author has given him. In other words, he has to be naive. I think there cannot be any other attitude on the part of the actor but humility towards the author. It is the main task of the stage director to help the actor, and to relieve the burdensome load on the way up to the identification with the spirit of the author—to help him along and to guide him. The difficult and rather subtle process can only be accomplished if there has been established confidence between the actor and the director and respect for their individual artistic personalities. The main burden, as I have said before, will always have to be carried by the actor. The part that the director has to play is that of a guide, not the part of a task-master. Because of the specific psychological makeup of the actor, nothing can be accomplished by force, anyway. The result will have to be to guide the actor to find himself, to make him secure, and to help him learn how to use all of his artistic means to their best advantage. Till the very end of the rehearsal time, he must be kept in a state that he can feel the identification with the part he is playing. The best director makes his actors feel secure and eager to act in a complete feeling of freedom.

A theatre-goer wants to see a play and not direction. The best director is one who remains in the background, anonymous, an artist with 'magic' and power to bring to life, with the help of his actors, the line the author has written.

As soon as I assemble the cast, I start immediately with rehearsal *onstage,* which means I don't talk about the play or discuss the characters at a table, *á la Italienne,* as both the Russians (sic!) and the French label this method. I do not theorize. I start immediately with blocking the scenes, because I am of the opinion that all difficulties which eventually arise can be solved through the lines of the play, but not by comment and analysis.

Often we may find the characterization of one role in the lines of dialogue of his partner, even if he is not present when a character or characters talk about him. Therefore, it is very important for an actor not only to know what *he* says himself, but also to know what the other characters say about him. The simplest, the fastest and the best way to play one's part is to be within the scene from the very first moment, listening to oneself talk and noting how the other actors react.

If he listens to *their* lines, if he questions and seeks answers, then he will learn what they have to communicate to him. The sooner an actor discovers that he is a part of a totality, that he is not only playing his part, but the play, the easier it will be for him to solve his personal and specific task as actor. Only then will he be able to recognize and comprehend all the nuances and subtleties of the play and his role in particular. To start with nuances and subtleties of a play is to put icing on the cake which has not been baked; to build a house, starting with the roof.

The actor has disguised his own self to reveal the character of his role. My actors and I jump head over heels right into the play and into the "scenes."

This method, which is no method at all, is the basis of any creative work in the theatre. The actor should read and re-read the text constantly. The words give him everything.

The actor must allow his powers of receptivity, his suggestibility, to come through in his work on a play; he must have confidence in his ability to stay on the track, and not wander in different directions. It is what the character *would* do, and that is the important thing.

I want the actor to act the moment-to-moment feel of the lines. The lines that the author has written may sometimes appear very difficult to speak, but they give a different impression when they are in the mouths of the actors, as spoken lines.

A director directs the production the same as if conducting an orchestra. More rehearsal time is needed to make the characters human beings, not puppets.

In my own case, I can speak as director and designer, and this relationship is of a personal union. Sometimes I avoid the tensions and the frictions between the two, (both being myself), but I can assure you a dialogue with one's self is sometimes not easier than with someone else! The first and most important task of the set designer is to transform the spirit of the work into the realities of the three dimensions of the stage. An example is SAINT JOAN by George Bernard Shaw and SAINT JOAN by Friedrich Schiller. Both are concerned with the same girl; both plays are of the same period. Would it be possible to use the same set for both productions? On the one hand we have the play of the ironical Shaw and on the other hand, the romantic Schiller. As designer, I show the unique spirit of the play, which demands the kind of set to use. If the designer pushes his way to the forefront of the picture, works for himself instead of working in relationship with the others concerned, a play can be ruined by the designer; e.g. overdoing the pictorial aspects of the production. A designer has to exercise humility; his signature on a production will be read even if he puts himself in the background of the production.

That the space on stage not be crammed full with sets is important. Sometimes an empty stage can exercise magical power. As with the set, well-designed costumes are overlooked and underestimated. Audiences and critics very often pay little attention to sets and costumes.

The designer depends on the help he gets from the technical staff. A sketch on paper is nothing. Team work is a necessity. The man behind the lighting equipment is as important as a leading lady. If he fails, she would be in the dark and could not go on playing!

In the Schiller Theater of Berlin, I present a floor plan to the technical staff and they build a neutral setting; walls, doors, windows. The setting is designed and decorated as the play is rehearsed, so that the needs of the actors and the contribution of their physical understanding of the text determines the completed theatrical entity.

LOVE AND INTRIGUE, as directed by me for IASTA, is mainly based on a concept of diagonal tensions, lines that lead the eye to many different infinities. To keep the audience from being too disturbed by the constant asymmetric design in each scene, there is the use of flowing movements of actors and deliberate use of parallel moves of the actors within a given diagonal. In the last moment Ferdinand's father, the wily President, gives Ferdinand an ultimatum and leaves, walking upstage to disappear off-stage. The passageway is on an acute diagonal. Ferdinand walks down stage simultaneously, in the exact same line. This is effective because the two actors are walking the same line, but their paths are quite different. It creates a harmony of movement within a dramatically unharmonious and tension-filled scene.

I select certain important gestures for a character to repeat in variations throughout the play. A character, full of his own conceit, confident that his future is assured, spreads his arms out and turns around in a full circle to display his newly-acquired clothes. Later, the same character, threatened with disgrace, is emotionally disrobed by dramatic events and once again spreads his arms wide . . . with the difference that he is now a lifeless puppet, ruined. The gesture is to remind the audience of his previous state and point up the contrast with his state, heightening the dramatic effect without resorting to histrionics for scenes of disgrace and ruin.

Ferdinand, the doomed young lover, expresses himself with wide sweeping gestures: to express love for Louisa, to protest before his father a forced engagement, to denounce Lady Milford. He expresses love of life and determination to save his love. Then, Louisa's fatal letter is written, and in the last scene Ferdinand enters the stage with his hands deep in the pockets of his great coat. His wings are clipped. (And so, by the way, is his dialogue.) He only removes his hands to take, dramatically, the lying letter from his pocket and throws it at Louisa's feet. His hands are no longer the warm wings of love, but the claws of death with which he poisons himself and Louisa. His hands have become weapons. Visual repetition italicizes and concretizes the text.

Now, after six weeks of strenuous work, I know that what I have demanded and expected from my cast with this method which, in my eyes is no method at all, is the basic fundamental of any creative work in the theatre. I try to retain flexibility and to be agreeable to trying changes, but I block this play at once.

'Get up and do' method as opposed to 'sit down and discuss.'

Q. Are most plays about particular people at a given time in a certain relationship?

Schmidt: Yes. A director has to study the spirit of the times out of which the play has been born. He has to familiarize himself with the point of view and the ideas of the playwright. A German play of the 18th century belongs to the classic heritage of our literature. It cannot be interpreted with naturalistic means.

The wonderful possibilities the theatre has! The theatre is able to connect the times of various periods during one evening, to show locales of many regions, using its wonderful means of dance, mime, music and all the other ways of expression. Tradition is important but not the tradition of the museum.

Q. Is a knowledge of the manners of the period important?

Schmidt: Yes, of course.

Q. How important to a production of a classic is authenticity of dress?

Schmidt: My recent production of Goethe's TORQUATO TASS in Berlin became a success in spite of the reviewers missing a "modern" interpretation of Goethe's drama. May I confess to you, I have no idea what I have to do to be "modern."

During my whole life (and I am in my 70th year now), I have tried to serve the *verity* which I hope is independent of any "modernness."

Q. How important is a knowledge of the physical form of the theatre for which the play was written?

Schmidt: Schiller's stage seems to me not too different from the familiar proscenium stage of the 19th century and later. Theatre is not a naturalistic medium. If Art is like life, boundless, diffuse, without form, and unmanageable, it is not Art. The dramatist has to concentrate the formless content of life into two or three hours on the stage.

GERMAN ROMANTICISM: SCHILLER

FILM

"German Theatre: Brecht and Schiller" (includes scenes from Schiller's "Love and Intrigue"): obtainable, for rental and purchase, through the Institute for Advanced Studies in the Theatre Arts (IASTA), P.O. Box 1106, Radio City Station, New York, NY 10101 or Gil Forman, 310 W. 56th St., #1B, New York, NY 10019.

SELECTED BIBLIOGRAPHY

Bentley, Eric. *The Classic Theatre, Volume Two, Five German Plays.* New York: Doubleday Anchor Books, 1959.

Friedenthal, Richard. *Goethe: His Life and Times.* New York: The World Publishing Company, 1963.

Schiller, Frederick. *The Works of Frederick Schiller.* London: George Bell & Sons, 1875.

MATERIALS AND BACKGROUND

Erick, Herman. *The Germans.* New York: Stein and Day, 1980.

Fuch, Peter Paul. *The Music Theater of Walter Felsenstein.* New York: W.W. Norton & Company, 1975.

Schiff, Gert and Waetzoldt, Stephen. *German Masters: Paintings and Drawings from the Federal Republic of Germany.* New York: New York Metropolitan Museum, 1981.

MUSIC

Concerto in B flat for 2 lutes and strings (Handel) RCA Records ARL-1-1180.

Beethoven: Trio in E flat, Op. 38 for Piano, Clarinet, Cello DG ARC-253318.

BRECHT

"the familiar made strange" *

* "verfremdungseffekte"

Traditionally, German dramatists have been intensely concerned about whether literature should be pure or *engageé*. That is, remain aloof or be involved with the events of its time. Schiller called the theatre a "moral institution," and the majority of German dramatists have shared his opinion. Even Brecht, who rebelled against so many other conventions, felt obliged to follow in this tradition and turned his poetic genius to become a "teacher of the people."

There has been much discussion about the Asian theatre's influence on Brecht. It is certainly significant, but it is overrated. The archaic Asian forms, such as those which distinguish the Chinese theatre, were fundamentally alien to him, for they express a conservative, traditional culture. By contrast, Brecht remained rebellious throughout all his plays— so revolutionary at times that many of his pronouncements became involuntarily anti-Communistic, as the Party platform grew rigidly conservative. More significant were the influences of the preclassical German writers, the STRUM UND DRANG period, Büchner, Wedekind, and particularly the German and Russian directors of the twenties as well as the AGITPROP (Agitation-Propaganda) theatre.

To fully grasp the range of Brecht, however, it is not sufficient to investigate the stylistic influences that he observed. Almost more important for scholars of Brecht is a knowledge of German dialectical materialistic philosophy as in Hegel, Marx and Engels; German idealistic philosophy as in Kant; and the Bible, all of which Brecht utilized. However, these influences are evident only in parodied form.

Most modern writers write for a select audience. It was the outside audience, the simple working people, that Brecht wanted to reach. He wanted to attract to the theatre those people who were not interested in literary works but who enjoyed musicals and popular entertainments. THE THREEPENNY OPERA, 1928, was his first successful example of this popular type. It was not until his third period, with plays like MOTHER COURAGE; GALILEO; THE CAUCASIAN CHALK CIRCLE; THE GOOD WOMAN OF SETZUAN that Brecht again reached such a wide audience.

In his early works, from his first period to about the time of THE THREEPENNY OPERA, Brecht was a nihilist. Brecht presented a world without ideals and without God. Life is meaningless; people are helpless, and trapped by their animal instincts. Brecht wears the mask of a cold observer, but behind the mask you see his lyrical feeling of bitterness and sorrow.

From about the time of THE THREEPENNY OPERA on, Brecht's world changed. He began to agitate for communism, but his early communism was more like anarchy. The communists Brecht wanted to please noticed this immediately and criticized him very harshly. At the same time, he shocked the conservative German middleclass so much that they were afraid he was helping to start a communist revolution. To them, Mac the Knife was a mixture of Lenin, Stalin, and Marx. But to the communist dictators, Mac the Knife, a gangster, was not a very acceptable hero of the proletariat!

In the works of the second period, during which Brecht wrote didactic and anti-Nazi plays, Brecht tried to write plays that would be completely acceptable to the party. In this period his poetry is as remarkable as in other periods, but his political ideas were mostly incorrect and very naive.

In the plays of the third period, Brecht became wiser. Only rarely do we find him writing communist propaganda—and only in minor scenes or in isolated lines and verses.

Nevertheless, even though Brecht does not agitate for communism, his plays of the third period are written from a Marxist point of view. He remained an idealist who was disillusioned by Christian idealogy and the limits of humanitarianism; he substituted communist ideals in their place. His writings became purely dialectic. That is to say, his plays posed questions, but did not answer them. He left the answers open, with the expectation that his audiences would leave the theatre with these questions in mind.

Brecht looked for a new style and a new definition of the theatre. The results of this looking, both as a writer and as a director, became the Epic Theatre. He developed, in his dramaturgy, in his dialogue, in his poetry, and also in his use of scenery, costumes, props, and music, and in his style of acting, a new concept of theatre.

We can only speculate as to what Brecht's fourth period might have been. On his return to Berlin from exile he once said he wanted to write an attack on the nihilism of WAITING FOR GODOT.

GERT WEYMANN, a native of Berlin, has been deeply involved in Brecht's Epic Theatre style. In addition, he has directed numerous works by Wedekind, Sternheim, and Kaiser representing the Expressionist theatre as well as Strindberg, Sartre, Gorki and Shakespeare.

Mr. Weymann is also a well-known German playwright. His most successful play, GENERATIONS, won the coveted Gerhart Hauptmann Award. THE GOOD WOMAN OF SETZUAN is the first play Mr. Weymann directed in a language other than German. The IASTA performance occurred in 1963 and the interview took place in the Fall of 1978.

Q. How do you choose and define the style for a Brecht production?

Weymann: By studying the play and the productions which have been authorized by the author, by some directors who have worked under Brecht. By studying the period, and the lives of the people on whom the characters were based.

Q. What are the elements of this style?

Weymann: Brecht's style? I think you are referring to characters who are "in a scene" and then are "out of scene." The actor playing a Brecht character is never completely in the scene because the emotions are always interrupted or broken. Emotions in a Brecht play do not flow as in an Elizabethan play.

The elements of Brecht's style are typical of the German style: Sturm und Drang (storm and stress). Before Goethe, for example, compare DER HOFMEISTER (THE TUTOR), 1774 by Lenz, of which Brecht wrote a variation that is not very far from the original play. Then you will see what I mean: classical German theatre is miusunderstood Shakespeare. The Germans did not understand Shakespeare; they saw, in this period, his plays as a completely free, wild, chaotic way of writing.

Thus we find in Brecht a bringing together of scenes as if they were singled out with a spotlight. The plays are episodic, fragmented scenes, put together as was common to all German playwrights for generations.

Brecht wanted to be didactic, to teach through theatre, to teach new ideas. These attitudes contributed to Brecht's style.

In Brecht's early plays expressionistic elements are strong, of course: we have a fusion of "storm and stress;" an historical style, coupled with the desire to use the theatre as if it were a church or school. This is not so surprising since Germany for two hundred years has had a theatre that has been subsidized with public or state funds; monies came, in early times, from Princes, and now from the government, and sometimes even from labor unions and political groups. Therefore, German playwrights, and in the case of Brecht as well, were under obligation to present the points of view of the groups which were subsidizing their theatres.

"Paying the piper" was true of Goethe (1749-1832) in those early times; he was a great humanist and a great poet, but even in his play IPHIGENIE, with a Greek classical theme, he voiced a message that *all* humans need to get along together, to co exist. Goethe accepted the theatre as an instrument of the ruling classes, the German Princes, the aristocracy and the upcoming bourgeoisie of the period of "enlightenment."

Q. Do you feel there is a tangible national theatre style? A German style of theatre?

Weymann: I think there is. The German theatre style came later than either the English Shakespearean style or the French theatre style, both of which greatly influenced the early

German theatre. There were two traditional influences, the one coming from France, and the other from England, most particularly Shakespeare.

At the beginning of the national German theatre, at the time of the playwright Lessing (1729-1781), influences mingled, French-English, but were also in conflict. There was a strong feeling against Shakespearean and pseudo-Shakespeare theatre as "storm and stress;" and on the other hand, against the classical French theatre of Cornielle and Racine. Goethe's GOETZ VON BERLICHINGEN is a typical "storm and stress" play; Schiller's (1759-1805) DIE RÄUBER (THE ROBBERS), 1781, was influenced by Shakespeare. German playwrights thought Shakespeare's plays each had a series of scenes, a pattern of short scenes, and so they wrote plays in what they thought was Shakespeare's style. But in reality Shakespeare had worked out a dramaturgy, not of scenes, but of continuing action. Early German writers didn't know the true nature of Shakespeare, believing that he just wrote one scene, then another: a violent scene, scenes of different locations, from the streets, perhaps to a palace of a Prince, suggesting changes of sets.

Early plays of Goethe, "storm and stress," are wild in style. Beginning with Lessing, playwrights learned from the French classical theatre of Molière, Corneille, and Racine; French classicism and Shakespeare were mixed up. Goethe wrote GOETZ VON BERLICHINGEN (influenced by Shakespeare) and IPHIGENIE (close to the classical French style), or he mixed both elements as in EGMONT. Schiller did the same thing, for in his DON CARLOS, each act is like that of a French tragedy, but the whole conception is more his idea of Shakespeare. This mixed national style continues down through the centuries to the style of the romantic; Tieck (1773-1853) and Grabbe (1801-1836) are more "Shakespearean," later on, Hebbel (1813-1863) and expressionism in theatre. Although Brecht is more of the "storm and stress" school, he was influenced by expressionism, dadism, and early 20th century philosophies.

I would say the German theatre has a national style, but in the beginning of the German theatre the style had two faces.

Q. Does each play have its own style or a correct style? Are plays about particular people at a certain time in certain relationships?

Weymann: In answer to the first question, I think that depends: if the writer is less strong, his play has the style of tradition and the period; but if the writer is strong, he creates styles and develops them so that each of his plays may have *its* own style: perhaps not too far from the tradition of the period. If the writer is strong, he has added personal things to the style, and he always tries to go one step further to the next period, to the next style, making the play in his own style. Ibsen's early plays are in one tradition; then his middle period gave us THE DOLL HOUSE; later, his last plays are mystical. Each has to be performed in a different, but appropriate, style. A minor author toasts the same bread throughout his whole life!

Q. Brecht was a strong individualistic writer. Did he have different styles?

Weymann: Brecht's early period, (before 1932 and before THREEPENNY OPERA), and his later plays are, of course, very different. Some groups of Brecht's plays have their own style, which is different from the other groupings.

Brecht is not a writer who is like a factory making plays for entertainment. Personally, I can think of no better writer. And, of course, he is very different from other great writers for theatre.

Q. Is part of Brecht's style didactic?

Weymann: I would not say that of his early plays. They were very very much "storm and stress," very emotional, chaotic, "dadaist." Later on, with the rise of Hitler, Brecht chose Marxism as a way to demonstrate against Hitler. Earlier, in the 1920s, Brecht lived very comfortably as an intellectual, an artist; he didn't think too deeply about the actual political situation. Later, in exile, he re-wrote much of what he had written in the 20s for example, TROMMELN IN DER NACHT or MANN IST MANN. THE GOOD WOMAN OF SETZUAN and other didactic plays, he wrote in exile, aimed to educate an audience.

All this came very late, and when he returned to Germany with these plays and produced them, they seemed artificial, because time had passed them by. Hitler was now dead; the Russians were in Germany; everything was different. Brecht's clever solution was to create a very high style, a perfected, even insulated style. I question whether or not this theatre was truly a didactic one, because the social situations he analyzed were typical for the time before Hitler and not for the Germany after the Second World War.

Q. You and I observed rehearsals at the Berliner Ensemble in 1959. Later that year in Moscow at a seminar on Russian theatre, I remember remarking "Where are the plays of Brecht?"

Weymann: I can tell you. The Russians had their revolution many years ago, and their new middle class doesn't want Brecht. They like Chekhov, Pushkin, opera or *new* plays in the traditional style of the Stanislavski theatre. In East Germany today, there's a new middle class also, and they like Brecht as a "classical."

Q. I think our Russian friends in 1959 found Brecht too

276

revolutionary. In "THE GOOD WOMAN OF SETZUAN," the heroine opens her little shop to the poor, and suddenly the poor exploit her! Does Brecht show the other side of the coin, i.e. poor people can exploit as well as be exploited?

Weymann: Not in the future of which Brecht is dreaming. Of course, Brecht wants to show how the capitalistic system makes people evil. If he presents the poor people of the working class also as capable of evil, he shows that to be just and not to be boring as an artist. At the same time, he tries to show that it is the system which induces the evil; in reality they are good people.

Q. I remember your directing the scene where the barber had broken the carpenter's wrist, and the carpenter wants to make the most of his injury. Is this the dramatization of a social situation?

Weymann: Yes, the carpenter needs money, and like every capitalist he is making the best of what he has. A carpenter has to try to make something out of his broken hand. Brecht would say that if a social utopia is realized, the carpenter would not need to do that. But now-a-days, he is in need and the system forces him to fight for whatever he can get.

Q. To what extent is tradition important in the production of a classical play?

Weymann: I would say the director should really try to be true to the tradition, to the style, and to bring out the play's ideas as written. That is best. If the director is strong, fresh, and modern enough to bring out consciously his view of the play, and an attitude of the society in which he is living from within the play, then this is the best combination. It is like rebuilding or remodeling a classical building today so that people can live in it and find in it something for themselves as well. The phoney thing or wrong thing, as in Germany at the moment, is to think we have to make everything new and arresting; e.g. Desdemona has to be 60 years old! This is to destroy the play; one doesn't bring out some new aspect of the play, but only a personal, subjective mood and caprice. In short, study the tradition, try to respect it, and to make it fresh enough to be vital, to bring to it without foolishness a fresh, new insight in the tradition.

Q.   Is a classic an affirmation of life?

Weymann: Yes, that's good. To come back to Brecht in East Berlin: The Berliner Ensemble gives very good performances but the productions are getting more and more chalky, like walls; they are devitalized. Brecht's daughter is living; his widow, Helene Weigel, is dead. In rehearsal, the directors and their teams discuss the old style of Brecht from morning to night in order to keep it alive. If they were to try something new with Brecht, that would be good, but they won't risk it. There is that tradition. That's why Brecht is relatively dead at the moment: the old Brecht students create his plays more or less in the same way he did twenty years ago, and it doesn't work. Respect for his style is fine, but after twenty years one must bring to it a fresh and new attitude.

Q.   Of what importance is it to know the physical structure of the theatre for which a playwright wrote a play?

Weymann: I think it is not as important as many people think. If the stage isn't extremely small, one can do practically all things from different types of theatre. One can do Shakespeare in the Deutches Theater of Max Reinhardt. One sees Shakespeare on his traditional stage, and Elizabethan stage, too.

I am of the impression that the more that one tries to reconstruct Sophocles' classical stage or the Elizabethan stage under modern conditions, the more apt it is to fail. Because the dimensions of our modern theatres are too big. Actors speaking Sophocles' verse with "method" acting of Stanislavski will find a large part of the audience unable to understand or even hear. To perform Attic tragedy in an old Greek theatre, actors have to have voices or the masks with the megaphones which scholars say the old Greek actors used. In the Expressionistic period of the '20s, there were plays, for example, where actors spoke through megaphones to reach their audiences or to underline or to enlarge the effect of their words and its message. The problem is to be able to follow without strain and without loss of concentration what is spoken and acted. If the audience is able to see change of expression on the face of the actor, then, of course, Sophocles in an arena theatre is surely more fascinating.

I prefer Shakespeare's apron stage. It gives a fluidity. I would choose to work in the style of the stage for which the play was written.

However, today I find the dimensions and shape are wrong. I can't stand that anymore. In Germany, in the woods, even beside wonderful rocky mountains, they produce festivals of classical plays. One sits there and, whether you like it or not, you see and hear the audience better than the actors! This situation you sometimes find in some of the modern big theatres. So, the size and shape have to be right in relationship to the audience. Always it should be small audiences in small places. How many people were sitting in Shakespeare's theatres? By our present standards, I'm sure the audiences were quite small. Trouble begins when you increase the size of the original theatre. Otherwise, you can use the original stage.

Q. Brecht gave the characters of "THE GOOD WOMAN . . ." Chinese names. What do you think of a director who

279

pulls up the eyebrows and the eyes of non-Chinese actors to give them almond-shaped, Chinese eyes?

Weymann: No, no, no. I don't know why a director would do that! A tobacco shop in Berlin in the '20s could have had the same problems that occur in THE GOOD WOMAN. To bring in the other world of China in this play through traditional Chinese costumes and makeup would defeat Brecht's intention. Brecht's style is certainly not Chinese; and the actors certainly need not appear to be Chinese.

Q. Elizabeth Hauptmann explained *verfremdungseffekte*, not as alienation, but to make familiar things appear strange. A strange milieu for the familiar calls our attention to the familiar. In other words, poverty, in an exotic setting, tends to have us realize poverty rather that ignore it.

Weymann: Yes, all of that's true. Also, stylized costumes are appropriate, but the actors' faces must not have makeup that makes them appear Chinese: the natural faces of poor people, whether Chinese or British, is all we need to see. For all Brecht's plays, actors' should use as little folklore-type makeup as possible. Of course, Brecht used makeup. He liked to give his actors other noses, etc. if he thought it fit the character.

Q. For your production of "THE GOOD WOMAN . . . ," you used newspaper as scenery: it was like Chicago in the Depression.

Weymann: Yes, yes, Brecht liked to show his idea of Chicago. His ST. JOAN OF THE STOCKYARDS shows his idea of Chicago. Even the early dadaist plays were sometimes set in Chicago.

Q. What about Brecht's later period?

Weymann: There was the great period of Brecht in the '50s. So impressive, so right, so exact; one must study that. But, one has to adjust the Berliner Ensemble style of the '50s to the present. One has to make a lot of adjustments. More so in a foreign country where you have Brecht in translation.

Q.　What advice do you have for an actor playing a Brecht character?

Weymann:　The actor playing a Brecht character is never really completely in the scene because the emotions of the character always stop, are broken repeatedly. Even in the acting, the emotions don't continue, don't flow as in an Elizabethan play. For an element of Brecht's style, compare Lenz's DER HOFMEISTER with the Brechtian variation of the same play. Brecht does not stray far from the original DER HOFMEISTER. His style is quite clear.

BRECHT'S THEATRE, THE BERLINER ENSEMBLE

The Berliner Ensemble rehearses daily six days a week from approximately ten in the morning until two in the afternoon. It is customary to have one short rehearsal break, during which time the actors get coffee or some take their lunch in the canteen.

In this ornate Biedermeier theatre, with nude caryatids, the boxes on balcony level at the side were used for sound and for accommodating musicians. The red hangings were closed on the upper boxes; in third-tier boxes lighting equipment had been set up, but sometimes they were used for an overflow audience when the house was sold out.

The theatre has a revolving stage; the turntable is used for most of the productions; also the stage is raked at a steep angle. The forestage extends into the house about seven feet from curtain line. The proscenium stage boxes at stage level have been used for *"proscenium"* entrances. For some productions they restore part of the box, but for most of the productions these stage boxes are used as proscenium doors.

A program provides the following statistics: The Berliner Ensemble am Schiffbauerdamm, founded in 1949, is a repertory theatre and consists of 219 members including 60 actors. In his capacity as chief advisor and producer, Bertolt Brecht guided the work of the actors, producers, writers, and stage designers.

Rehearsals last from two to five months. As a rule, the company plays seven times a week, with a month's holiday each year. The theatre seats 727; seats costs from one to ten marks. There are single and group subscriptions at reduced rates. Financed out of state funds, the Berliner Ensemble has a free hand in choosing plays and engaging artists.

Brecht's plays involve a great many characters; therefore, cast and technicians are a challenge for the directors. It is informative to see at an early stage in rehearsal that the actors have platforms and levels to work with; they already use certain props; actors work with hats, some with guns.

A theatre, this early in rehearsal when they do not know as yet when they are going to give a public performance, has so many elements of the production for rehearsal. Impressive, to say the least, the extent to which they have stagehands, electricians, prop men, and all technical personnel (in the now familiar white coats), present and working the rehearsal.

There is a relaxed and casual atmosphere as people move in and out of the auditorium during the rehearsal. There are no tense nor temperamental nor pretentious actors or directors. They seem adjusted to observers moving in and out of the house, quietly. They seem to take as a matter of course having strangers in the auditorium observing rehearsals.

Some days later, we went to the Berliner Ensemble to pay a last visit to Elizabeth Hauptmann, a woman who had worked with Brecht for thirty years. She tells how Brecht, forming and shaping his company The Berliner Ensemble, had communicated his style and theory of acting.

"Brecht was an expert theoretician, but he was, after all, first and foremost a practical theatre man. He communicated his concept of acting through rehearsal. Brecht was aware that often actors do not read through the play they are performing in. Or if they read it, they read it superficially. He was concerned in working with his actors that they read the play and get beneath the surface of the play—that they know it thoroughly. He saw his job as director to take them into the depth of a play."

BRECHT

FILM

"German Theatre: Brecht and Schiller" (includes scenes from Brecht's "The Good Woman of Setzuan"), obtainable, for rental and purchase, through the Institute for Advanced Studies in the Theatre Arts (IASTA), P.O. Box 1106, Radio City Station, New York, NY 10101 or Gil Forman, 310 W. 56th St., #1B, New York, NY 10019.

SELECTED BIBLIOGRAPHY

Brecht, Bertolt. *Helen Weigel—Actress*. (Translated by John Berger and Anna Bostock.) Veb Edition Leipzig, 1961.

Brecht, Bertolt. *The Messingkauf Dialogues*. (Translated by John Willett.) London: Methuen & Co. Ltd., 1965.

Esslin, Martin. *Brecht: The Man and His Work*. New York: Doubleday, 1960.

Lyon, James K. *Bertolt Brecht in America*. Princeton: Princeton U. Press, 1980.

Willett, John. *Brecht on Theatre: The Development of an Aesthetic*. London: Methuen & Co. Ltd., 1964.

Willett, John. *The Theatre of Bertolt Brecht*. Norfolk, Conn.: New Directions, 1959.

MATERIALS AND BACKGROUND

Erick, Herman. The Germans. New York: Stein and Day, 1980.

Schiff, Gert and Waetzoldt, Stephan. *German Masters: Paintings and Drawings from the Federal Republic of Germany*. New York: New York Metropolitan Museum, 1981.

MUSIC BOOK

Brecht, Dessau. *Leider und Gesange*. Berlin: Henschelverlag, 1963.

MUSIC

Kurt Weill and Bertolt Brecht. The Three Penny Opera. Columbia O2S 201.

Kurt Weill. Mahagonny Songspiel. Deutsche Grammophon 2740153.

POLISH: WYSPIANSKI

"nationalism as theatre"

L.T.M.

Has Poland ever been a country of great drama? Has she ever made her mark in this field in the sense in which England and France, or in certain historic periods, Spain, Scandinavia, Russia, and Germany have; or in the sense in which the U.S.A. is making her mark today, thanks to the dynamic impact of her distinguished dramatists?

The answer lies in the fact that a significant feature of Polish drama, a feature that accounts perhaps for its greatness as well as for its limitations is its involvement in the political scene. Our earliest significant play, THE DISMISSAL OF THE GREEK ENVOYS, by Wojciech Boguslawski, was, in fact, referring to the political situation of the time and was intended as a call to military campaign. It was, in short, a political play.

At the close of the eighteenth and the beginning of the nineteenth century, the Polish theatre and drama were distinguished by the activities of this man whom we consider the father of our modern theatre. Actor, dramatist, teacher and director—Wojciech Boguslawski wrote, among other things, a work of crucial importance to the Polish theatre: a national comedy-opera. In it the stylized folklore of the Polish mountaineers and of the peasants of the Cracow region is set against a background of Rococo music à la maniére Italienne, with a rich sprinkling of Polish folk music.

This simple story about a purely regional feud between the Cracovians and Mountaineers, fighting for a girl, held for the contemporary playgoer an unmistakable reference to the struggle between the Poles, determined to defend their country, and the Russians, determined to seize it.

Poles heard in this highly artistic and highly political play the initial call to the Kosciuszko uprising of 1794, just as some people distinguish in LE MARIAGE DE FIGARO the initial call to the French Revolution.

From the time this play was written, all that was great and important in Polish drama was invariably connected with the country's political tragedy, i.e. with its partition among the three powers, which deprived it of its political and economic independence, and in consequence hampered its cultural growth.

ERWIN AXER

Since 1949, Erwin Axer has been Artistic Director and Head of the Teatr

286

Wspolczesny or Contemporary Theatre in Warsaw. For three years, beginning in 1954, Mr. Axer was also Artistic Director of the Polish National Theatre. In the early days of the Berliner Ensemble, Mr. Axer directed for Bertolt Brecht. He is a frequent visiting director in the Soviet Union, Austria and West Germany. Mr. Axer is the author of two books bearing the same title, LETTERS FROM THE STAGE. In recognition of his significant artistic accomplishments, Mr. Axer was awarded, in 1955, the highest honor by the Polish Government, the National Prize, 1st Class.

On April 12, 1962, Mr. Axer presented the Institute for Advanced Studies in the Theatre Arts' actors in the Polish classic THE WEDDING at the IASTA Theatre, New York. The interview was conducted in Vienna in May, at the time Mr. Axer was directing a Polish classic at the Burgtheater.

Q. Can you tell us something about the author of THE WEDDING?

Axer: Stanislaw Wyspianski appeared on the scene of Polish drama at the close of the nineteenth century. This highly original genius: poet, painter, producer and reformer of the theatre, who was trying to work out a synthesis of dramatic art, following the example of Wagner or Gordon Craig (whom he did not imitate, by the way), is so tied up with historical and philosophical ideas and symbolism, and is so immersed in Greek and old Slav mythology that the majority of his plays are accessible today only to well-educated people with a good literary background. To fully understand the rich historical associations and to feel all the emotions embodied in this play THE WEDDING would pose difficulties even for a well-schooled Pole.

Q. Does Polish theatre have a distinct style?

Axer: The briefest answer to that question is a statement from Roman Szydlowski's THE THEATRE OF POLAND: "A theatre's rank is its style and Poland's style, among others is 'an education in patriotism'."

Q. Do you feel there is a tangible National Theatre style in regard to acting?

Axer: Max Reinhardt believed, as Thomas Mann has recalled in an essay, that the abundance of acting talent in Austria, in particular in Vienna, was due to the mingling of cultures and races which has taken place in the Danube Basin: Slavs, Italians, even Greeks, Hungarians, and of course, Germans. When he moved to the United States, Reinhardt ascribed to similar sources the extraordinary vigor and versatility of theatrical skills which he found in your country at the time.

If we look at the opportunities of Polish actors in these terms, we can see that they are equally fortunate. We are a country which lies at the crossroads of the East and the West. The Romans came here, and we have had visits from the Turks and Tartars. We seem to have assimilated the culture of humanism fairly completely; for a hundred years we have had inter-communication with Germany, and we live next door to Russia with its Byzantine cultural heritage.

Like the Austrian, the Polish actor's flexibility—a gift which can be ascribed to the cultural melting-pot that Poland has been over the centuries, is, I think, a very important attribute.

Q. What kind of actors does one see in cities like Warsaw, Cracow, or Katowice?

Axer: One may come across two or three actors of the very oldest generation, the successors of "the age of stars," a characteristic of the theatre in Poland at the turn of the century. It would be wrong, however, to imagine that in style they are all of a piece. Of course, they do have some characteristics in common apart from their venerable age: a gravity of approach to their trade, the habit of not learning their lines until after the blocking has been done, and a distrust of modern (which means 20th century) stage design. Apart from these things, they are all different. Among them you can find perpetuators of the naturalistic convention, the painstaking social portraits, blood-and-thunder romantics full of fire, and also cool, correct actors of the academic type. Some are excellent speakers of verse; with others it's not so much that they can't do it but that as a matter of realistic principle they are incapable and unwilling to take any notice of rhyme or rhythm.

Among the actors in their fifties there will certainly be some from the "Reduta" company, which played an enormous role in the growth of our modern theatre. The spirit and discipline of the Reduta were monastic, undoubtedly the right word since the company did not boggle at mysticism. They worked on each play—incidentally they produced Polish writers almost exclusively—for many months. Their method of analysis was a little different from Stanislavsky's: they went to enormous pains to dissect the off-stage life of the characters and even the props in each play. There is a famous story of how Limanowski speculated on the geological structure of a certain river mentioned in one of the plays. Though this is hardly surprising, in view of his being a trained geologist.

Parts were learned by heart, purely mechanically, before rehearsals started. They were written out by the actors themselves with no punctuation marks or periods.

This and lots of other things helped to create in the "Reduta" an atmosphere of absorbed, devout industry, and if these rituals were not a short cut to the goal, at least they were not too much of a detour. And the whole operation was consummated by the genius of Osterwa, a coach and teacher with a unique touch. He could take a player of very mediocre abilities and with the simplest of methods—a startlingly lucid explanation of the key to the character, some practical hint, a few pats on the back, followed up by some discreet suggestion which turned the interpretation inside out (often without the offender notic-ing it) or, if need be, with some ingenious exercises—he could coax out of this actor the sort of rounded perform-ance we are used to seeing only from the very great. I, myself, once saw him running for hours round the theatre garden with a young actress who had been drooping all over the stage, making her recite, as she ran, an important soliloquy. I roared with laughter and I stopped laughing only when I saw the results on the first night.

Actors who worked in the "Reduta" can be recognized today by their natural delivery—and a host of supersti-tions. They are best in realistic and psychological dramas on which they were brought up and they can never have enough rehearsals.

Actors under fifty have had training in the pre-war State Institute of Theatrical Art which had an Acting and Pro-ducing Department, which also trained designers.

The thirty-five to forty age group of actors in Poland has a very strange background, found nowhere else. Their apprenticeship was served not on the stage or in a theatrical school, but in the cramped rooms of private apartments where, hidden from the Gestapo, they were initiated into the secrets of their craft. There was no room to develop gesture or voice. At the beginning of their careers the technique of these actors was very shaky, though they know their theory well. So it took much longer than usual, ten, sometimes fifteen years for some real artists to emerge from this generation. The younger actors come now from the state schools in Warsaw and Cracow and the one in Lodz which works in close partner-ship with the film school there.

There is one other phenomenon I should touch on. As a result of the enormous upsurge of interest in the theatre in provincial centers and even in small towns (there are many more theatres now than before the war), a large number of amateurs poured into the theatre just after the war despite the protests and precautions of the professionals. Men, in particular, were able simply to walk in and get a contract. Except in the more well-informed theatrical centres the broad public was not so discriminating yet as to have sent them packing. They have since been required to take the state exams which every actor must pass before he is allowed to join a theatre or appear on the stage. Many of this group who would not ordinarily have passed because of their faulty diction and crude technique were granted their licenses so that they could continue in the work that only the exigencies of postwar circumstances made possible in the first place. The examining board was apparently more impressed by the predicament of the new actors than by the predicament of the public.

Q. How do you rehearse?

Axer: Rehearsals in Poland follow a number of different patterns depending on whether the plays in the repertory are popular successes, whether we are putting on something about which we know more or less how it should be staged, or whether we are looking for some original, distinctive form for it. My theatre, for example, is not very big. The company numbers thirty actors of whom more than half have worked together for more than ten years and some for more than fifteen years. I consider myself fortunate in having the artisitc and administrative direction of my theatre for seventeen continuous years, a rare occurrence in Poland where managements spring up and fade away in the course of two or three seasons. We stage at least three and not more than five plays each year. The theatre's board—made up of designer, two literary consultants, composer, head producer and artistic director, and some of the actors, meet regularly on something like a family basis to discuss the theatre's affairs. We rehearse each play a minimum of two, sometimes three, four, or in exceptional cases, five months. I personally like to rehearse three to four months. I, myself, do a maximum of two plays a year; sometimes I do only one; once I did four. We don't rehearse on Sundays and Mondays, and often on Tuesday we have to go back to where we left off on Thursday. We start at ten in the morning. We used to work up till three or even four in the afternoon. Now, we have to break up promptly at two. Everyone has some sort of engagement, radio, television, film or maybe even worse. We rehearse very loosely. Time is not so precious for us as in America. If we don't feel in the mood, we are quite likely to stop and sit down over a cup of coffee for an hour and talk. We arrive punctually in the morning, but if we feel like it, we spend twenty minutes or even longer swapping jokes. Nevertheless, the discipline is there, though it is far from coercive. In all my time I have not had to impose fines more than ten times, and half of these I waived.

In the old days actors came to rehearsal much better prepared. Now, films and television are making inroads on their time and energy.

Once I used to arrive at rehearsal with my homework carefully done. Later when the actors ceased to frighten me I began to plan only the main outlines of the production. The rest we fill in together on stage: we improvise a great deal, we discuss, we analyze and immediately check the results. So rehearsals are more like explorations than training sessions in which we go over a pre-arranged routine. The rhythm of our openings permits us this luxury. Of course, it would be impossible if the actors in the rehearsals were not closely knit and sure of each other. It would be fatal if they were worried about making mistakes in front of the others or the director. For his part, the director does not have to be omniscient or pretend to be omnipotent. His authority can only be established by his record over the years. At rehearsal he can be baffled, make mistakes, change his mind, fumble, just as long as he keeps going. This method will not do for large and quick productions, but it often produces results. It stops us from getting stale and leaves us free to be constantly on the lookout for a more original and more appropriate form for a new subject.

We spend a great deal of time over the sets and costumes; we start work with the designers before the beginning of rehearsals and we keep it up throughout the first weeks and even months of rehearsal. When we discover some new insight in a play or change the conception, the designer and composer have to adapt themselves to the new plan. We try to avoid wasting their work and our money and throwing away finished sets and costumes, but if the welfare of the production calls for such a step, we have no qualms. We never open until we are really ready. In contemporary, straight plays the actors start to work in their costumes and makeup a week before the first night; with more difficult plays, two or even three weeks earlier. During the three or four days prior to the opening of a new production, we will not give performances of our other plays—so that if necessary we can rehearse around the clock.

We are familiar with Stanislavsky, we have seen Brecht for ourselves and we have read Diderot. We try to keep up with the times, not let oursleves be carried away by passing fashions, and follow the prompting of our common sense, taking our main cue from our subject and our playwright, through whom we want to speak to our public. We picture our public at least as intelligent as ourselves. For an actor to think of the audience as more stupid than himself is the most dangerous and most pernicious trap into which he can fall.

Q. What is the position of the Polish dramatist?

Axer: On the whole, Polish drama has made little impact on the world stage. We have dramatists whom we believe to be very great artists indeed—and yet we are denied general recognition of their greatness.

The reasons for this is that the history of the Polish nation has narrowed the subject matter of our drama and the interests of our poets, keeping them within the bounds of Poland's political tragedy.

The finest Polish stage works are written by poets. The Polish theatre until recently evinced little enthusiasm for narrow realism and domestic drama. Wyspianski and his poetic theatre, the dramatic style and ideas of an epic theatre, projected its image into the 20th century.

Q. How does the contemporary dramatist operate?

Axer: I don't think there is much difference between the situation of the Polish dramatist and the situation and customs of the profession all over Europe.

Our authors offer their work straight to our theatres, though they can do it via our Ministry of Culture. Directors take a very long time in telling the author if his play is worth anything. Sometimes they put the play on, more often they don't. If they do, the play is a success—or it's a flop. If it's a success, the author makes some money on it, rarely big money. He thinks it's his doing, the theatre thinks it's all it's doing. The public, of course, couldn't care less whose doing it is. If the play is a flop, the author blames the theatre and the theatre blames the author and the author remains the life enemy of the theatre. If the play is rejected, the author remains the enemy of the theatre until he writes a new play.

However, strange as it may seem, our plays don't vanish altogether—the good ones, at least. They are being published, along with outstanding foreign plays. Journals, in addition to two or three plays in each issue, bring essays and criticism as well as extensive information about drama everywhere. Some plays are published *before* they are produced. Many a Polish playwright owes his success to publication in a journal, and many foreign authors—to mention only Beckett, Ionesco, Genet, Duerrenmatt, Pinter—have been introduced to our theatres this way.

Q. Does each play have its own "correct" style? Is THE WEDDING about particular people at a certain time in a certain relationship?

Axer: THE WEDDING is a symbolic work based on an actual event. On a November day, 1900, in a small village not far from Cracow, the daughter of a local peasant married the famous poet, Lucian Rydel. At the wedding party, artists, intellectuals, members of the upper bourgeoisie mingled freely with peasants. This event reflected the mood of an era in which the intelligentsia's interest in the peasantry became a "fashion." There were some, however, who firmly believed that a power born out of the physical and moral health of the peasants would redeem and liberate Poland, partitioned at the time among Germany, Russia and Austria. One of the guests at the wedding party was Stanislaw Wyspianski. Shortly afterwards, he wrote THE WEDDING, a play dramatizing the immaturity, the romantic notions and the weak foundations of this peasant-intelligentsia alliance.

Q. How important to a production of THE WEDDING is authenticity of dress?

Axer: All the costumes by Ali Bunsch for the IASTA production were borrowed from Teatr Wybrzeze, Gdansk, Poland. These costumes were copies of the regional costumes worn by the peasants and by the bourgeoisie in the village of Bronewice, near Cracow, where the real-life wedding took place in November of 1900.

Q. Do you feel the IASTA production provided our actors with an insight into this work?

Axer: IASTA'S performances, the result of six weeks of rehearsal-cum-seminar work, was just the end of a certain stage; to explore all the facets of the play would require much more time. Still, the original form and style of the work, combining in the most unusual way poetic semi-naturalism with drama, provided—in line with IASTA'S aim—eloquent material for the study of a foreign and difficult theatre style.

POLISH

SELECTED BIBLIOGRAPHY

Nelken, Halina. *Stanislaw Wyspianski*. Warsaw: Arkady Publications, 1959.

Kirby, Victoria Nes. "World Festival of Theatre". *The Drama Review*, Vol. 17, No. 4. New York: December, 1973.

MATERIALS AND BACKGROUND

Losz, Czeslow. *History of Polish Literature*. New York: Macmillan, 1969.

MUSIC

Chopin
Polonaise for Cello and Piano, Op. 3 Tel. 642184

Chopin
Polonaise Fantasie, Op. 61 3-Ang. S-3723.

CHEKHOV

"reality as theatre"

D.C.

To bring up an artist—to give him unity of thought and feeling, this was the task that Stanislavski put before himself.

Chekhov is the author who offers this opportunity to the actor to an enormous degree; rather, more correctly, he *demands* it of the actor. You cannot play Chekhov in a superficial manner.

Actually, according to Stanislavski, according to Chekhov, you should not play the *characters* but, rather, you should play what happens between people in their interrelationships. This Third Dimension—what happens between—creates the world of human relationships.

One of the great actors of the Moscow Art Theatre, Leonidov, a man of enormous temperament, used to say that Stanislavski was very sly, that he invented the Method for himself because he was fighting his shortcomings; but as Stanislavski's shortcomings happened to coincide with the shortcomings of most of the others, his Method proved generally usable. In reality we know that an actor gets bored with playing. And this shortcoming of an actor Stanislavski studied very carefully, for it was his own. Stanislavski studied not how to *portray* a character but how to *become* a character.

YURI ZAVADSKI

Yuri Zavadski, IASTA's visiting director from Russia, a People's Artist of the U.S.S.R. and head of the Mossoviet Theatre, worked with Vakhtangov from 1915 to 1924 and Stanislavski from 1924 to 1936. He was thus able to acquaint us first hand with the final developments, as well as the present interpretation in the Soviet Union, of Stanislavski's Method.

Working with his own troupe in Moscow Mr. Zavadski would have taken at least three months to stage CHERRY ORCHARD. In the six weeks of his visit to New York in 1960, he preferred to concentrate on two of the four acts of the play. Even so, in a certain psychological sense, the results, in Mr. Zavadski's opinion, were forced and rushed. Nevertheless, he shed new light on and deepened our understanding of CHERRY ORCHARD stressing, as he did, the Russian as well as the universal elements.

INTERVIEW WITH YURI ZAVADSKI

Q. Mr. Zavadski, is there a Chekhov-style?

Zavadski: The problem of style is very complicated because style is often confused with manner. Style is something very significant; whereas manner, which is occasionally presented as style, in reality is only external mannerisms. True style is determined by the time, by the period, by the complexities of human interrelationships, by the particular author and what is most important to him. One has to determine style somehow from within.

One can interpret style through signs, external clues, or, one can interpret style as the essence of something deeper. One can define Chekhov's style as a slowing down, pauses, or something like that, but that would not be a deep understanding of Chekhov. How does one look for it? In art, it is difficult to separate subconscious feelings from conscious feelings; the conscious somehow reflects the subconscious.

When I study a play, the feeling of its style comes not as a literal definition, but it is expressed through visual images, through sounds and rhythms. I begin to understand, at first dimly, the shape of the production. The uniqueness of character relationships as they unfold dictate the style.

Q. What is the style of CHERRY ORCHARD?

Zavadski: The scheme of time passing goes through the play. The desire to hold on to time—to stop it—is the inner rhythm of the play. Our task is to make the audience believe the words are thoughts as they are spoken. Chekhov demands this, Chekhov is very musical and poetic; therefore every word is important. Any theatricality would be wrong here. We approach the play very slowly but it doesn't mean the whole process is slow. Each character is a succession of actions.

The whole play shows a lack of communication between people. The play is really about the flow of time; how people change, how youth passes.

Q. Is there a theatre style unique to Russia?

Zavadski: What gives me the right to speak about theatre in Russia? A very complicated, interesting, unique autobiography. I started with Vakhtangov as an actor and I was with him until his death. Then, I moved over to the Moscow Art Theatre, where I concentrated on directing. For 12 years I worked next to Constatin S. Stanislavski, absorbing his teachings as I had absorbed Vakhtangov's, Stanislavski's closest disciple. Meyerhold's influence on Vakhtangov was enormous. Meyerhold was a remarkable artist, and in time we have come to understand the importance of the contrasting juxtaposition of Stanislavski and Meyerhold, especially in the initial years of the revolution. Stanislavski and Meyerhold represented two sides of one and the same coin. Meyerhold actually said, "We have dug a tunnel from two different sides. Stanislavski worked from the inner to the external, and I work from the external to the inner. We were destined to meet some place in the depths of this tunnel." Vakhtangov's greatness was that he understood this; he dreamed that in a workshop he would utilize both Stanislavski's and Meyerhold's method. He felt that it was his mission to reconcile these two seeming contradictions, and toward the end they had actually begun to draw together.

Even in his early preoccupations and exercises, Stanislavski stressed that you can't consciously will the experience of heat, for instance, but if you begin slowly and accurately, to wipe perspiration from a seemingly sweaty face with your hands convincingly, then you and the audience will believe that you are perspiring. That is to say, the relationship between the psychological and the physical is inseparable.

Today we need to extract, from both men's work, the most important revelations in order to continue developing theatre! That is our duty.

302

Q. What problem did Stanislavski give himself to solve while creating his method?

Zavadski: He wanted to raise theatre to the level of great Russian literature. Tolstoi, Pushkin, Dostoevski, and Gogol are names of world artists of the written word. Fortunately, these literary giants were actively interested in the theatre. Gogol was the first, perhaps, who formulated the concept of the director when he said that the actor who directed the troupe has to take as *his* goal the performance of the play as a whole.

Dostoevski spoke of the artistic discipline required of each actor that he should play no more and no less than what he's required to play. He also said a playwright considers a play as yet unfinished until the theatre finishes the play when it is reincarnated by the actors.

Pushkin expressed Stanislavski's whole method in his little tragedy STONE GUEST. The character, Laura, has just finished her performance, and Pushkin has her say, "Today everyone of my gestures, and words worked. I freely gave myself up to inspiration. Words flowed as if they came not from memory, but from the heart." Here is the whole Stanislavski method.

Q. What is your understanding of Stanislavki's method?

Zavadski: Stanislavski based his method on the culture of the past; he always stressed that he had not discovered his method, that he had not invented anything; simply codified the experiences of generations of actors. In giving examples of the right kind of playing, he uses, not himself and his colleagues, but artists of the past, Salvini, Duse. These people did not know the Method as we understand it, but through their creative genius, had it in them and used it in their acting. In a certain measure, Stanislavski wanted to channel the forces of genius and intiution into conscious awareness. I'm quite sure that now all actors know this, because this is the Stanislavski formula: conscious awareness to reach the subconscious creativity; it is very important to understand it in its totality because in the understanding of the Method there is sometimes a leaning too much to one side or the other. Some make the Method into a cold and dry calculation and they say, "You've just got to play; what do you mean by the Method?" Others consider the Method as just the art of feeling and experiencing, leaving calculations and awareness aside.

We cannot imagine a pianist sitting down and playing Beethoven immediately. If we are to approach the theatre arts seriously we must create an artist who is a master craftsman.

Q. How do you incorporate Stanislavski's method into your directing?

Zavadski: The whole work in directing should be to make the text of the role the actor's own. I believe it is very important to create the production jointly with the actors. A play is created through the creation of each part; as each character unfolds, the play unfolds. It is very important that each individual part be only a part of the whole we are trying to create. Each person is the sum of his thoughts, his feelings, his actions, and his inner world. My first task as director, therefore, is to help the actors create the inner world of the part.

The actor, according to Stanislavski, must always play from desires, wishes, motivation. In life one has a relationship to what one is saying; it is the subtlety of that relationship which the actor has to explore, and not a single phrase is accidental. We must be able not so much to play the text as to react to it. One plays, not individual parts, but the interrelationship between people. A person only says part of what he thinks and each sentence is surrounded by a lot of unspoken thoughts. An actor must know how to talk and also how to listen.

We have to organize methods which help the actors understand the theatre as a unit, an ensemble. It is easier for the actor to play when he knows who and where he is—when he is sure.

Stanislavski was interested in the expressiveness of the spoken word and in the laws of speech as well as a person's thoughts, feelings, desires and actions, the inner life of the character and of the time, and of the meaning *under* the meaning of each line.

The last idea of Stanislavski was the unity of the physical and the spiritual. A childlike spontaneity is needed for the artists we are trying to become—the complete joy in playing. Play, in a double sense.

Sometimes I look only for the pantomime of the performance, for elements of the character in movements, gestures and in *mise-en-scene*. Translate each day's rehearsal into truth.

If I stop to tell the actor something, he is not to come out of character to be himself. He stays in character; listens to me in character on stage, and during the entire rehearsal remains in character. All actors listen to everyone; one talks and the others listen; all hear everything and all react. Only then will the company of actors create an ensemble.

The actor's goal is to be sensitive and quick to respond to both the present emotions required by the scenes and emotional memories used in the scenes. As director my goal is to evoke this extreme sensitivity to the essence of life—to make all of the senses of the actors in varying degrees responsive to both the external life and the inner life of the character. Each part is not a straight line but a line with ups and downs, with contradictions. These contradictions are very interesting to develop within the role.

The actor must search for a line of uninterrupted existence—where the character is coming from and where he is going. Actors and director must all think of the act as music. Each actor has his own rhythm but within the rhythm of the scene.

At some point, I go up on the stage and 'act out' without words the parts which are read by the actors themselves. I do this only to hint at the intensity of the intention and the rhythm. Not just to state facts but to concentrate on the inner *subtext* for the action. My job is not only to introduce the actor to Chekhov's world but to rebuild his mechanisms so he'll be more creative.

Stanislavski himself said, "The art of the Moscow Art Theatre is such that it requires constant renewal, constant, persistent work on itself!" For this type of art a special technique is necessary, not the effect of studied theatrical forms but a technique to develop one's intuitiveness, one's creative possibilities in every performance. You have to work so that the difficulties become habit, the habit becomes easy, the easy becomes beautiful. When you are sure, the audible and visual, and the inner music of Chekhov's art will come through.

Q.   When you direct in your own theatre in Russia is your approach similar to your work with American actors?

Zavadski: I have to do less with Russian actors because most of the troupe of the Mossoviet Theatre are my students who have had this preparation under me. But still in every new production one has to look at the actor in a new way. And maybe twist him a little bit—turn him the right way.

Q.   Does the Mossoviet Theatre, like the Moscow Art Theatre, have its own school?

Zavadski: It is not a permanent school. But periodically I will collect a group, train them, and bring them into the theatre. I now have a special problem of enlarging the theatre and of giving it a larger scope. I want it to become one of the best theatres in the country. I say it with humor: I am a living museum, for I am the only one left who had direct contact with Stanislavski, Vakhtangov and Meyerhold. Theatrical art today becomes an enormous inner strength. In other countries, some may have religion, but in Russia the whole spiritual life is concentrated in art. I want audiences to remember for the rest of their lives that they have encountered in my theatre an experience with mankind.

I always trust the spectators to have taste and comprehension. I have faith in my actors. Productions come about and are perceived as the natural result of a friendly merger of the efforts of the director and the actors. Such co-authorship gives the production the naturalness of breathing; the actors do not appear as performers but as inventors, creators, poets of their parts, real masters of the stage.

Q. What problems did you encounter with the IASTA production of CHERRY ORCHARD?

Zavadski: It was important for me to find the inner style of Chekhov's period and time, and to show the American actors this understanding. While casting for CHERRY ORCHARD, I saw that they were very close to an understanding of Stanislavski's method. They were free on stage, they were organized, they communicated, they talked an understanding of Stanislavski's method. The whole problem was that they had no deep understanding of that world in which Chekhov's characters lived. The actors were contemporary Americans who were more or less familiar with the text, but they had not penetrated into Chekhov's epoch. It was my job to lead them and to recreate for them Chekhov's world, to explain the rela-

307

tionships within the play. If a young actor today looks at the relationships between men and women in Chekhov, they may be incomprehensible to him; for only in terms of that specific period can these characters be understood. Looked at from today's liberated point of view, their actions may not seem justifiable and cannot be understood. Still, my job was to penetrate into Chekhov, and it seems in ways I was successful. That is the job of a teacher, a director who loves his actors, and who finds approaches to actors to make the actors gradually an ensemble.

I did not coerce the actor's artistic world; I awakened his imagination to lead him on bit by bit, slowly, slowly, and without his realizing, day by day he came close to understanding Chekhov. The actor remained himself but at the same time was becoming somebody else. Very frequently, actors play their parts superficially, not deeply. Ours was a process of organic growth in the part. One can talk of artificial growth: to play the part immediately as one sees it. But no, one has to do it gradually so that a character like Trofimov emerges slowly, so that the actor didn't know how he became Trofimov.

The great actor, Ivan Moskvin of the Moscow Art Theatre, was first to interpret and create the character Yepihodov in CHERRY ORCHARD, under the direction of Stanislavski. His 'choreography' if you will, was and is definitive. For a production of CHERRY ORCHARD, it was only necessary for me to teach my American actor Moskvin's movements and gestures. The actor and I worked, of course, together on the interpretation.

Q. Is knowledge of the manners of the period important? Authenticity of dress?

Zavadski: It is not enough to know the art of the clothes of a period; one must understand why such clothes were worn. How they reflected peoples' behavior. How they moved in these clothes. Here I would like to substitute another word, because many might "know," historians might "know," an ethnographer might "know," a scholar. But an artist has somehow to understand from within that which he "knows." He must understand, how should one say it, as if he were reincarnated into the period, so that his knowledge is special. Here the question is whether it is imperative to have costumes match the period. There are these experiments when Shakespeare, for instance, is done in modern dress. I doubt whether Shakespeare should be played in historically accurate costumes, because when he writes that the action takes place in Venice, for instance, in reality, he is camouflaging because we know perfectly well that Shakespeare always wrote of his people, Elizabethans. That is why his historical accuracy is relative. For that reason in our country, as in yours, we can shift him in time a bit and even deprive him of historical accuracy. But, as regards to bringing the play completely into a contemporary setting, it seems to me I have not seen a successful solution of this plan. There is always created some kind of contradiction between contemporary clothes and the characters portrayed. They were, after all, different people. They were not just different clothes, but different people. So that when Shakespeare's characters put on contemporary clothes, they seemed to be in costume, at a masquerade, so to speak, dressed up. This does not bring the play closer, but makes it strange. It does not help, in my opinion, in the appreciation of Shakespeare.

Q. How important is a knowledge of the physical form of the theatre for which the play was written?

Zavadski: Knowing the kind of theatre the dramatist knew when he was writing the play is, of course, important. Shakespeare wrote fast, continuing action without scene changes. If we, today, don't take this into account, and play each scene with a curtain, with stage waits, we break the rhythmic thrust of the play. That is a mistake. One must understand what differentiates the style and theatre of one author from the style of another. Style is a core thing; it is the essence of the play.

THE MOSCOW ART THEATRE

The Moscow Art Theatre is grounded in the training and theories of theatre education as taught by Stanislavski. This is basically technique plus Stanislavski's theories of reincarnation of the character by the actor. The second thing is that the Moscow Art Theatre is an ensemble theatre! The actors have been playing together for years, and some plays have continued in the repertory forty years. Thus, an unbroken tradition has been passed on without interruption from older actors to younger actors. The fact that they are an ensemble, rehearsing, acting, and teaching together for many years makes it easier for them as actors to create an illusion of reincarnation of character and reality.

Rehearsals begin at eleven and run customarily until three p.m., five times a week. Sunday is a matinee day, and Monday is the "day off" for actors.

During a break in rehearsal of a new contemporary play, stage director Stanitsyn said that rehearsals of this play had begun in January. When asked if he had used early in the rehearsal improvisation before giving the actors the text of the play, he said, "No, since this is a contemporary play and the characters are close to the actors themselves there was no need for improvisation." He added, "Some directors use improvisation more; some directors less. I feel that improvisation may be good for a period play far from the lives of the actors." He quickly stated that it was of great importance in MXAT's school for training the actor but not needed so much for the mature actor in rehearsal.

When asked if he blocked the play before coming to rehearsals, he said, "Frankly, as a director, I like to have a clear idea of what the scene is going to look like—the action and the crosses. But sometimes actors are dis-

tressed by this, so I have to slip the plotting of the action in unobtrusively."
At the same time, he made it clear that as a director (based on his own experiences both as a director and actor) he wants the actor to be comfortable in the scene both in his actions and in his spatial relationships with the other actors. Therefore, he gives them in early rehearsals a freedom to change and to experiment with the action and details of stage business.

Curious about backstage practice, and having seen him in Gorki's *Lower Depths,* he was asked if while he was offstage in the wings of the theatre he maintained his character and the mood of the play. He laughed and said, "I've played that role (the bibulous Policeman) for so many years now that it's not necessary. When it's a new play, for the first few performances it's a good idea."

We also asked him if he came to the theatre early and warmed up his voice and body with exercises and reconstructed the role he would play that night through concentration on it. Again, he said, "This is indeed from Stanislavski, but it's an individual matter with the actors of our theatre. Some may choose, when they are new to a role, to come early and to concentrate and to work on warming up." He went on to say that *he* did not need usually to do so.

MXAT's school has an enrollment of 130 students and a faculty of 70 professors. Approximately 100 students are students of acting; in all four years they get instruction in voice quality, diction, musical training of the voice, listening to music, and responding to rhythm; 30 students are enrolled for a two-year period of instruction as technicians (stage managers).

The school is financed by the state, and all students have a stipend. It is like salary; it not only includes tuition but also provides living expenses. At the end of the four-year period, from among those who get diplomas, four to six students are chosen to become members of the company of the Moscow Art Theatre. The third and fourth year all students have had professional experience. A few advanced students are given character parts with lines, while others are used in crowd scenes. Thus they have played on stage with the MXAT troupe. Of the twenty or more who graduate, those who do not go to the Moscow Art Theatre to become members of

311

the troupe usually go to theatres in other cities.

In any one year of the four years there are only twenty students, and the ratio of men to women is thirteen men to seven women. For the first, second, third or fourth year group of twenty students, there are two classes so that one acting class on a particular day at a particular hour under a professor will not exceed ten or twelve students.

To recruit students of acting, MXAT's school sends a commission to twenty-five places in Russia. Here they hold auditions. For the first audition there are usually seventeen hundred candidates. By the second audition there are only a thousand, and by the third audition there are sixty. Twenty are chosen for the first year of study at MXAT's school. Some months before the young people take these auditions, there are consultations for advising them on material to prepare for auditions. At the auditions they recite poems and perform short scenes. Their voices are checked. These candidates are also give a written examination in history, for they must have had a secondary school education. Training in the MXAT school is considered higher education by the state and is financed as such by the state.

The director of the school said, "Their study load is very heavy; we want to lighten it." The students take courses in history and literature of world theatre and of the national theatre. There is some instruction in a foreign language of the student's choice: French, German or English.

A Soviet theatre school resembles the continental European *vocational* school, for the curriculum does not provide a broad liberal education of a college or university, Soviet or Western European or American.

During the first year of instruction the students spend nine hours a day, six days a week at school; they arrive at nine in the morning and study and rehearse until seven in the evening. Later on towards the end of their four-year period of training they may be at the school from nine until eleven at night. During the four years, most time each day is devoted to acting. There is always one class in movement each day and also one in voice, so there is a balance between movement and voice. But most time is devoted to acting.

There is no specialized training in musical theatre. They study vaudeville technique and thus get some experience in working with music, which often plays an important (and to some observers—intrusive) part in dramatic productions.

The first year is devoted to improvisation some times with the words improvised, at others with pantomime only. First, the instructors try to get the actor to improvise in terms of his own person, and then they take him on to more difficult characters away from his own personality.

Students do improvisations of animals and even inanimate objects to sharpen perception while observing animals and objects and also to stimulate the imagination of actors.

By the second year students start on scenes from plays. The MXAT school not only trains them for the character type they are likely to play later if they are taken into the troupe, but also attempts to develop the total actor. To accomplish the latter objective teachers have the students play a wide variety of characters in scenes from plays and even in the important student productions. In these acting classes students work first with period plays of a variety of types: comedy, farce, tragedy. Thus they begin instruction in acting with the classics.

By the third year they are performing in full-length plays. These are performed only for invited audiences, "papa and mama audiences."

Fourth year students at MXAT's school, rehearsing Gorki's final play, *Last People*, had been in rehearsal for two months and it was now to be rehearsed from beginning to end for two weeks or a month more. A performance would be given then by these diploma students. If it were found good enough, it would be transferred to the downtown Moscow Student Theatre.

The director of the student production of *Last People* was S.K. Blennikov, a People's Artist of the USSR. His schedule seemed rather taxing in that he plays three times a week on the stage of the Moscow Art Theatre and was rehearsing in the production of *Battle on the Road*. Thus, Blennikov is an active member of the troupe performing on certain evenings; he is engaged in rehearsal as many as five days a week (if needed at rehearsals for the role he is playing); he is also a professor in the MXAT Studio School.

So, reinforced more recently by the rehearsal procedures of Yuri Zavadski at the Institute for Advanced Studies in the Theatre Arts, New York,

Russian directors do not indulge actors in rehearsal or in performance by permitting inaudibility, license to wander, to re-write the dialogue, or to alter radically the pace and line readings, but concern themselves with maintaining their ensembles of actors playing in repertory.

CHEKHOV

FILM

"Chekhov and The Moscow Art Theatre": obtainable, for rental and purchase, through the Institute for Advanced Studies in the Theatre Arts (IASTA), P.O. Box 1106, Radio City Station, New York, NY 10101 or Gil Forman, 310 W. 56th St., #1B, New York, NY 10019.

SELECTED BIBLIOGRAPHY

Bristow, Eugene K. *Anton Chekhov's Plays*. New York: W.W. Norton & Company, Inc., 1977.

Gorchakov, Nikolai M. *Stanislavsky Directs*. (Translation by Miriam Goldina.) New York: Funk & Wagnalls Company, 1954.

Gorchakov, Nikolai A. *The Theatre in Soviet Russia*. New York: Columbia U. Press, 1957.

Houghton, Norris. *Moscow Rehearsals*. New York: Harcourt, Brace and Company, 1936.

Komissarzhevsky, V. *Moscow Theatres*. Moscow: Foreign Languages Publishing House, 1959.

Nemirovitch-Dantchenko, Vladimir. *My Life in the Russian Theatre*. (Translated by John Cournos.) London: Geoffrey Bles (N.D.)

Sayler, Oliver M. *Inside The Moscow Art Theatre*. New York: Brentano's, 1925.

Stanislavski, Constantin. *Stanislavski's Legacy*. (Translated and edited by Elizabeth Reynolds Hapgood.) New York: Theatre Arts Books, 1958.

MATERIALS AND BACKGROUND

Houghton, Norris. *Return Engagement*. New York: Holt, Rinehart and Winston, 1962.

Mitchell, J. D. and Drew, G. and Mitchell, M. P. "The Moscow Art Theatre in Rehearsal". *Educational Theatre Journal*. December, 1960.

Mitchell, J. D. and M. P. "The Theatre in Russia". *Today's Speech*, Vol. VI, Number 2. Pennsylvania: Pennsylvania State U., 1958.

Hingley, Ronald. *The Russian Mind*. New York: Scribner, 1977.

Simmons, Ernest J. *Chekhov, A Biography*. Boston: Little, Brown and Company, 1962.

MUSIC

Scriabin Concerto in F sharp for Piano and Orchestra Lon. C732.

Tchaikovsky Serenade in C for Strings Op. 48 Ang. S-36269.

THE FUTURE OF THEATRE
AND THE SEARCH FOR STYLE

Thus, twenty styles have been explored in depth; they are among the major styles of world theatre. Classical dramas have survived through the ages in all cultures because they have dramatized an affirmation of life. They reinforce the traditional values of the society for which they have been written. They are humanistic and positive in their outlook.

The search for style does not end, however, for there are world playwrights whose works deserve to be in the repertories of our theatres. Some are performed; many are not performed. Too often the true style may elude directors and actors, or the style may be only dimly realized.

"I would like to suggest that the works of the past survive only if they have style, which means quality."[*]

The Institute recognized, among many, as important playwrights: Ibsen, Pirandello, and Sean O'Casey. These three playwrights of Norway, Italy and Ireland, respectively, are of such a stature as innovative playwrights that the search for the style requisite to their plays should be taken up.

Learning a language is learning a culture. The style of a play is imbedded in the language and the culture of the author. A stage director or actor of Norway, of Italy, of Ireland is rooted in the culture and the language of his native land. As a recognized master of theatre by his compatriots he has something special to share with actors and directors of a country who are eager to produce the play. This is particularly true for any country where the classical play is to be performed in translation. (It goes without saying that being of the language and of the culture is not enough; the director from abroad for Ibsen, Pirandello, O'Casey, etc. must be a master, first and foremost.)

Dimitrios Rondiris has given us clues as to the way to recapture the style of ancient Greek tragedy. Are not the Greek playwright Aristophanes and the writers of Roman comedy: PLAUTUS and TERENCE deserving of our learning their style?

---

[*] Saint-Denis, Michael. *Theatre: The Discovery of Style.* New York; Theatre Arts Books, 1959.

PLAUTUS, alone, has contributed much to theatre of the Western world. Immediately comes to mind Shakespeare's THE COMEDY OF ERRORS, Molière's THE MISER, and more recently the delightful American musical comedy A FUNNY THING HAPPENED ON THE WAY TO THE FORUM written by American Burt Shevlove and Larry Galbart, with lyrics and music by Stephen Sondheim.

Before leaving the ancients, the writer is prompted to commend the National Theatre of England for its exploring the style of that Roman playwright of tragedies, Seneca. Scholars had long relegated the tragedies of the philosopher Seneca to the library, as static plays. Peter Brook's production of Seneca's OEDIPUS won over audiences in London and suggested that Seneca, among the ancients, may be a neglected playwright.

The English director, E. Martin Browne has said, "The Medieval is a huge world of theatre which is just beginning to be explored. My own pioneer efforts to show that Medieval theatre was theatre could claim no sort of authenticity of style. What I've achieved is to set the next two generations going along the paths of discovery in the world of Medieval theatre."

Johan de Meester and E. Martin Browne, each, had explored for a style for the religious plays of the middle ages. Were efforts to continue to reconstruct a style for the York and Chester cycle of English mystery plays might not the productions be meritorious in their own right, but also they would contribute to the evocation of a style appropriate to the plays of T.S. Eliot; e.g. MURDER IN THE CATHEDRAL and other religious plays.

William Shakespeare is head and shoulders above his fellow Elizabethan playwrights, but had there been no Shakespeare, we would recognize immediately the value to the repertories of our theatres of Christopher Marlowe, Ben Jonson. Collaborators with Shakespeare: Francis Beaumont and John Fletcher created a style. Their entertaining play THE KNIGHT OF THE BURNING PESTLE comes to mind immediately. From this period one turns as well to Thomas Dekker's THE SHOEMAKER'S HOLIDAY.

Mozart and Molière are but two who had turned to the legend of Don Juan. We are told that the Spanish continue to produce EL BURLADOR DE SEVILLA by Tirso de Molina. In view of the vitality of Tirso de Molina's play as a progenitor of a legion of Don Juan's down through the century, would it not be of value to invite a master Spanish director to share with us the style for this Spanish classic which ranks with the monumental works of Lope de Vega and Calderon.

France is a treasure house of plays. The French for more than 300 years, as stage directors Charon, Manuel and Deiber, have pointed out, have a reverence for masterworks, which French actors perform in their national theatres *and* in their commerical boulevard theatres.

The style for the tragedies and comedies of Pierre Corneille are deserving of a search for their styles. Victor Hugo, better known to us as a novelist, set in motion a great style in the 19th century: romanticism. Most of us only know something of Victor Hugo's theatre through Verdi's HERNANI (and other operas) a play which at its premiere prompted dignified Frenchmen to rip their seats up from the orchestra floor and hurl them at each other and onto the stage. The style of neo-romanticism of Edmond Rostand may be found in his play CYRANO de BERGERAC, which when produced in France achieves the 'hit' status of a Broadway musical.

In the 19th century, England developed a style of play which is very difficult to recapture unless handled with great sensitivity. This style is that of the 19th century sentimental comedy. If it is treated as exaggerated melodrama, it fails. If the play CASTE by Tom Robertson is approached with sincerity and sympathy its vitality is discovered.

The plays of the 19th century playwright Dion Boucicault delight audiences with their geniality. Boucicault's plays exude an infectous good humor. Also, the texture is right for actors: he has the inborn knack of keeping a play on the move and yet allowing enough room for an actor to move about inside it and create a great performance.

A London critic Hugh Leonard writes of the value of repertories of classical plays, even the minor classics. "Boucicault's LONDON ASSURANCE is not only a happy occasion in itself, but it marks the discovery of a vital missing link in the genealogy of farce. In LONDON ASSURANCE there are echoes of Vanbrugh and of Goldsmith".

Less than 50 years after the premier of LONDON ASSURANCE, the French playwright Eugene Labiche was to write CELIMARE LE BIEN-

AIMÉ, a farce concerning an aging *roué*. The gentleness of Labiche was toughened by Pinero, and Pinero's plays were refined, chilled and re-rendered with magnificent precision by the incomparable Feydeau.

Playwright Pinero's style is enchanting. Before the style is lost and forgotten by a generation of actors and directors in England, it deserves to be taught. The style is Edwardian, and its best known exponent is Oscar Wilde. Wilde's THE IMPORTANCE OF BEING ERNEST has never ceased to be performed throughout the world. It is even an acting exercise for student actors in Budapest; it is a play much admired.

Shaw's plays are Shaw, but they are progeny of the Edwardian era. A failure to know the etiquette and manners of this period can result in a mauling of the plays of George Bernard Shaw. This can be a grave loss to theatres around the world.

Playwrights Somerset Maugham and Noel Coward were inheritors of the Edwardian style. The witty, crisp and at times impudent style of their plays is readily accessible as yet to our theatre. It would be unfortunate within a generation to have lost that syle.

"Theatre is perhaps the most accessible and immediate of all the performing arts—accessible because its medium of communication is language; immediate because the audience is an active element of every performance and without whom the theatre simply cannot exist."*

High comedy *is* language—manners. The American theatre came of age early in the 20th century. A style which it developed to a point of perfection is its high comedy, the comedies of manner of Philip Barry, George Kelly, S.N. Behrman and others.

Recent efforts to revive these entertaining plays show that the style of these prewar comedies is vanishing, for a style is an evanescent thing. Within a generation, it can be lost.

It can also be recalled. Before it is too late, the directors and actors who had worked in the style should be recruited to teach a generation of today's actors and directors the style, *and* a training in techniques requisite to the

---

*Lasch, Christopher. *The Culture of Narcissism*. New York: W.W. Norton and Company, Inc., 1978

style. Training in voice, movement, etiquette of the period, as the foregoing chapters have often indicated, is fundamental to achieving a unique style.

What may be needed is an 'actors ladder,' a series of seminars and workshops committed to recapturing the style of American comedy of manners.

Plays and authors of Eastern Europe which come to mind are Russia's Tolstoy and Ostrowski.

Hungary's Ferenc Molnar. Today, actors and directors of Budapest in several of its many theatres are recapturing the style for such Molnar comedies as THE GUARDSMAN, THE SWAN and LILIOM.

Roumania has its master playwright Ion Luca Caragile. Their national theatre's production of Caragile's THE LOST LETTER won international enthusiasm at the Théâtre des Nation, in Paris.

THE INSECT COMEDY, R.U.R., and THE MACROPOULOS SECRET (which is seen and heard today throughout the world as an opera) remind us of Czechoslovakia's playwright Karel Capek.

Ludwig Holberg is reffered to affectionately as Denmark's Molière. A statue of Holberg stands before the entrances to Denmark's imposing national theatre in Copenhagen. His plays deserve to be performed.

Austria's Johann Nestroy wrote a series of unique farcical comedies. The American playwright Thorton Wilder turned the famous Nestroy comedy *Ein Jux Will Er Sich Machen* into THE MATCHMAKER, which later became the basis for the successful American musical HELLO, DOLLY. Production of Nestroy's prototype of THE MATCHMAKER, as produced by the National Theatre of Vienna reveals style. It is a viable theatre piece.

Plays reflect a people, their temperament, and their time. Some exploration has begun into the styles of theatre of Africa, of the Middle East and of Latin America. More needs to be done.

The Western inspired contemporary plays of some Asian countries are deserving of consideration for presentation in English translation in our theatres. The theatre of Shanghai in China early in the century developed some remarkable playwrights, among them are Lao Shih, Tsao Yü, and dramatizations of the 20th century novels of Pa Chin.

Japan has developed a vigorous and dynamic contemporary theatre.

The playwrights are numerous and are deserving of research and exploration for texts for performance in today's American theatre.

"One should realize that without the experience of the Japanese woodcut, Degas would never have perfected the off-hand, sawn-short,
asymetrical compositional devices that give so deceptive an air of non-
chalance to many of his best pictures.

"As for the Post impressionists, Gauguin and Van Gogh were deep in
the dyes of Japan. Whistler, Toulouse-Lautrec, Mary Cassatt, Pierre Bon-
nard, and Edouard Vuillard all underwent the same initiation, and all took
from it what they needed most. Monet first learned of Japanese prints in
The Netherlands, when they were used as wrapping paper; he later built a
Japanese garden in his house in Giverny."*

The Theatre Department of the University of Hawaii continues to explore Asian forms of theatre as far afield as the Thai and Indonesian dance
theatre forms.

The Japan Society and the Asia Society, through its performing arts
program, bring troupes of theatrical performers from Asia to heighten
awareness and diversity of theatre around the world.

The critic Kenneth Tynan observed that the American stage was preoccupied with sex. He raised the question: Why not plays about money?
Why not dramas of politics?

With the end of the cultural revolution, in Peking and in Shanghai contemporary political plays in a Western style of theatre prove to be provocative, involving, and entertaining for audiences.

As well as doing Chinese plays, might not American plays of the future
explore the American political scene and themes of the relations of the individual and money?

"Where are the world's classics being performed? In the last three
decades there has been a decentralization in the United States of theatre.
There are an impressive number of regional theatres throughout the country. There are 152 professional regional theatres. These 152 theatres spent
$79,233,500.00 producing 1,368 plays. Ninety four of these institutions

---

*"How Japan Influenced French Art." Russell, John. New York Times. Wednesday,
January 15, 1975.

were founded in the last 10 years, the fact which underscores the enormous expansion of the professional non-commercial theatre in the United States in recent years.

Shakespeare was still the most frequently produced playwright, as well as Shaw, Coward, Molière, Chekhov and Ibsen."[*]

Add to the above impressive number of regional theatres the more than 1,500 university and college theatres, as well as substantial community theatres in the United States and Canada.

Another facet of decentralization in recent times has been the productions of foreign and vintage American plays at the Kennedy center, Washington, D.C., and the performances there by visiting national theatres from abroad.

In this century, the City of Baltimore had not been thought of as a center for creative activity in theatre. Baltimore built a performing arts center and in 1981 sponsored an international theatre festival of major theatres from more than seven countries.

Stratford, Ontario, Canada, has become a theatre center of international stature, not only for its productions of the plays of Shakespeare, but also for its revivals of classical plays of other nations.

It is unfortunate—admirable as these theatres are—that too many of our regional theatres, our college and university theatres, and our off-Broadway theatres "keep toasting the same bread."

Might they not be advised to examine the repertories of world theatre? How often does a community in Minneapolis or Los Angeles or Baltimore or Atlanta wish to see, great as they are, frequent repeats of each of the four or five plays of Anton Chekhov? Other classical playwrights of Russia, as well as of France, Germany, Spain, Italy, Asia have been cited and attention has been called to their intrinsic and extrinsic merits. They would provide American audiences everywhere with, not only a fresh experience, but also aesthetic pleasure through insights into diverse—largely unknown—cultures.

In advance of looking into the future to determine what may be the themes of the theatre in the future, let us consider what had been some of

---

[*]THEATRE PROFILES/3. New York: Theatre Communications Group, Inc. 1977.

the themes in the recent past. A dominant theme of American plays in the '30s and 40s could be characterized as "momism"[*] or "now Eve plays all the parts." Typical American plays of the '30s and '40s were ones in which woman is all-knowing, all-powerful, all-loving, and largely triumphant over the male. American plays ran the gamut of situations in which the female was the disguised "hero" or the real power behind the throne on which the playwright had placed a paper-maché hero.

The most successful plays of more than 20 seasons showed that on the average 8 out of 10 plays lacked a clearly delineated hero. During this same period in American stage history, the majority of the plays which received production on the professional stage depicted women in competitive conflict with men. Covertly or overtly, the women of these dramas were depicted as triumphing over men.

The most indigenous form of American theatre, the musical comedy for the era, in varying degrees, reflected in part or whole tensions which existed in American culture between men and women. Typical are the heroines of musical comedies of the '40s; e.g. ANNIE GET YOUR GUN. This ANNIE ran for over two years on Broadway (1,147 performances) and was highly successful commercially on tour throughout the United States. The title alone of the musical comedy was provocative of analysis and symbolized pointedly the male-female competitive struggle which was at the heart of the piece.

The stage has always mirrored the character of the audiences it entertained. "In a period of social decay and confusion, theatre can never go very far and never affirm more than husks of values."[**] The ponderance of authors who wrote for the stage, television, and radio in the '30s and '40s were men, but, unlike in the Elizabethan age, the plays were written largely about women for women. Characterizations of heroines were as aggressive, competitive females.

"Even a rational understanding of the techniques by means of which a

---

[*]Gorer, Geoffrey, *The American People: A Study In National Character*. New York: W.W. Norton, 1948.

[**]Brook, Peter, "Interview: The Drama Review." Volume 17 #3 (T-59) September, 1973.

given illusion is produced does not necessarily destroy our capacity to experience it as a representative of reality."*

Nihilism as a theme in plays began in the '50s in France with Ionesco and Beckett. The loose form and the elements of fantasy and the negativism of these plays spread to the United States. By the 1960s the plays in the United States had become the *status quo* and the middle class, *and* they were marked by revolt against form.

"A living respect for form, sensitivity to poetical colour and to rhythm, are essential to the kind of intensified drama which a classical actor, faced with character, has got to create."* *

All of these plays were children of the Norwegian playwright Ibsen of the 19th century. Ibsen created realism to develop his themes of man, the individual, in conflict with society. Thus, entered a hero as a revolutionary.

Ibsen said of his work: "The illusion I wished to create was that of reality. The effect of the play depends a great deal on making the spectator feel as if he were actually sitting, listening, and looking at events happening in real life."

The contemporary playwright had abandoned the effort to portray coherent and generally recognized truth and presented the poet's personalized intuition of truth.

The absurdist theatre of Albee, Beckett, Ionesco, and Genet centers on the emptiness, isolation, loneliness, and despair experienced by the borderline personality.* * *

As we examine the theatre of the future have there been negative tendencies, counter to the affirmation of man and the enhancement of life to be found in classical theatre?

It has ever been that expertise in the magic of theatre and its fantasies which invite identification on the part of audiences can be both constructive and destructive of the spectators. The heroes of television, films, cartoons, and theatre become role models.

Certainly one commends the inventiveness and the brilliance of the stag-

---

*Lasch, C., *ibid*

* *Saint-Denis, Michael, *ibid*

* * *Lasch, C., *ibid*

ing of the American musical: EVITA, CHORUS LINE, ANNIE, SWEENEY TODD, 42ND STREET *ad infinitum*. The critical acclaim and popular success of the musical EVITA has propelled it around the world. It is brilliantly staged. There are seven companies in all. Its gross receipts have been 83 million dollars.

It is performed nightly in New York, London, and Madrid, Australia and South America. As a role model, Evita Peron tops all *success* stories: through whoring, murdering, exploiting the masses, she attains not only the goods and abundance of this world, but sainthood as well. Can anyone dispute that this is an obscene fantasy? As a theatre piece it energizes an audience's fantasies to approve, even to adopt, destructive and self-destructive means to realize the American dream of success.

"In earlier times, the self-made man took pride in his judgment of character and probity. THE HAPPY HOOKER stands in place of Horatio Alger as the prototype of personal success."*

The future of the unique American musical will continue to be toward integrated musical theatre. Some suggest that it is moving in the direction of an indigenous form of opera. This is positive.

The phase of late of permissiveness in respect to language and morality in the performing arts may have done some good, as we look to the future. Nevertheless, it is evident that the public is weary of smut and the four-letter words. Although this period of license may have liberated language and diminished hypocrisy and repression in the depiction of stories of human relationships, " the characteristic devaluation of language, vagueness as to time and place, sparse scenery, and lack of plot development evoke the barren world. . ."*

The emergence of black theatre throughout the country is a very positive aspect of American theatre. The Negro Ensemble Company has been attracting audiences with serious plays on black themes. Productions like THE WIZ, a black musical version of THE WIZARD OF OZ and AIN'T MISBEHAVIN' appealed not only to youth but to ethnic audiences.

This positive trend should counteract a negative tendency for some sub-

---

*Lasch, C., *ibid*

sidized theatres to exploit a minority's old grievances, feelings of injustice, and hatred toward other elements of American society. Certain of these theatres have passed from the scene, and they deserve it since it is not appropriate to theatre to finance art by digging into the government pork barrel and in a sense exploit the minorities for government subsidy.

"Positive affirmation, for example, really depends on the possibility for a poet not to be just an individual speaking from his own private world, but to be like the Greek dramatist a recognized spokesman, heard and understood by everyone, who finds things that they feel deeply but cannot put a name to."*

There was a tradition in the past to honor the creative people of the theatre by naming theatres after them; e.g. The Ethel Barrymore Theatre, The Helen Hayes Theatre, The Golden Theatre, etc.

It is a negative tendency for theatres to be named for eminently forgettable people simply because they are real estate developers or they have contributed large sums of money to build or to rehabilitate a theatre. How much more appropriate for New York's performing arts center to have been named, at least, for a great president, Lincoln.

Theatre managers' quoting the praise of critics for their new productions have created Frankenstein monsters, critics, who have turned on them. This has made of critics, largely forgettable on their own merit, household words. This negative phenomenon has educated a public to look to the critics for what they should seek in the way of education and entertainment.

A New York theatrical critic, now retired, did not read his own reviews. He dismissed Bertolt Brecht's play; e.g. GALILEO. A decade or more later he cited Brecht as a great playwright of the 20th century. He is one of the forgettable people for whom a theatre has been named!

To increase circulation for a magazine, its publisher tolerates John Simon's spiteful, personal, and destructive reviewing of New York theatre.

In Europe, advertisement is a small part of the budget for play productions, and since the advertisement space is small for plays, the critics are

---

*Brook, P., *ibid.*

not quoted and made into household words.

Two of Broadway's most successful producers point out that the impact of what reviewers have written about the plays, for good or for ill, diminishes and largely disappears after two months. The play or musical continues to attract audiences through word-of-mouth. The audience is the final arbiter of what succeeds, what is good, and what deserves to survive in memory.

The loss of hearing the true timbre of the human voice, whether the performer is singing or acting, is, indeed, a true loss. Among the negatives of today's theatre—and it is destructive of style—is the increasing use of amplification in our much too large theatres. Perhaps the proliferation of national regional theatres, off-off-Broadway and off-Broadway theatres which are very small may communicate to the builders of theatres and to the producers in large commercial theatres the dangers to the future of that kind of theatre if they continue to utilize amplification.

Communist countries have subjected theatre and the classics to distortion to promote idealogies. Theatre as propaganda fails to be art and theatre, and of late in America there has been a regrettable tendency to vulgarize the works of classic writers. Not only have commercial theatres been guilty of this but subsidized theatres; e.g. Shakespeare in the Park, the Public Theatre in New York. Broadway's THE PIRATES OF PENZANCE may help support Joseph Papp's Public Theatre, but the Messieurs Gilbert and Sullivan, as lyricists and composers, are no longer able to defend themselves; their works are no longer protected by copyrights.

It violates Shakespeare's plays to turn verse into prose. The plays of Shakespeare are poems, dramatic poems, and the actors must heed the verse.

Speaking of the verse which Shakespeare employed in his dramatic works, an English director says, "One of the things the actor has to be most careful about is not allowing himself to destroy the structure, because the structure of the language is very firm. The actor must respect the verse. What the playwright has put down for the actor does much of the work for the actor. The wise actor respects the language and, if it is verse, he plays the verse."

Thus to alter Shakespeare's plays, to reduce the verse to prose, or worse, to maul the text for propaganda and political ends or to use actors not yet equipped to perform the classics in order to get public funds for one's theatre is reprehensible. Productions in which the verse and style are obscured or obfuscated by heavy, foreign accents, or 'black-English' is a negative tendency on the part of some subsidized theatres.

A great author, long dead, cannot defend himself. Shakespeare's prayer is carved in stone in the church in Stratford-upon-Avon urging that his bones be not disturbed. Out of respect for the world's greatest playwright, stage directors, producers and actors should pause and heed that mild request.

Regional American theatres are producing the plays of Molière, of Ibsen, of Pirandello, etc., in translation into English. The English author Andrew Porter had brought closer to English-speaking audiences the operas of Wagner through his translations of THE RING and other operas by Richard Wagner.

Great poets of other lands have translated into their languages the dramatic verse of William Shakespeare. The son of Victor Hugo comes to mind, as does the French author André Gide; each has enabled the French language to bring the plays of Shakespeare to French audiences. It has been the good fortune of the writer to have seen, perhaps for him, the best production of TWELFTH NIGHT, performed in German, in Salzburg, Austria, by the Burgtheater of Vienna; KING LEAR, in German at Deutsches Theater in Berlin; Sheridan's THE SCHOOL FOR SCANDAL performed by the actors of the Comédie Française in Paris. Directed by a British guest director, for the writer, the finest production of RICHARD III of Shakespeare was in French at the Comédie Française.

Let a classic style be a catalyst. But a Noh or Kabuki theatre's style a la the playwright Yukio Mishima or the off-Broadway theatre group, La Mamma, easily become rootless parodies of the older traditional and classical forms of theatre and fail. Performances of classical plays, productions derivative of these styles, must respect the integrity of the original style, which is a distillation of generations of dedicated, creative artists: actors, writers, directors, teachers. We might emulate the Chinese painters who seek and find originality within an established discipline and infuse old conventions with renewed energy.

"Full human development requires that the pursuit of pleasure and enlightenment be at one with the drive for economic and physical security. Training in, about and through the arts is essential to learning both how to live and how to make a living."*

Civilization is a fragile thing. Anti-heroes are hardly role models for succeeding generations who need to keep afloat that fragile bark we designate as civilization.

"References, which formerly penetrated deep into everyday awareness, have become incomprehensible, and the same thing is now happening to literature and mythology of antiquity—indeed, to the entire literary tradition of the West. The effective loss of cultural traditions on such a scale makes talk of a new Dark Age far from frivolous."**

It may have been inevitable that in recent years the focus and emphasis of plays on reality and the rebelling individual would reach at the bottom of the barrel the individual as mental or physical defective, the criminal, the under-privileged and the terminally ill. One has only to cite the following award-winning plays: ELEPHANT MAN, CHILDREN OF A LESSER GOD, SHORT-EYES, WHOSE LIFE IS IT ANYWAY, SHADOW BOX. Despite its Pulitzer Prize, SHADOW BOX failed at the box office. The public has begun to weary of the anti-hero. Realism with its focus on the *common* common man has become stale.

The impact of television and now more recently cable television upon films would seem to be drastic. The box office receipts for films seem to reveal that the American public prefers to watch its films in the comfort of their homes rather than as a member of a group seated in a darkened auditorium.

In 1972, the average age of a Broadway patron was 55, according to the New York Times.

---

*Rockefeller, Jr., David. "Wanted, a new policy for the arts in education." *The New York Times*, Sunday, New York: May 22, 1977.

**Lasch, C., *ibid.*

However, hits like HAIR, Peter Brook's unconventional staging of MID-SUMMER NIGHT'S DREAM, GREASE, PIPPIN, CANDIDE influenced by television and film techniques, full of lively young performers attracted a new young public.

It is possible that television has stimulated, particularly among the young, an interest in theatre, ballet and opera. Not only are attendance records being broken for plays, for ballets, and for operas and concerts, but audiences are filled with young people casually dressed in blue jeans.

The popularity on television, for example, of Masterpiece Theatre, is a harbinger of a renaissance of enthusiasm for stories with a beginning, a middle, and an end.

We may look forward to the return to the theatre of narrative and craftsmanship in dramaturgy. The future of theatre lies in a return, as well, to the *uncommon* man as hero.

A contemporary play which had the trappings of a classic was voted in 1980-81 the best play here and abroad. In New York it won four additional awards. It is AMADEUS, a complex, literate play depicting two highly diverse uncommon heroes, the Italian composer Salieri and the genius Mozart. AMADEUS is the retelling of a rebel and his revolt against heaven, but more importantly it reveals what a wonder is man in his creativity.

May not the success of AMADEUS encourage playwrights for survival to develop themes in plays which enhance life, plays of heroes, leaders, who provide great role models? The success of AMADEUS also suggests that once again there is a public hungry for language of eloquence and elegance.

The amount of money in box office receipts does not tell us the whole story of the health of the American theatre, but it is a measure of the important role that it has come to play in the lives of the American people. Broadway entertains more than 200,000 people weekly, according to statistics prepared by the League of New York Theatre owners and producers. Between June and November in 1980, 5.5 million people attended Broadway shows, compared with 4.4 million the season before. Ticket sales have reached 92 million; 7.7 million people attended road shows, paying $101 million for tickets.*

The long held assumption that the theatre is frequented only by the 'carriage trade' is no longer valid. Such a limited sector of the population outside New York could not account for the 12,000,000 admissions in 75 American towns and cities for these 152 theatres, filling them to more than 82%, of seating subscribers, people committed enough to their particular theatre to purchase a ticket not just to one play, but to an entire season of plays.**

A challenge for the future for all creative people in theatre is to eliminate the present feast or famine syndrome. As one looks to the future, money will have to come for the performing arts once again from the private sector. Of late, corporations have joined the foundations and individuals in supporting cultural events to an impressive degree. It is hoped that once again both foundations and corporations and individuals will be encouraged and be able to continue to foster and support the performing arts.

When it is businessmen who are supporting theatre, there will be need for training in arts managements. Cultural centers and theatres need to be on a sound business basis.

Today, it is not a question of the future of theatre and the future of the *search* for style. The future of the theatre *is* in the continuing search for style.

---

*Croyden, Margaret. "The Box-Office Boom," THE NEW YORK TIMES MAGAZINE, June, 1981
**Theatre Profile/3